Venturing in International Firms

This book gives students a new perspective on entrepreneurial venturing in an international context. By analyzing the dynamics in international companies, they will be armed with the skills they need to build successful strategies for entering new international markets.

Williams presents a framework built around four contexts for international venturing: headquarters-driven through internal capabilities; subsidiary-driven through peripheral capabilities; headquarters-driven through external capabilities; and subsidiary-driven though external capabilities. Through this, students gain insight into the conditions that enable venturing in different types of MNEs, the mechanisms by which MNEs pursue international opportunities, and the leadership and managerial challenges of developing entrepreneurial capabilities across borders. Following a definition and analysis of each context, the book synthesizes the outcomes in an integrative way, providing implications for strategic leaders in international firms as well as for researchers and students. These contexts are used to frame the literature and engage with eight topical cases, which are also published in full in the Appendix of the book.

With case studies from around the world that focus both on smaller and larger enterprises, *Venturing in International Firms* will give students of international entrepreneurship, corporate entrepreneurship and international business an edge when venturing internationally in the real world.

Dr. Christopher Williams is Associate Professor in Management at Durham University Business School. He worked for nearly 20 years in international firms before entering academia. He is an active researcher and case writer and has published in a range of journals.

"The book provides refreshing insights into how organizations balance and approach the challenges associated with international growth and technological investment. Definitely an interesting read of any business leader that is looking at ways to excel in today's highly competitive international landscape."

Jaap Vossen, *Swisscom*

"Professor Williams packs a great deal of important research into a surprisingly readable and compact format. The book is an outstanding piece of work regarding the different types of international venturing that are clearly described and scrutinized – with vivid illustrations to make this come alive. Where articles normally lack in the big picture, this book provides an astonishingly easy way to understand current and future research on international venturing. The many accompanying cases make it a very useful text for teaching as well as for practitioners wanting to get a comprehensive overview of the current state-of-the-art on international venturing."

Torben Pedersen, *Bocconi University*

"*Venturing in International Firms* provides a timely and inspiring analysis of entrepreneurial dynamics in the international firm. Seeing the firm as a guided heterarchy, Christopher Williams integrates insights from international entrepreneurship, international business and knowledge-based research streams to develop an original approach to international entrepreneurial venturing. His approach puts the concept of entrepreneurial knowledge in the international firm at center-stage. He discusses and integrates ideas from different perspectives, including headquarters-driven and subsidiary-driven venturing, as well as internally-oriented and externally-oriented forms, and illustrates his arguments with real-life case studies of a range of firms in high-tech industries. This book is a must-read for students, academics and business practitioners aiming to advance understanding of international venturing within the tech landscape of an ever-changing global economy."

Ana Colovic, *NEOMA Business School*

Venturing in International Firms

Contexts and Cases in a High-Tech World

Christopher Williams

NEW YORK AND LONDON

First published 2018
by Routledge
711 Third Avenue, New York, NY 10017

and by Routledge
2 Park Square, Milton Park, Abingdon, Oxon, OX14 4RN

Routledge is an imprint of the Taylor & Francis Group, an informa business

© 2018 Taylor & Francis

The right of Christopher Williams to be identified as author of this work
has been asserted by him in accordance with sections 77 and 78 of the
Copyright, Designs and Patents Act 1988.

All rights reserved. No part of this book may be reprinted or reproduced or
utilized in any form or by any electronic, mechanical, or other means, now
known or hereafter invented, including photocopying and recording, or in
any information storage or retrieval system, without permission in writing
from the publishers.

Trademark notice: Product or corporate names may be trademarks or
registered trademarks, and are used only for identification and explanation
without intent to infringe.

Library of Congress Cataloging-in-Publication Data
Names: Williams, Christopher, 1966- author.
Title: Venturing in international firms: contexts and cases in high-tech
world/Christopher Williams.
Description: 1 Edition. | New York: Routledge, 2018. | Includes
bibliographical references and index.
Identifiers: LCCN 2017037264 (print) | LCCN 2017057724 (ebook) |
ISBN 9781315189000 (eBook) | ISBN 9781138731387
(hardback: alk. paper) | ISBN 9781138731394 (pbk. : alk. paper) |
ISBN 9781315189000 (ebk)
Subjects: LCSH: Venture capital. | Capital investments. | Investments,
Foreign.
Classification: LCC HG4751 (ebook) | LCC HG4751.W53 2018 (print) |
DDC 658.15/2–dc23
LC record available at https://lccn.loc.gov/2017037264

ISBN: 978-1-138-73138-7 (hbk)
ISBN: 978-1-138-73139-4 (pbk)
ISBN: 978-1-315-18900-0 (ebk)

Typeset in Bembo
by Sunrise Setting Ltd, Brixham, UK

Contents

Preface		vi
Chapter 1	Introduction	1
Chapter 2	'Context A' – Headquarters-driven Venturing: A Strategic Direction for Internal Capabilities	23
Chapter 3	'Context B' – Subsidiary-driven Venturing: Unleashing Peripheral Capabilities	39
Chapter 4	'Context C' – Headquarters-driven Venturing: Accessing Strategic External Capabilities	54
Chapter 5	'Context D' – Subsidiary-driven Venturing: Local Embedding to Drive Change	70
Chapter 6	'Across the Contexts' – Strategic Integration and Leading the Firm in International Venturing	85
Chapter 7	Summary and Conclusion	116

Appendix: *Cases of Venturing in International Firms*	121
References	275
Index	293

Preface

My interest in entrepreneurial dynamics in international companies and international settings spawned out of my experience in industry. Between 1986 and 2007, I worked for a number of international firms that had their assets spread across multiple countries while at the same time being pro-actively engaged in exploring new – and in many cases risky – technological and commercial opportunities in the hope of achieving growth. I always seemed to have been involved in projects that were international *and* had an innovative nature. These two themes took center-stage in my PhD dissertation and in the research, case-writing and teaching that I have done since embarking on a career in business schools.

But looking back, I think I was inspired much earlier growing up in 1970s London, one of the world's most international and creative cities. I avidly watched two television programmes: *Whicker's World* (on independent television in the 1970s), and *Tomorrow's World* (on the BBC). The former traced the adventures of journalist, writer and TV icon Alan Whicker as he traveled the globe documenting a diverse range of social, political and economic issues across the planet[1]. The latter charted innovation and latest developments in science and technology at that time[2]. I later found out that the elements of these two worlds collide and coalesce on a daily basis . . . in international firms.

This book provides an analysis of entrepreneurial dynamics in firms that have embarked on a journey of internationalization. I hope the book will be useful for business students at undergraduate and graduate levels who want to pursue a career in international firms *and* who want to be part of an environment where innovation, risk-taking and proactivity are ever-present. The book is primarily targeted at you. From my own experience I can say that these career elements make life stimulating and rewarding in so many ways.

I hope the book will also be useful for experienced managers and consultants dealing with international firms (either as employers or clients) *and* the question of change and rejuvenation of those organizations. This 'and' is important and central to the argument put forward in this book. In modern times, most, if not all, international firms seek out advantages by undertaking entrepreneurially-oriented activities across borders. No longer is the home country seen as the only source of fresh technological and commercial ideas and opportunities. Globalization has moved us all on from the ancient times when this may have once been the case. Indeed, in this book we take it as given that international firms of all shapes and sizes, from small born-globals to the large giants, and from those starting out in developed countries to those from newly emerging economies, will continually *need* to venture internationally in order to win. The question is not whether they should, but rather how they should. The reality is that the twenty-first century already is on track to becoming the century of Venturing in International Firms.

The book provides:

1 A *new perspective* on entrepreneurial venturing involving international firms.
2 Knowledge of *conditions* that enable venturing in different types of firms and *mechanisms* by which firms pursue international opportunities.
3 New insights into the managerial and leadership challenges of *developing strategic entrepreneurial capabilities across borders*.

In the Introduction chapter we look at why people and organizations venture across borders. We look briefly at mankind's proclivity to seek out newness and to learn and understand about what happens in different parts of the world. The Introduction lays out the main thematic structure of the book, defines the central concept of 'entrepreneurial knowledge' and argues that this type of knowledge lies at the heart of international venturing by firms. The structure we adopt in the analysis follows four thematic areas. Each of these thematic areas relates to a separate 'context' for venturing. In each context, international firms can create and share entrepreneurial knowledge. While there is academic literature that we use to discuss and debate these four contexts, we also use examples, and in-depth insights from published cases to reinforce our learning about what goes on in each of these contexts. I have been very creative and have labeled these contexts: A, B, C and D. I thought about some other labels but for the purposes of this analysis held these labels in place. But please note: I have never heard a manager in an international firm talk about contexts A, B, C or D. These simply are labels for our analytical purposes and ones that you are free to change and adapt as you see fit!

Once we have established our understanding of these four contexts, we consider the strategic challenge of integration across and between entrepreneurial contexts in international firms, and what this means for the 'Venturing Workforce' and the leaders of these companies. Think of each of these contexts as a separate optical lens. It is when we line up all of the four lenses that we see the phenomenon clearly. It is this that allows us to fully appreciate how international firms are the world's most powerful – and fascinating – entrepreneurial force.

A word of caution: this book is not (and cannot be for space reasons!) an exhaustive and comprehensive literature review. There has been such a tremendous amount of academic research and writing on the topics discussed in the book and I deliberately draw on a wide range of literature to support the core arguments and learning points. I have selected literature that I have found most inspiring, insightful and useful; research that aligns with the key points in each chapter.

I also draw on my own research as well as eight cases on technology-intensive companies that I have developed with co-authors in different countries and used in classes with business students in different countries. These eight cases are real-world situations of various types of private-sector international firms based in various countries. None of them are anonymized and the cases are reproduced in full in the Appendix. Teaching notes for all of the cases are available through Ivey Publishing. Each case required a decision to be made about how to pursue a specific opportunity in an international setting. Apologies in advance if I have not cited your work or case and please do get in touch if you feel your work could be cited in any future editions of this book. At the end of each chapter in the book I also suggest other cases that can be used in class or in individual analysis to explore the themes of the chapter.

I have presented the eight cases in order of size, starting with the smallest in terms of numbers of employees (at the time the case was written), up to the largest. In the smallest case, *Expatica*, we have an opportunity to get inside the strategic thinking of a Dutch born-global firm at the precise moment in its evolution when the owner-founders needed to decide on how to balance internationalization and product development in order to get beyond a break-even point. The case should resonate with those who have moved countries in their careers, as the firm's mission was to provide information and services to expatriates living abroad. The case also highlights the challenges of aggressive international entrepreneurship, and the issues in balancing many commitments in terms of geography and product lines with limited resources. In the next case, *Roq.ad*, we get insights into challenges facing a fast-growing German-based firm seeking to compete in the rapidly-expanding ad-tech industry. One of the main questions facing the leaders of the firm was how to evolve the core business model from an agency model towards one based on the technology being developed. The firm had set up a near-shore operation in neighboring Poland in order to drive technology development. How should the leaders of the company plan the path forward in terms of international expansion?

In the *Time Out Group* case, a new CEO to the UK-headquartered company has led significant changes in organizational and business systems. He had successfully led the firm to an initial public offering (IPO) but was facing numerous challenges in how to return the company back to profitability using international resources and international opportunities springing up around the world. The firm had embarked on a digital transformation strategy and had allocated a significant proportion of the IPO proceeds for this. But it also had seen impressive growth in foreign initiatives that involved providing hospitality experiences directly to clients. How to balance these initiatives going forward in a highly competitive global environment?

The next two cases on *Infusion Development Corporation* and *Infusion's Greenfield subsidiary in Poland* are clearly about the same Canadian-based company. However, they take very different perspectives on the evolving international strategy of the company. The first Infusion case looks at the 'big picture'; how the company quite literally went from zero to 50 million US$ in revenue (and over 300 employees around the world) within a ten-year period. International venturing was a central theme in this journey as the company grew initially from the United States to Canada, and then to India, Dubai, London and Poland. Alongside the trials and tribulations during this journey, the leaders had to grapple with the issue of how to implement an organizational management layer that would provide a platform for the company to win ever-larger deals in foreign markets. The second Infusion case on Poland is set a decade after the formation of the company and charts the specific sequence of events before, during and after the company's establishment of a new Green-field subsidiary in Poland. What is really interesting here is how the leaders of the company were able to learn from their experiences in international venturing over the previous decade when planning and executing their strategy for Poland. Of critical importance to the success of the Polish investment was top-level management's attention to the environment 'on the ground' in Poland in terms of human capital and skills pools that the company wanted to tap into. Furthermore, the leaders were personally involved in orchestrating an induction and integration phase to make sure the new recruits would be able to deliver global projects while also helping to grow the subsidiary in the near term.

Moving along, the *Tesla* case takes a focused look at one aspect of the US-based company's venturing in South and East Asia. In particular, the case examines the circumstances surrounding the company's decision to enter Singapore, as well as the decision to then pull out of Singapore less than a year later. Given that the circumstances for making a success of an investment in Singapore seemed favorable, it is very interesting that the company then put a spotlight on China as a target for investment, where the circumstances appeared – on paper at least – less favorable. However, the company was able to use its entrepreneurial spirit and its learning and know-how from other markets to make a go of it in China.

The final two cases concern much larger, older and more established international firms, 3M and Xerox. Despite the fact that these firms had had 'winning formulas' that had clearly worked well in the past, in different ways they both found themselves facing critical decisions in how to develop new capabilities in order to continue to be competitive in international markets. In the case on *3M in Taiwan*, the country manager for the company in Taiwan has been alerted to an opportunity in the host country for re-developing one of the company's existing technologies for a new product line. However, there was a lack of experience in how this could be achieved, knowledge of the market was very patchy, and if the country manager took on the initiative but failed, the subsidiary could damage or lose its reputation. Despite these issues, the case also highlights aspects of the corporation's organizational systems and culture that would facilitate risk-taking and innovation by managers in foreign markets a long way from the corporate headquarters. And finally, in the case on *Xerox Innovation Group (XIG)*, the challenge is very much a strategic one. The corporation has sensed the need to develop new competences in the area of providing advanced services to global accounts. As a traditionally product-oriented firm, the question is: how should the company realize these ambitions? The role of the company's Innovation Group is center-stage and, indeed, new capabilities in customer-centricity and services-orientation are challenges faced by the group. On top of this, the company is aware of new opportunities for expanding its innovation capabilities around the world into new locations, and wonders if this can be done as part of spearheading its continued drive into services. This case can lead to an interesting reflection and discussion on related vs. unrelated diversification and of how to assess the best way of venturing into new industrial segments for clients that are themselves global.

When analyzing each of these cases please ask yourself: what would you do if you were the key manager in the situation? And, why would you take that route of action?

I hope the concepts and ideas put forward in this book will help you develop approaches for answering these questions and deal strategically with the issues confronting the companies in the cases. Moreover, while the ideas put forward are there to be thought-provoking, they also are there to be discussed and challenged. I hope you will read with a critical and open mind and come up with some new questions that have been overlooked by the academic community after engaging with this book. It would be wonderful if some new research questions, themes and topics for business school research and dissertations arise as a consequence of the ideas and case material put forward here. Similarly, managers and consultants may look at their employers and clients in a new way after reading this book and it is hoped this will lead to improved competitiveness and performance for these companies, as well as for the careers of the individuals concerned.

I trust you enjoy the book as much as I enjoyed writing it. I am grateful for the gracious comments made by some current and former colleagues and students on the perspective I put forward. It is no coincidence that these people all live and work in a different country to that in which they were born. They are true international venturers. This book is dedicated to all who venture abroad in search of entrepreneurial knowledge, to the memory of Antoine van Veldhuizen, to the countless managers and leaders in international firms who have given their time to talk with me over the years and also to Alan Whicker and *Tomorrow's World* many moons ago for making such inspiring TV. I express my gratitude to the staff at Routledge and also to Ivey Publishing for permissions to reproduce the eight cases used in this book. All author royalties from this book are donated to UNICEF.

Christopher Williams, Durham, Spring 2017

Notes

1 For a fascinating listen to Alan Whicker's adventures you might like to listen to the audiobook: 'Journey of a Lifetime', A. Whicker, 2009, HarperCollins Publishers Ltd.
2 For an historical (and fun) insight into this you may like to refer to Raymond Baxter and James Burke. *Tomorrow's World*. Edited by Michael Latham, 1970, British Broadcasting Corporation or numerous clips on YouTube.

1
Introduction

In Search of a Better Deal

Over the course of history, man has never stood still. There is something about us that drives us to travel to far-off lands in search of a better deal. From the legendary travelers of the ancient Greeks and Polynesians, through the traveling merchants of the silk route between China and Europe, and on to the Vikings, Muhammad al-Idrisi, Marco Polo and Columbus, human beings have taken it upon themselves to seek out new pastures in a quest for scientific advancement, knowledge, profit and/or power (Obregón, 2001). And this is not just restricted to powerful peoples and those with military strength. A former colleague of mine, Richard Reed, once drove a Land Rover Defender around the planet. Along with friend, Dwyer Rooney, they drove from London to Sydney, taking in 25 countries in 12 months. They converted a second-hand Defender from mode of transport into a combined vehicle + sleeping space + cooking and dining space, crossing Iran during heightened tension around the country's nuclear plans, weaving through Pakistan during political unrest due to the murder of a local tribal leader, navigating the relentless bureaucracy of China, and journeying into Myanmar at the time of the ruling junta's house arrest of Aung San Suu Kyi. Why did he do it? Let's ask him:

I was once told that travellers are either running away from something or trying to find something, and it's probably true. With every exploration it has provided perspective, and no more so than the journey from London to Sydney. In our cramped and un-air-conditioned sweat-box, every day we experienced something new, and depending on your outlook, on your own constitution, it could be utterly breathtaking. You can read or watch the adventures of others, but discovering with your own eyes, drawing your own conclusions from your own experience is priceless. On most journeys, paradoxically, you're discovering yourself: your capacity for constant flux; problem solving; vastly different social and environmental interactions that test your fortitude; and the realisation of how immensely fortunate you are. Even from this paragraph, my mind is transported from my desk in Australia all over the world on previous adventures, and these snippets of life mean more to me than any physical asset I could ever possess[1]

Richard Reed (April 2017)

People don't stay in one place. And neither do organizations, especially ones of a competitive nature. Firms have found out that they can compete better by seeking and exploiting new opportunities at great distance from their initial physical starting point. As part of Richard and Dwyer's adventure from London to Sydney, they visited Land Rover dealerships and mechanics in every country they drove through. As they went they wrote monthly updates for *Land Rover Monthly*, a Land Rover enthusiasts' magazine, sharing their story with other Land Rover fans around the world. It turns out that Land Rover (the company) had got to these locations first! The Land Rover company had already internationalized, taking its products, technology and brand with it. As a result of the company's internationalization, customers and dealers around the world became loyal to the brand; there was global diffusion of the underlying technology, and global sharing of know-how related to the use of the technology in diverse driving conditions (Chapman, 2013). Indeed, dealers had sprung up in all kinds of fascinating places. In one sense, Richard and Dwyer's drive around the planet was an exploration of this particular global community, the creation of which had already been spearheaded by a private sector, for profit, company.

Indeed, it was over half a century earlier that Land Rover had pursued *international entrepreneurship*. It had *ventured into international markets* with its first official launch at the Amsterdam Motor Show in 1948. But what do we mean by these terms? What do we mean by international entrepreneurship and venturing? Academic definitions of these constructs have evolved in the past 25 or so years as the research literature has grown (Coviello et al., 2011). Back in 1989, Patricia McDougall spoke about international entrepreneurship in terms of the study of "international new ventures or start-ups that, from their inception, engage in international business" (McDougall, 1989: 387). Oviatt and McDougall (1994: 49) continued in this vein, defining an international new venture as a business organization that "from inception, seeks to derive significant competitive advantage from the use of resources from and the sale of outputs to multiple countries". Zahra and George (2002: 261) described the wider phenomenon of international entrepreneurship as a "process of creatively discovering and exploiting opportunities that lie outside a firm's domestic markets in the pursuit of competitive advantage". Oviatt and McDougall (2005: 540) described international entrepreneurship as: "the discovery, enactment, evaluation, and exploitation of opportunities – across national borders – to create future goods and services".

We have, from those earlier definitions, the notion of the international new venture itself, as well as the notion of the phenomenon of entrepreneurship in an international context from which specific international ventures arise (Coviello et al., 2011). Some of the technology-intensive companies we discuss in this book, such as Expatica and Roq.ad, were small-sized companies that indeed sought resources and/or sales in international markets at or soon after inception. Other cases we will discuss, such as 3M and Xerox, were much larger, well-established and highly internationalized companies, but still initiating and co-ordinating new projects to hunt down and exploit opportunities in international markets. And in between these poles, we will discuss cases of companies that were neither big nor small, such as Infusion Development Corporation and Time Out Group. In these cases, the companies had started to internationalize into a few select countries but faced various strategic and organizational pains. They were confronted by significant challenges in how to maintain an entrepreneurial spirit, develop their technology and grow internationally.

In their review of the international entrepreneurship field, Keupp and Gassmann (2009: 617) note how "none of these [previous] conceptual foundations of entrepreneurship depends on firm size – opportunities can be recognized and exploited by both small and large firms". I agree and will use this point throughout this book. Our notion of venturing in international firms extends from small, new ventures seeking international advantage from the outset (da Rocha et al., 2017), through to small- and medium-sized enterprises (SMEs) with a narrow but established presence in international markets (Dimitratos et al., 2010; Turunen and Nummela, 2017), through to the large, highly internationalized giants. I will use the term 'multinational enterprise' (or 'MNE') and international firm interchangeably in this book to refer to all of these categories of firms as long as they have assets in more than one country. Across the spectrum, we find international firms (MNEs) seeking to create future goods and services in new areas while extending beyond existing geographic markets where they had a presence.

In Search of Better Theory

Various theoretical frameworks have been used in research on how firms venture in international markets. These indeed can be used to analyze aspects of the phenomena we discuss in this book and the situations in the cases in the Appendix. They include resource-based theory (Barney, 1991; Penrose, 1959), transaction-cost and internalization theories (Buckley and Casson, 1976; Hennart, 1982; Rugman, 1980; Williamson, 1991), evolutionary theory (Kogut and Zander, 1993; Verbeke, 2003), institutional theory (North, 1990; Powell and DiMaggio, 2012; Scott, 1995), social network theory (Zhou et al., 2007), principal-agent theory (Eisenhardt, 1989a; George et al., 2005) and others. Despite all these tremendous contributions to human thinking, there is no single unified theory that explains all things entrepreneurial *and* all things international.

Consequently, the field of international entrepreneurship has not been without criticism. As Dimitratos and Plakoyiannaki (2003) and Jones et al. (2011) pointed out, the field is fragmented, but it is still relatively young and is growing. Jones et al. (2011) documented a comprehensive inventory of research in the field of international entrepreneurship – based on work published between 1989 and 2009 – to help with theorizing in the field. They identified three domains: entrepreneurial internationalization, international comparisons of entrepreneurship, and comparative entrepreneurial internationalization. Entrepreneurial internationalization relates to studies concerned with entrepreneurship that crosses international borders. The focus here has been on venture types, internationalization patterns and influences, networks and social capital, organizational issues and entrepreneurship per se. International comparisons of entrepreneurship consists of research examining country differences pertaining to entrepreneurs and entrepreneurship. It also encompasses research on cultural differences of entrepreneurs, looking at these differences across countries. Work on comparative entrepreneurial internationalization examines venture types and patterns of internationalization but comparing these across countries. The logic and ideas of this book fall squarely into the first domain identified by Jones et al. (2011). Our principal aim is not to compare entrepreneurial phenomena across countries. But we will examine internationalization, networks, organizational issues and entrepreneurial dynamics in different types of firms.

While we fall squarely into the first of Jones et al.'s (2011) categories, where do we stand in terms of core theory in our discussion? Will we be as fragmented as the literature is? In short, no. Instead, we will be developing one central theoretical perspective throughout the book – that of the internationally venturing firm as a *guided heterarchy* (Hedlund, 1994; Lee and Williams, 2007; Nonaka et al., 2006). In essence, there is a knowledge-based underpinning to all we do in this book. According to the knowledge-based view, firms specialize in the creation and transfer of knowledge. Their efficiency in so doing relative to other firms is a key factor when making strategic choices (Kogut and Zander, 1993). We will draw from, and build on, concepts related to 'heterarchical' organization, as well as on a knowledge-based view of the entrepreneurial process as it pertains to international venturing.

The starting point for this approach is embedded in the broadly accepted definition of the field of entrepreneurship research developed by Venkataraman (1997) and Shane and Venkataraman (2000). This is given as "the scholarly examination of how, by whom, and with what effects opportunities to create future goods and services are discovered, evaluated, and exploited" (Shane and Venkataraman, 2000: 218). What is embedded in here is the notion of entrepreneurship as a process of discovery, evaluation, and exploitation of opportunities (Shane and Venkataraman, 2000). What is not captured here is the international nature of what we are looking at. Both process and international elements were later captured by Oviatt and McDougall (2005: 540), as noted above: "the discovery, enactment, evaluation, and exploitation of opportunities – across national borders – to create future goods and services".

So why a knowledge-based stance? I argued in my PhD and in various academic articles published since that a particular type of knowledge will underpin this entrepreneurial process. Harnessing and managing this type of knowledge in international firms deserves careful appraisal and analysis. We will refer to knowledge that underpins the entrepreneurial process as *entrepreneurial knowledge* (Lee and Williams, 2007; Williams, 2009; Williams and Lee, 2011a). Not to put too fine a point on it, entrepreneurial knowledge is gold dust for international companies.

In Search of Entrepreneurial Knowledge

In order for entrepreneurial knowledge to underpin the entrepreneurial process it must provide some benefit to that process. It provides benefit by allowing awareness of untapped opportunities to be shared, by allowing potential solutions to opportunities to be developed, and by allowing learning from outcomes to take place across the company (Williams, 2009; Williams and Lee, 2011a). Furthermore, managers in all types of firms need to understand *international* entrepreneurial knowledge as they develop and deploy capabilities in search of growth. Globalization and the growing interconnectivity of nations and people (Dunning, 2002; Ghemawat, 2011; Guest, 2011) provides the environment for international entrepreneurial knowledge as it is created, shared and exploited by international firms.

First, *knowledge of untapped international opportunities* is needed. This forms the basis for sharing awareness of what an opportunity is and even why some people perceive it as being an opportunity in the first place, while others might not. Without a shared awareness of new opportunity, its evaluation within the company cannot effectively take place. Decisions about whether to allocate resources to pursuing it cannot be made. All of the cases highlighted in this book require some kind of decision to be made about specific opportunities. Scholars have highlighted the need for entrepreneurial theory to consider characteristics of opportunities in addition to actions of people involved in entrepreneurship. Indeed, it is the nexus of entrepreneur and opportunity that creates the foundation for new goods, services and methods of production to be developed (Eckhardt and Shane, 2003; Venkataraman, 1997). In the international firm, an opportunity with the potential to become a new and commercially viable good or service may exist in different places. It may only be an idea in the mind of the CEO based at headquarters. Or an alert individual located in an overseas subsidiary unit may spot the new opportunity for the first time. Time-honored research has shown how various actors then become involved in influencing the sharing of awareness and understanding of what the opportunity actually is (Burgelman and Sayles, 1986; Kanter, 1983). Later work argued how social networks become important mechanisms by which knowledge of opportunities is shared and then appraised (Ardichvili et al., 2003; Lee and Williams, 2007).

In the case of Toronto-headquartered *Infusion Development Corporation*, the company faced a crisis when Lehman Brothers, its primary client in New York at the time and the source of the majority of the company's revenues, decided to end its relationship with Infusion in favor of an offshoring strategy using companies in India. This could have been a disaster for Infusion, but the company did not see it as a disaster. It was seen as an opportunity, not as a doomsday scenario. Despite having no resources in India, no experience of delivery out of India, and no experience of recruiting talent in India, the company managed to convince Lehman Brothers that it could join it in its transition to India. It persuaded its most important client that it could accompany it on its own global journey. This was not without risk, but the company had limited choices at that point. More importantly, Infusion had recognized Lehman's move as an opportunity and pursued this opportunity full on.

In the case of Berlin-based *Roq.ad*, a job advertisement placed by the company alerted a technical team in Poland to the need the company had for software and programmatic solutions in the ad-tech industry. The ad-tech industry had become a global and fast-moving industry with many leading, international companies with large resource pools competing in global markets. For a company to compete in this market, technology and knowledge of cutting-edge (but legal) ways of linking users across multiple devices was needed. I personally, still find this fascinating: you can search for a product or service on one internet-connected device, and a short while later companies in that industry are advertising to you on other devices. In the Roq.ad case, the Polish team contacted Berlin, and the company responded by recruiting the whole team rather than just one individual! The company's near-shoring strategy was born. Roq.ad saw the Poznan team as an opportunity for enhancing the company's core technological competence and it also – just like Infusion in India – pursued the opportunity full on.

In the case of *3M in Taiwan*, the overseas subsidiary manager in the Taiwan office was alerted to the potential application of hydrocolloid dressing to treat acne. The corporation had ownership rights over the hydrocolloid dressing technology which previously had been developed centrally within the company. However, the company had never manufactured the product in a format that could be sold 'over the counter' to acne sufferers in East Asia. The product would normally come in jumbo-sized rolls, totally inappropriate for use on customers' faces! And it had not been tested for this purpose or marketed for this purpose in any of the 3M subsidiaries around the world. The subsidiary not only identified this opportunity, but it spearheaded an initiative to develop the new product and market it in East Asia.

Second, *knowledge of international solutions to international opportunities is needed*. Resources and capabilities spread out across borders need to be harnessed in new ways in order for international firms to seize new opportunities. Clearly, not all newly identified opportunities can be – or should be – pursued. Some may be inappropriate and inconsistent with the strategy of the company. Others may be deemed too risky. Yet others might be seen as too expensive to finance or incurring an opportunity cost that the company is not willing to bear. But without knowledge about how an opportunity might be pursued, and what resources and capabilities the company will need to harness the opportunity, the company will not be able to effectively decide whether the risks are worth bearing, whether benefits outweigh the costs and whether the pursuit of the opportunity aligns with the current and future strategic direction of the company. Hence knowledge of solutions matters. This relates to how the allocation of resources for exploiting a specific opportunity might be achieved, whether resources predominantly should be sourced from inside the firm (i.e., internal resources) or from outside the firm with partnering firms or other organizations such as universities, non-governmental organizations (NGOs) or governments (i.e., external resources). The task of finding solutions to problems has been high-lighted by researchers as a central aspect of entrepreneurship within established firms (Ahuja and Morris Lampert, 2001; Hsieh et al., 2007). Schumpeter's (1934) seminal work on innovation referred to the 'new combination' in this respect. Knowledge of any solution first needs to be created and, second, needs to be shared within the firm in order for the firm to establish feasibility and viability. For large-scale opportunities, this inevitably involves knowledge transfer across international borders and across organizational levels.

In the case of *Expatica Communications*, an opportunity for the company to enter the online dating space was identified. The company had not previously competed in this space, having initially been set up as a service provider of information and assistance to expats living in The Netherlands. After expanding to over ten countries, including other Western European countries as well as South Africa and Russia, and having learnt a tremendous amount about expats and their needs, the company identified online dating as a potentially lucrative opportunity.

The solution to the opportunity lay in partnering with a global player in online dating, and forming a strategic alliance that would ultimately allow the company to reach over 100 countries in a short space of time. This was an order of magnitude greater in terms of numbers of countries from where the firm originally sought revenue. Pursuing this opportunity with internal resources at a time when the company was struggling to break even in its traditional lines of business would have jeopardized attempts to refine and hone those scarce internal resources for use in activities that would support the core business.

Third, not all opportunities are given a positive evaluation by managers. The vast majority are indeed not pursued, albeit after careful consideration. However, those that are, such as Infusion's move to set up in India to service Lehman Brothers, or 3M Taiwan's initiative to develop an acne dressing for the East Asian market, will end up as sources of vital knowledge for the company. The third element of entrepreneurial knowledge that we will refer to is *learning from outcomes*. When companies learn from outcomes of entrepreneurial initiatives across borders, they are, in effect, recognizing and sharing experiences of the effects of utilizing new combinations of resources (as 'solutions') to risky entrepreneurial opportunities.

Companies ask themselves inter-related questions: What worked well within the process of pursuing an entrepreneurial opportunity, and conversely, what did not work well? Why did outcomes occur the way they occurred? This reflection and objective sharing of knowledge to do with outcomes is critically important. First, it allows the firm to be responsive to new opportunities in the future (Corbett, 2007). Responsiveness matters because of the never-ending competitive threats in markets around the world. Second, it helps the firm overcome future 'learning traps' (Ahuja and Morris Lampert, 2001). Learning traps occur when firms become inhibited in their strategic learning, creativity and innovation; their learning is adaptive rather than generative (Minocha and Stonehouse, 2006; Senge, 1990). Third, feedback information interacts with how psychological feelings of 'grief' among those who have experienced a failed venture encourage individual entrepreneurs to apply their learning in new ventures (Shepherd, 2003). The recognition of grief after a failed venture is something that can apply to small-sized born-globals as well as managers who have become attached to ventures within larger organizations. Fourth, learning from outcomes helps guide the organization in future uncertain situations; failure is informative

(Minniti and Bygrave, 2001). Situations such as the ones faced by Infusion as they planned to enter India to service Lehman Brothers, 3M Taiwan's considerations for launching an acne dressing product, and Tesla's contemplations before entering China, are all inherently uncertain. Learning from outcomes of prior initiatives is vital in helping to deal with these uncertain situations.

We see an interesting development in the *Infusion* case, where the senior management team set up a 'Dragon's Den' initiative with the University of Waterloo in Canada in order to gain exposure to new opportunities arising through presentations made by students who were based, quite literally, on their doorstep. Only a small handful of all pitches were selected for further consideration and only two were mentioned in the case as having eventually received serious attention from Infusion's management and resource commitment. Similarly, one of the company's engineers providing support for Microsoft's mapping business approached Infusion's top management team with a proposal to develop Infusion's own capabilities in this area. The company became exposed to these opportunities in a relatively uncomplicated way. Those that then were pursued were done so in a way that generated a wealth of new knowledge from international markets. The company had a high learning orientation and was prepared to learn from outcomes of entrepreneurial initiatives.

Entrepreneurial knowledge can be seen as distinct from what we can refer to as production knowledge, i.e., knowledge about how to make and market existing goods and services. There are at least two important differences. First, entrepreneurial knowledge is not applied by the company to manufacture existing goods and services for current consumption by an existing market. Instead, entrepreneurial knowledge encompasses the knowledge underpinning the company's efforts to create future goods and services. Hence entrepreneurial knowledge is a precursor to production knowledge; without entrepreneurial knowledge underpinning the process of entrepreneurship, production of a new good or service will never take place, and production knowledge will never come about. While this is consistent with the definitions of international entrepreneurship given above, it also emphasizes a passage of time between phases of exploration and exploitation (March, 1991). As the senior management team at Infusion prepared for their expansion into Poland through a new Greenfield subsidiary in Krakow, they spent considerable time and effort collecting data from various alternative locations, visiting the country, networking and connecting with the .NET community in Poland. During this period, nothing was produced by resources in Poland for the company. The management team was investing in the generation of entrepreneurial knowledge.

Second, the aspect of entrepreneurial knowledge related to knowledge of opportunity and knowledge of solution to opportunity has no immediate financial value for the company. It cannot easily be sold as a product or service offering from the company to a buyer. Most entrepreneurial knowledge is tacit by nature. Admittedly, if the company is acquired by another, and the individual managers and employees all become employees of the new company, then entrepreneurial knowledge – as shared among them through prior explorative activities – also will be passed to the new owner. But the knowledge cannot be disentangled and sold by the current or new owner in the same sense that a product or service can. Indeed, in the case of Infusion's entry into Poland, the revenue-generating activities of the new team in Krakow did not start immediately after the decision was made to enter Poland with a Greenfield investment. Following months of effort on recruitment, a training and induction program lasting over two months took place. This involved all of the new recruits in Poland being sent to Toronto for training and mentoring. Only after this had taken place could the new capabilities in Poland be used for new revenue generation.

Controlling the Unpredictable: Heterarchy and Entrepreneurial Knowledge

So if we can appreciate that international firms constantly need to develop entrepreneurial knowledge across different countries, the question arises on how, organizationally, this can be achieved? What structures, managerial processes and control systems will be most effective at allowing an international firm to build capabilities in generating and harnessing entrepreneurial knowledge? We can approach this by looking at an international organization as both heterarchy and hierarchy. The heterarchical view suggests that international firms are networked organizations, even though they may have formalized hierarchical report lines and structure. The stream of literature underpinning this emphasizes dynamic heterarchy as an *alternative* to static organizational hierarchy[2].

A number of features are salient in a heterarchical form. First, there is an enabling of subsidiary co-participation in strategy formulation and innovation (Morgan and Whitley, 2003). Second, normative integration is used as the basis of control. This is where individuals are controlled and incentivized to act in the interests of the wider organization by sharing the same norms and values as managers in headquarters. This is often achieved by investment in rotations and socialization among managers and employees in different countries (Ghoshal and Nohria, 1989; Nohria and Ghoshal, 1994). Third, heterarchy allows for autonomy of work units, with authority emerging laterally (Stark, 1999). The emphasis within the heterarchical view is very much on informal organization and tolerating autonomous initiative and strategic thinking within all types of overseas subsidiary. In the case of the international firm, this means that overseas subsidiaries are given the rights to make important decisions for themselves without having to rely on headquarters (Williams and van Triest, 2009). Fourth, a heterarchical international firm has many and different kinds of international centers, with the potential for many of the company's foreign subsidiaries to play a key role in shaping strategy of the overall company. Last but not least, heterarchy supports experimentation and testing out new ideas within the firm (Hedlund and Rolander, 1990).

Given these characteristics, the idea of heterarchy has important implications for how we can understand entrepreneurial dynamics in an international firm. For example, autonomy provides a basis for overseas subsidiaries to become embedded in internal as well as external networks and to make their own decisions about how they become embedded and who they become embedded with. Autonomy also allows the subsidiary to make its own decisions with respect to how it develops its own capabilities (Young and Tavares, 2004). These are themes we see in the 3M Taiwan case in this book. Linking these two points, Garcia-Pont et al. (2009) described subsidiary embeddedness as a resource which subsidiary managers are able to influence on a day-to-day basis by manipulating resource dependencies and exerting lateral influence.

While heterarchy allows for foreign subsidiaries to adopt a strategic role (Hedlund and Rolander, 1990), top-level managers in headquarters also see their roles changing, becoming catalysts for knowledge sharing and transfer of re-combinable knowledge elements around the firm (Hedlund, 1994). Recent work has shown the importance of headquarters' involvement in enhancing the innovation impact of MNE units around the world (Ciabuschi et al., 2011). Such roles are still intrinsic to the N-form view of the international firm. In the N-form view, ". . . 'N' stands for 'new,' and 'novelty'" (Hedlund, 1994: 82). This N-form provides a basis of effective knowledge management through *combination rather than hierarchical division*, and therefore stands in opposition to the traditional M-form ('M' stands for multi-divisional) (Hedlund, 1994).

The heterarchical view provides a viable basis on which to understand entrepreneurial knowledge in the MNE. In other words, knowledge of opportunity, knowledge of solution to opportunity, and learning from outcomes, flow throughout the MNE because there are lateral networked relationships between managers in different countries (Haas and Cummings, 2015). The heterarchical view criticized the hierarchical nature of the strategy-structure paradigm[3] (Chandler, 1962) and shows that the diffusion of knowledge and innovation throughout the MNE happens because it is organized and governed as a network.

Nevertheless, these heterarchical and network structures represent a more complex control problem than traditional hierarchical structures suggest. While heterarchy displaces static organizational forms with flexibility and the potential for foreign subsidiaries to adopt strategic roles (Hedlund and Rolander, 1990), the MNE as a networked organization creates a great deal of scope for control problems to arise (Song, 2014; Williams and Lee, 2009b). Research has shown how foreign subsidiaries can become isolated and, when controlled in an inappropriate way given their role and the nature of the external environment, may end up as a burden to the MNE (Monteiro et al., 2008; Williams and Nones, 2009).

Hedlund's (1980) early study of six large Swedish MNEs showed how integration between headquarters and subsidiaries can be accomplished in an informal way when foreign subsidiaries are involved in strategic decision-making. Hedlund (1980) suggested eight ways to achieve this: (1) de-ritualizing the planning process, emphasizing dialogue with subsidiaries; (2) top subsidiary managers being more involved in formulating corporate strategy in specified areas; (3) regional, divisional or corporate-wide meetings and conferences being given strategic content; (4) communicating assumptions about environment conditions; (5) subsidiaries having a personal channel to headquarters; (6) transferring of personnel, rotating between headquarters and subsidiary; (7) managing directors sitting on boards of other subsidiaries; and (8) clarifying the role of subsidiary board directors (strategic decision-making or formality).

These – and similar – themes were extended in later work on knowledge integration and control within the MNE. For example, in Ghoshal and Nohria's (1989) study, the relation and governance style that is appropriate between headquarters and a subsidiary will be dependent on the specific environmental conditions and resource endowments in the subsidiary. Similarly, for Nobel and Birkinshaw (1998), the control mechanism used for an R&D subsidiary and the focus of communication (internal or external) will depend on the specific role of the subsidiary. Williams and Nones (2009) found that experience levels within the headquarters and subsidiary, and the use of training and rotation practices by the subsidiary, all act to counter isolation. Thus we see many of Hedlund's original ideas reformulated in later studies and portrayals of MNE organization (Song, 2014). For the purposes of our current analysis, integrating subsidiaries appropriately (and countering isolation) is essential to avoid situations where knowledge gaps and miscommunications arise between managers in different parts of the organization. For us, it is critically important to avoid situations where the flow of entrepreneurial knowledge around the firm is hindered.

While heterarchy provides an appropriate basis to understand how MNEs can control entrepreneurial activity and harness knowledge related to new opportunities, we must be careful not to go along with the line that heterarchy provides the only organizational solution for controlling activities in international venturing. Recent research highlights the importance of hierarchy and, in particular, the role of headquarters' managers within the MNE promoting innovation, facilitating knowledge flows, and guiding new ventures (Ambos and Mahnke, 2010; Ciabuschi et al., 2011; Egelhoff, 2010). The cases discussed throughout this book reveal that hierarchy does not need to be displaced and, indeed, should not be displaced.

In the smaller companies, such as Expatica, Roq.ad and Infusion, owner-founders and C-suite managers were instrumental in the decision-making process related to how the company's core technology needed to be developed and how new international opportunities were pursued. They were personally involved in developing knowledge of solution to opportunities and keen to learn from outcomes. Their involvement was a critical determinant of the ultimate outcome. This, you may argue, is something we might expect in smaller companies. However, in our cases, we also see C-suite managers making their presence felt in their company's international venturing efforts. In mid-size companies such as Time Out Group, the CEO was directly involved in all stages of the entrepreneurial process as it pertained to new international ventures and the use of the company's technology in new ventures. This required a lot of travel time and high commitment by the CEO and colleagues. And in the even larger cases, such as Tesla and Xerox, we see direct and personal involvement of the top management teams throughout the process of international venturing. They influence the ways of thinking about problems, the ways solutions to problems can be formulated and how the broader organization can learn from the firm's involvement in international venturing.

Thematic Structure of the Book

There is a multitude of ways for an international firm to set about identifying, valuing and capturing opportunity and developing entrepreneurial knowledge as it does so. In this book we use a framework of four contexts with which to analyze this venturing process. These contexts are defined by two dimensions. First, the venturing process may be driven by actors in a wide range of geographic locations. Some will be in the home country, some will be overseas. So the first dimension we consider is the driving force for the entrepreneurial process either being headquarters or dispersed/overseas subsidiary unit. Second, while large international firms tend to have deep pockets with which to undertake entrepreneurial projects, smaller international ventures and born-globals are more constrained. Nevertheless, both types are able to use externally-oriented alliances in addition to developing capabilities in-house when pursuing new opportunities. The second dimension for framing venturing in international firms relates to the primary resources used in entrepreneurial endeavor and whether these are internal or external to the firm.

The framework brings together various research streams relating to entrepreneurial phenomena in MNEs. Prior research has been restrictive when dealing with entrepreneurial phenomena involving MNEs, leading to a fragmented literature. In one thread, 'corporate' entrepreneurship is guided by strategic leaders of the firm (Dess et al., 2003; Guth and Ginsberg, 1990; Prahalad and Doz, 1981), emphasizing international venturing as a central feature of the company's strategy, espoused from the corporate headquarters (Dess et al., 1997; Ireland et al., 2003). Another stream of literature has explored 'dispersed' entrepreneurship in international firms. This examines how overseas subsidiaries engage in venturing and initiative-taking (Birkinshaw, 1997; Birkinshaw and Ridderstråle, 1999; Ghoshal and Bartlett, 1988; Lee and Williams, 2007; Verbeke et al., 2007). Looking at our second dimension, a stream of literature has emerged on internally-oriented venturing (Burgelman and Sayles, 1986; Garud and Van de Ven, 1992), while others have emphasized an external dimension to corporate venturing (Keil, 2002; Miles and Covin, 2002).

While these contributions have indeed been focused and insightful, any narrow approach comes with limitations. How do they explain the evolving story in companies such as Expatica where the emphasis for venturing shifted over time from an internal one to an external one? How do they explain the situation that evolved at Time Out Group where a subsidiary-driven initiative that was deeply embedded in a local host country was used in combination with headquarters-driven initiatives to turn the company around? I argue there are significant limitations in taking a narrow focus when studying venturing in international firms. First and foremost, narrowness leads to a lack of appreciation of the full extent of entrepreneurial capability within an organization as diverse as the international firm. Second, narrowness leads to an exclusion of the complex dynamics of the 'bigger picture' of venturing in international firms.

International firms, despite many being mature and large, need to engage in entrepreneurially-oriented strategy on an ongoing basis in order to rejuvenate and create new options (Hitt et al., 2001; Stopford and Baden-Fuller, 1994). For this to happen, the firm can emphasize entrepreneurship as part of an espoused, centrally-driven strategy. It can also happen by allowing entrepreneurial competences to be developed in locations around the world. Thus some aspects of international venturing may emanate from the center, as part of a prevailing headquarters-driven global strategy. And some aspects arise de-centrally, with opportunities being seized in foreign subsidiaries. We combine the dual questions of 'who drives international venturing?' and 'where do they get their resources to pursue international venturing?' to define the dimensions that form the thematic framework for our analysis in this book. Figure 1.1 shows this framework.

Introduction

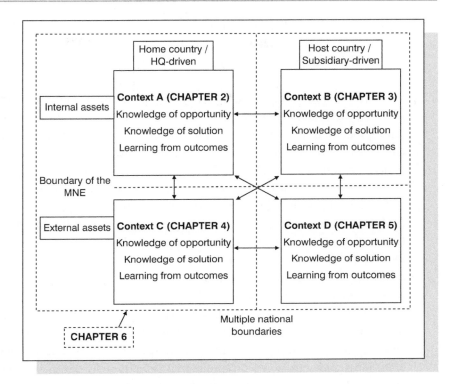

Figure 1.1 Thematic structure of this book (adapted from Williams and Lee, 2011a)

The Driving Force: Who Instigates the Search for Entrepreneurial Knowledge?

Much of the literature on venturing in large corporations has focused at firm – or corporate – level. The corporate entrepreneurship literature has shown how industry, organizational, leadership and performance factors combine to influence firm strategy in terms of emphasis on strategic renewal (Guth and Ginsberg, 1990; Zahra and George, 2002). The literature on strategic entrepreneurship has emphasized the importance of innovation, risk-taking and proactivity in corporate strategy, and argued that above-normal performance can be achieved when these elements are present in corporate strategy, especially when the firm is facing uncertainty and turbulence in its environment (Dimitratos et al., 2010; Hitt et al., 2001; Meyer and Heppard, 2000). This emphasis on innovation, risk-taking and proactivity at corporate level asserts that established firms can use corporate entrepreneurship as a deliberate way

17

of renewing themselves and turning themselves around (Miller, 1983; Miller and Friesen, 1982; Stopford and Baden-Fuller, 1994).

This deliberateness is also emphasized in the literature on entrepreneurial orientation (EO). This literature argues that firms can be analyzed in terms of their position on a notional continuum of entrepreneurial postures, or stances, ranging from passive (conservative) to aggressive (entrepreneurial) (Covin, 1991; Fombrun and Ginsberg, 1990; Lumpkin and Dess, 1996). These postures are carefully considered and intentional stances adopted by the strategic leaders of the organization as a way of providing direction for the organization. This extends to international EO, and has been shown to apply to small- and medium-sized enterprises (SMEs) as much as it does to much larger corporations (Knight, 2001). In this view, entrepreneurial initiatives are centrally-driven (Prahalad and Doz, 1981; Williams, 2009), aimed at competing on a global basis through direction from headquarters and a "transfer of knowledge from home base to subsidiaries" (Porter, 1986: 33).

On the other hand, research has shown how the process of entrepreneurship may arise in any location of the international firm. Managers and employees in overseas subsidiaries can spot new opportunities, generate ideas and start new entrepreneurial initiatives (Birkinshaw, 1997, 2000; Delany, 2000; Ghoshal and Bartlett, 1988). Birkinshaw (1997) defined entrepreneurial initiative as a "process . . . bounded by the identification of an opportunity at the front end and the commitment of resources to the undertaking at the back end" (Birkinshaw, 1997: 209). These 'subsidiary entrepreneurs' are embedded as much in the local host country as they are in the internal organizational environment of the MNE. In this sense, they operate in two worlds, in a *duality* (Kostova and Roth, 2002; Morgan and Kristensen, 2006; Nell et al., 2015). As Morgan and Kristensen (2006: 1467) noted: "within multinationals, actors are pressured to conform to the expectations of their home context whilst also being subjected to the transfer of practices from the home context of the MNE itself". Because of this unique position, they are able to act in an entrepreneurial way irrespective of any deliberateness in strategic entrepreneurship espoused by the corporate center. Subsidiary entrepreneurs take their own initiative.

According to Low (2001), entrepreneurship occurs "under conditions of uncertainty and tight resource constraint and is driven by individual initiative" (Low, 2001: 21). These conditions are typically encountered in distant overseas subsidiary units existing within a duality

(Kostova and Roth, 2002; Morgan and Kristensen, 2006; Nell et al., 2015); environmental turbulence and competitive actions make the situations uncertain, while the headquarters may prescribe tight budgetary and resource constraints. A phenomenon then arises whereby initiatives to exploit opportunities are started in one subsidiary, possibly for use only in that subsidiary. Nohria and Ghoshal (1997) referred to innovations of this type as 'local-for-local'. Alternatively, innovative initiatives can be started in one subsidiary and then diffused throughout the MNE for use in other parts of the MNE. Nohria and Ghoshal (1997) referred to this as 'local-for-global'[4]. We build on this to define dispersed entrepreneurship in the MNE in terms of initiative: i.e., *the outward diffusion of initiative from a subsidiary into the wider MNE*. This phenomenon is important as it provides a valuable source of new knowledge for building firm-specific advantages and altering strategic behavior (Andersson and Pahlberg, 1997). Initiatives act as a vehicle by which knowledge is created (opportunity identification) and applied (commitment and management of resources). Thus, a useful alternative way of analyzing the process of venturing in MNEs is at the subsidiary level, where mechanisms for knowledge creation and transfer across borders are in operation.

The Resources and Capabilities: How do we Create Entrepreneurial Knowledge?

Capabilities are the set of skills and competences needed by the firm to gain competitive advantage and outperform. In the current analysis we look at capabilities that will enable the firm to venture in international markets. These capabilities create entrepreneurial knowledge for the firm, allowing the firm to assess where new opportunities lie, how the firm may exploit them, and how the firm can learn from what happens next. Sometimes these capabilities already exist in the firm, waiting to be unleashed. Sometimes the firm needs to draw on them from external organizations and outside sources that are not directly owned or controlled by the firm. So this second dimension for analysis relates to the degree to which already-existing, internal resources and capabilities are utilized in the search for entrepreneurial knowledge in an international firm. The implication is that the firm has to consider how these assets might be used versus those available through various modes of collaboration and transacting with external actors (Chesbrough, 2006; Keil, 2002; Miles and Covin, 2002; Roberts and Berry, 1985).

In support of this, researchers have noted how the focus of venturing strategy can take two principal orientations: internal and external (Roberts and Berry, 1985; Miles and Covin, 2002). Large international firms have the financial means to undertake internal and external modes of venturing at the same time (Burgelman and Sayles, 1986), such as internal and external R&D investment (Narula, 2001). We see this in the case of Tesla for instance. But we should also not ignore the fact that smaller entrepreneurial start-ups are not prohibited from drawing on internal and external capabilities in the quest for entrepreneurial knowledge. Note the case of Expatica in this book.

Internally-oriented venturing is formed around existing organizational structures and resources (Burgelman and Sayles, 1986; Garud and Van de Ven, 1992). Burgelman's (1983) model of *internal corporate venturing* (ICV) in large firms highlighted interaction between multiple internal participants, particularly those from R&D functions under the control of the firm. Garud and Van de Ven (1992) described internal venturing in terms of employees persisting on risky projects despite negative outcomes, particularly when the level of ambiguity is high and slack resources are available. In this stream of literature, change is brought about because employees of the firm (including those involved in R&D) are encouraged to make discoveries, generate knowledge and then work towards the architecture of a new product–market future for the firm in conjunction, in the most part, with other employees.

On the other hand, externally-oriented venturing occurs where the primary focus for investment is outside of the firm's existing asset base. Scholars have highlighted the trend towards outward technology transfer and commercialization: *external corporate venturing* (ECV) is a way for an international firm to acquire new knowledge while managing risk, thereby acting as an attractive source of firm renewal (Keil, 2002). This includes modes such as mergers, acquisitions, joint ventures and alliances, corporate venture capital and disposals (e.g., Dittrich et al., 2007; Hayward, 2002; MacMillan et al., 1986; Narula, 2001; Rothaermel, 2001; Weber and Weber, 2007). One common reason for seeking entrepreneurial capabilities from outside is the lack of entrepreneurial capabilities inside. For example, Rothaermel (2001) showed how incumbent firms can benefit by collaborating with new entrants who bring new technology and know-how, and where incumbent assets are complementary, i.e., the incumbent contains assets that new entrants do not possess in terms of commercialization of new technology.

External venturing has benefits for firms that internal venturing may not be able to provide. As Roberts and Berry (1985: 5) highlighted: "In contrast to internal development, acquisition can take weeks rather than years to execute . . . [offering] a much lower initial cost of entry into a new business". A number of scholars have highlighted the performance advantages of various forms of joint ventures and alliances (Inkpen and Tsang, 2005; Lee and Beamish, 1995), and others have demonstrated the importance of acquisitions to firm development and growth (Anand et al., 2005). Koruna (2004) drew attention to the need for external acquisition of technology because of its increasingly complex nature. Weber and Weber (2007) showed how relational capital (consisting of social capital and knowledge relatedness) between corporate venture units and the external recipients of venture funds can influence the venture's performance.

Internal venturing had traditionally been given more attention by scholars than external venturing (Keil, 2002). Nevertheless, knowledge and resource acquisition has received increasing attention in the recent literature, particularly in the international context (Ethiraj et al., 2005; Nerkar and Roberts, 2004).

The preceding discussion leads to a thematic structure for this book. We will explore venturing in international firms using a framework having as axes: (1) the driving force for entrepreneurship being home-country headquarters or dispersed/overseas unit(s); and (2) the resources and capabilities used in entrepreneurial endeavor being internal or external. Each quadrant within this framework represents a distinct context – with its own idiosyncratic characteristics – and different implications for knowledge of opportunity, knowledge of solution to opportunity, and learning from outcomes.

Central to the framework is the idea that the components of entre-preneurial knowledge develop in various distinct contexts. They are not confined to one particular manifestation of corporate entrepreneurship, such as subsidiary initiative. The international nature of the MNE not only provides a basis for these contexts, it also raises the issue of uncer-tainty. Knowledge of opportunities cannot be predicted in advance, the outcomes from deploying any specific solution to an opportunity cannot be foretold, and a large part of the learning from outcomes will always be unforeseen. Each context can be seen as a solution space. Problems are paired with solutions, and knowledge sharing becomes concentrated (Hsieh et al., 2007).

Each context will warrant a different chapter in this book. Chapters 2, 3, 4 and 5 will explore Contexts A, B, C and D individually. Finally, the strategic issues of how to co-ordinate between contexts, how entrepreneurial knowledge may form in a given context that *might* be useful in other contexts, and the challenges of leadership and managing in international firms operating in all of these contexts will be discussed in Chapter 6. Chapter 6 will use an integrative approach to examine the implications for venturing in international firms across these multiple contexts.

Notes

1 You can read about Richard and Dwyer's adventures in "An Antipodean Adventure": www.smashwords.com/books/view/650125
2 Early work on heterarchy was critical of four assumptions made in the hierarchical view: (1) pre-specified and stable relationships; (2) instrumentality and additivity in parts; (3) uni-directionality and universality; and (4) the coincidence of action, knowledge and people hierarchies. These assumptions were criticized by Hedlund as an inadequate representation of the modern MNE; hierarchy becomes strained by: (1) the need to co-ordinate on product, geographical and functional lines; (2) control systems other than formal structure becoming more important (e.g., sharing goals, strong cultures); (3) the need for lateral communications between subsidiaries; (4) flexibility, competence becoming more important than internalization. More recent research has examined inter-personal knowledge flows in MNEs as an important strategic process. Haas and Cummings (2015), for instance, found that position-based structural differences between employees present greater barriers to knowledge flows in the MNE than those that are person-based (i.e., those based on demographic differences).
3 Bartlett and Ghoshal (2003: 270) referred to this as a "dehumanizing management paradigm."
4 Nohria and Ghoshal (1997) also discussed two other forms: 'center-for-global', where sensing and response are orchestrated at the corporate center but implementation is made in a wide number of units around the world; and 'global-for-global', where many organizational units are involved in sensing the opportunity, creating the response to it and then implementing that response.

2

'Context A' – Headquarters-driven Venturing: A Strategic Direction for Internal Capabilities

Context A is a domain for venturing in international firms where the driving force for venturing is predominantly headquarters and where the company seeks to develop and recombine its own resources and capabilities in order to accomplish the change and rejuvenation it wants. This context emphasizes two important themes. First, there is a role for top-level headquarters' managers in recognizing opportunities, assessing and evaluating them, and choosing new strategic options as a response to competitive challenges. Second, there is a reliance on pre-existing, company-owned and controlled internal resources and capabilities for exploring and exploiting new opportunities around the world.

In this context, entrepreneurship is a phenomenon where the ingredients of innovation, risk-taking and proactivity are present in the corporate strategy of the international firm. It is this that forms a basis for performance (Rauch et al., 2009). This is not just a phenomenon in large firms such as 3M, Google, IBM and Virgin Group. These types of firms were commonly used to develop and illustrate management thought on international corporate entrepreneurship. However, small firms and start-ups (Dimitratos et al., 2010), such as the Expatica and Roq.ad cases discussed in this book, also explored opportunities outside the home country under the direct guidance of their top management teams. The key point is that these strategic behaviors are directed and guided by central managers operating at the core (Ciabuschi et al., 2011; Hart, 1992; Isenberg, 2008) – normally the global headquarters – of the firm. According to Bartlett and Ghoshal (2003: 265), the primary value added of top-level managers involves: "creating and embedding a sense of direction, commitment, and challenge to people throughout the organization." According to McKern and Naman (2003), despite the need to delegate responsibility to strategic business unit (SBU) leaders in diversified, international firms, the degree of delegation does have limits. In other words, there are certain functions, even in these much larger firms, where the corporate center needs to retain responsibility and where its interventions matter because of 'market failure' at the SBU level (McKern and Naman, 2003).

Increasingly we see headquarters-driven venturing arising in companies in emerging and transition economies as well. Home-country managers within firms in emerging markets are becoming adept at using foreign-market knowledge to enhance innovative performance in their home country (Williams et al., 2016).

The Driving Force: Strategic Leaders Guiding Strategy with an Entrepreneurial Component

Context A relates to how the strategic leaders of the international firm develop the company's strategy with an entrepreneurial component (Bartlett and Ghoshal, 2003). Headquarters' managers, based in the home country of the company, are responsible for assessing the need for – and viability of – an entrepreneurial component to the company's strategy. They set the strategic posture for the company and make decisions regarding management structures, communication channels, budgets and specific targets for centrally-driven initiatives. In some instances this posturing and strategic preparedness can take many years to cement. In the case of Asahi Breweries of Japan, three successive regimes of leader (Murai from 1982 to 1986, Higuchi from 1986 to 1992 and Seto from 1992 to 1998) were involved in different ways in order to take the company from a purely home-country brand to one that is well-known all over the world (Williams et al., 2013). As this study showed, the transformational leadership provided by Murai formed the foundation for foreign direct investment made by the company over ten years later! In other situations, top-level headquarters' managers must respond to the situation confronting the firm more quickly. We see a formidable entrepreneurial component to the strategic direction set by Julio Bruno in the Time Out Group case in this book. Following successive years of financial loss, as well as an intensely competitive environment, entrepreneurially-minded strategic direction was necessary.

An entrepreneurial component to corporate strategy may relate to creating an entrepreneurial mindset in the company (Dess and Lumpkin, 2005), and emphasizing new products and services that need to be developed. It may also relate to internal process change and improving the efficiency of the company (Prahalad and Doz, 1981; Van de Ven, 1986). The point is that the authority for directing innovation and change resides with headquarters (Ciabuschi et al., 2011; Egelhoff, 2010; Hart, 1992; Prahalad and Doz, 1981) and this often is driven out on a global basis (Williams, 2009). Transformational leadership by headquarters' managers lies behind much of the change and rejuvenation we see in dynamically-evolving MNEs (Teece, 2014).

Headquarters' managers in the international firm will be closely in touch with the global environment; this defines the circumstances in which strategic decisions are made (McKern and Naman, 2003; Shepherd et al., 2015). Decisions made by headquarters in this context determine the overall entrepreneurial orientation (EO) of the company (Covin, 1991; Fombrun and Ginsberg, 1990; Lumpkin and Dess, 1996; Miller and Friesen, 1982; Shepherd et al., 2015). According to the EO view, any firm can be positioned and characterized on a continuum ranging from 'passive' (or conservative) to 'aggressive' (or entrepreneurial). When a firm is 'aggressive', it inherently has the ingredients of innovation, risk-taking and proactivity present in its corporate strategy (Lumpkin and Dess, 1996; Wiklund, 1999; Williams and Lee, 2009a). Covin and Miller (2014) showed how the field of EO has increasingly taken on an international dimension and how the role of the top management team's proclivity for innovation, risk-taking and proactivity has been adopted by scholars in research on EO in international contexts.

There are various manifestations of adopting an 'aggressive' EO in an international firm. Any or all of the following may be signs that headquarters' managers are pursuing an aggressive EO. First, headquarters may be seen – quite visibly – to be driving new global initiatives. Williams (2009) investigated headquarters-driven global initiatives, defining them as a process of opportunity identification and exploitation spanning many countries. A global initiative in the MNE is a new allocation of resources to meet an identified (but untapped) opportunity that spans many, if not all, of the countries in which the MNE operates. Thus a global initiative in the MNE has two key components: an identified opportunity that spans a large number of countries simultaneously; and a new allocation of firm resources to exploiting opportunity.

Second, headquarters may seek to orchestrate innovative assets globally. This can be done in various ways, including by establishing new formal R&D subsidiaries around the world (Kuemmerle, 1999) or expanding the formal mandate of existing subsidiaries to include responsibility for product development and R&D. The case on the establishing of SAP's R&D lab in China is an interesting example here; headquarters' managers ultimately had to make a choice between competing locations in China (Kumar et al., 2009). Kuemmerle (1999) showed that MNEs can seek to establish R&D operations in countries where there is a strong science base, this being a motive to develop new firm-specific advantages. These decisions are important strategic investments and will be driven by headquarters' managers; they are sensitive decisions that cannot be taken lightly because remote R&D operations in foreign countries are difficult to establish and oversee (Berry, 2014; Ecker et al., 2013). Headquarters can seek to set up and drive a new venture within the company, involving an R&D aspect and a commercialization aspect (Garud and Van de Ven, 1992). The 'sponsoring' by corporate managers may happen as a consequence of wider environmental changes and will take effect as a change in direction of a venture (Garud and Van de Ven, 1992). This also can involve a decision to exit a venture (Shepherd et al., 2015), as happened in the cases of Tesla in Singapore and Infusion in India in this book.

Third, the headquarters may drive change in the fundamental business model of the company. While scholars continue to disagree on a definition of 'business model', there is widespread agreement that a business model is distinct from a new product or service, and is not the same unit of analysis as a firm, industry or network (Zott et al., 2011). A business model explains "how firms 'do business'" (Zott et al., 2011: 1020). Developing and adapting a business model is a particular concern for small international companies, and something that is the responsibility of centrally-located founders and managers of the firm. This is a key theme in the Expatica and Roq.ad cases in this book. However, larger firms must also re-assess their fundamental business model from time to time, especially in times of crisis and intense competitive pressure – as was the case of IBM in the 1990s (Dittrich et al., 2007).

The Resources and Capabilities: Tangible and Intangible Assets to Underpin Strategic Aggressiveness

The emphasis in Context A is on how centrally-driven corporate strategy can utilize and develop internal capabilities in search of entrepreneurial knowledge. These capabilities may be located in the home country or abroad, and may include a range of different types of asset, including tangible and intangible assets. These assets are under the hierarchical control of the firm. An important literature in this respect emerged in the 1980s on Internal Corporate Venturing (ICV) (Burgelman, 1983; Burgelman and Sayles, 1986). ICV stresses the importance of large-scale entry into, and continued commitment for, new ventures and requires the allocation of dedicated venture managers and sponsors to new opportunities (Dess and Lumpkin, 2005). Change is brought about because employees of the firm are encouraged to make discoveries that have commercial potential. In a formal sense, the company establishes traditional R&D units, centers of excellence (CoEs) for product development and new cross-functional venture teams or venture divisions that are expected to seek out opportunities and develop solutions for them (Burgelman, 1983; Kumar et al., 2009). This resonates closely with the case of Xerox in this book where the company's own Innovation Group (XIG) was tasked with spearheading the strategic shift from products to services. A new opportunity may be exploited, for example, by developing and launching an innovative product, or product enhancement for a defined marketplace, or by making a change to the organizational system, effectively using assets under the control of the firm.

In an informal sense, top level managers may establish a culture for entrepreneurship within the firm and control entrepreneurial activities undertaken by employees of the firm by making sure these activities are consistent with the strategic vision of the company (Isenberg, 2008). Corporate culture is seen as an intangible, socially-complex asset that may be difficult to imitate among competing firms (Klein, 2011). This point about the deliberate use of corporate culture as a resource to facilitate international venturing applies to international firms of all sizes, not just well-known large firms (Dimitratos and Plakoyiannaki, 2003). Naldi et al. (2015), for instance, showed how entrepreneurial culture has a positive effect on international corporate entrepreneurship in SMEs, enhancing performance in new markets and performance with new products.

Building on Fombrun and Ginsberg's (1990) longitudinal study of two types of opposing forces (inertial and inductive) on corporate aggressiveness, Williams and Lee (2009a) linked the concept of corporate aggressiveness to international firms and their patterns of strategic resource commitments. Using terminology from the EO literature, Williams and Lee (2009a) viewed conservative (or passive) MNEs as emphasizing a lower resource commitment to developing new opportunities. The leaders of such companies are relatively risk averse in how they allocate resources to seeking and exploiting new opportunities internationally. Such leaders would be taking a stance arguing that entrepreneurial knowledge, while not altogether redundant, is not as strategically important as it would be in more aggressive stances. In Williams and Lee's (2009a) operationalization, conservative MNEs have a relatively low ratio of R&D spend to total sales – the exposure of financial resources to the uncertain process of entrepreneurial knowledge creation is minimized. In addition, following the line of reasoning emphasized by Burgelman (1983), Klein (2011) and Naldi et al. (2015), conservative MNEs are careful about deploying intangible and socially-complex assets, such as corporate culture, in order to legitimize risk-taking within the company. Aggressive MNEs, on the other hand, will have a greater depth of R&D resource commitment; often operationalized by researchers in terms of a higher ratio of R&D spend to sales. They take on greater risk when allocating resources to the process of opportunity identification, evaluation and exploitation. In terms of intangible assets, they have cultures that encourage employees to participate on projects that develop entrepreneurial knowledge for the firm on an international basis. The example of 3M Taiwan in this book is an interesting case to learn about this.

The Nature of Entrepreneurial Knowledge in Context A

In this context, *knowledge of opportunity* arises because of the alertness of headquarters' managers. This knowledge is likely to be annotated with input from other senior managers, subsidiary managers, subject matter experts and possibly external consultants. The key actors, though, are headquarters' managers, including the top management team, as these individuals make the final strategic choices and decisions to invest in new risky ventures. Egelhoff (2010) used an information processing perspective to describe how headquarters' managers, in this age of globalization and highly internationalized firms, still play a critical role in infusing innovation into corporate strategy. Ambos and Mahnke (2010) highlighted how managers from different types of headquarters (global, divisional, regional) play a role in challenging subsidiaries to constantly improve. These two examples highlight the sense of alertness to new opportunity that headquarters' managers possess and utilize in their leadership roles.

Similarly, *knowledge of solution* must involve headquarters' managers in Context A. When driving venturing from a position high up in the hierarchy of the firm, knowledge of solution will be articulated on a top-down basis. While the propensity to pursue international venturing in MNEs may be associated to the degree of entrepreneurship emphasized in corporate strategy, the effectiveness of such corporate entrepreneurship is linked to the factors that help or hinder the progress of initiatives at the level of specific business opportunities. Headquarters' managers must have some sense of the resource and capability implications of pursuing specific opportunities. Ambos and Mahnke (2010) showed how subsidiary managers perceive the value added by managers in global headquarters to include provision of guidance and advice. Not all headquarters' managers will be technical experts in all new technological areas; they will not have crystal balls and cannot predict all outcomes from international venturing. But they will have the ability to guide how the company can "pull together the dispersed information from all of the markets . . . subsidiaries participate in and centrally evaluate the opportunities" (Egelhoff, 2010: 424).

Finally, the *learning from outcomes* that takes place in Context A must involve headquarters' managers. Knowledge about the reasons for success and failure will be sought by headquarters' managers, particularly if the level of investment in the solution to the opportunity in question was high. In the cases of General Motors Overseas Operations highlighted in Doz and Prahalad's influential (1984) study, a top-down initiative stimulating global and local product development acted to "increase the influence of headquarters' executives over international operations sufficiently to make strategic control effective" (Doz and Prahalad, 1984: 67). Headquarters' managers need to be able to control these centrally-driven venturing initiatives such that they can directly learn from them. Interestingly, in Ambos and Mahnke's (2010) study, improving information flow was perceived as the highest area of value added by global and regional headquarters. Headquarters' managers play a critical role in sharing knowledge – and facilitating the sharing of knowledge between subsidiary units – relating to entrepreneurial initiatives driven by the headquarters using internal resources and capabilities.

Context A: Cases in Point

In the German-headquartered *Roq.ad* case, we see headquarters' managers grapple with the challenges of business model development and entrepreneurial growth. The new Berlin-based venture in the ad-tech industry was involved in the development of cross-device user advertising technology. A key question facing this company, and many other similar new ventures, was how to fund the core technology development. The founders drew on their prior knowledge and experience in the industry and made the decision early on to seek their own streams of revenue to fund technology development, instead of seeking venture capital. The founders decided to use an agency model for selling advertisements. This gave them more control over the business and allowed them to use initial contracts to build long-standing relationships with clients. This investment in social capital would be valuable once the time was right to switch over to the cross-device user recognition technology that was under development. This was a business model that itself was not intended to last beyond the initial start-up period. This was a deliberate decision initially to use a business model to generate revenues to fund new cutting-edge technology that then would allow the company to subsequently revise the business model! It was the responsibility of headquarters' managers to lay out the roadmap for business model evolution, and to nurture entrepreneurial knowledge that would inform the decision on when to shift the business model as part of a long-term venturing strategy.

In the case on UK-headquartered *Time Out Group*, the company undertook a wide-ranging set of strategic initiatives and change programs under the leadership of Julio Bruno, who joined the company in

September 2015 following consecutive years of financial loss for the company. A key thrust for the company was its digital transformation. Among the range of initiatives that accompanied this was a sequence of organizational changes led directly by Bruno aimed at improving the atmosphere inside the company. He wanted to inject an entrepreneurial climate into the company and bring it more in line with start-ups that he had experienced in the United States. As the case shows, he thought of the company as a "48-year old start-up." He established new organizational routines aimed at promoting a more entrepreneurial culture. He set up café/bar areas in the offices in London and New York and had external representatives from the entertainment and media sectors attending weekly to present and promote their offerings. He established new routines in meetings, such as "stand-up" meetings where employees would stand-up and give a verbal update to all attending on what they were working on. He instigated "shout-outs," encouraging employees to provide accolades to colleagues to acknowledge quality and impact of colleagues' work. In addition, "show and tell" meetings were used to host product demonstrations and showcase new technology from the product development teams. These types of new organizational routines were driven by the key headquarters' manager and were – in most part – executed using resources and capabilities already under the hierarchical control of the firm.

In the case on United States-headquartered *Tesla*, the company decided to enter Singapore with apparently clear motives for entry. In particular, the environment in Singapore appeared very conducive to an engagement by Tesla. There was a Transport Technology Innovation and Development Scheme (TIDES) set up by the government that ostensibly aligned with Tesla's own strategy and technology. The government also pursued an environmentally-friendly city policy, a policy that would provide encouragement for electric vehicles. There were also shorter driving distances in Singapore, compared to some of the other Tesla markets, such as the United States. However, there was intense rivalry from other international electric and hybrid manufacturers, and sales of Tesla products were disappointing. This led the company to make the decision to exit the country after little more than a year. This was a direct intervention by the corporate center (McKern and Naman, 2003). Exit decisions like this are made by headquarters' managers with deep knowledge of the opportunity, of how they wanted to pursue the opportunity and of what outcomes occurred.

The case then focuses on the question of whether it makes sense for the company to take its technology and product offerings to China. Does this make sense so soon after the exit from Singapore? If the company was to enter China, how should it do it? The local conditions in Singapore made that country attractive, and the company could not succeed there. What knowledge did headquarters' managers at Tesla have that would allow them to make a go of it in China, an environment for electric vehicles that in many ways seemed more problematic than Singapore? Potential problems extended beyond competitive pressures in the electric vehicle space in China. They also included a lack of infrastructure and supercharger stations, lack of brand awareness and customer loyalty to more established brands, practicality issues of charging at home and lack of tax credits for electric vehicles.

Elon Musk announced in January 2013 that Tesla would enter China. The company used the showroom strategy that it had pioneered in the home market (United States) and used elsewhere in the world (for instance in the UK). It set up a showroom in a strategically-located shopping mall in Beijing – close to central government and in a city that had a history of air pollution issues. These decisions were made by centrally-located headquarters' managers and they drew on the entrepreneurial knowledge gained in other markets around the world, such as Singapore and the United States. And the company used assets already developed and under its control in this new market entry strategy: its brand; its vehicle and battery technology; and its know-how in sales and marketing through the showroom model.

Challenges for Leaders, Managers and Analysts

This context for venturing in international firms presents various challenges for the leadership of an international firm. We see a need for the centralization of initiative and competence in leaders to direct change and growth initiatives in the firm (Prahalad and Doz, 1981). Key investment decisions become centralized and the overall stance towards investment needs to be established by leaders who, in making these decisions, are constrained by the size and degree of internationalization of the firm. These are factors that, in larger and older companies, come about through generation upon generation of previous leaders (Williams and Lee, 2009a).

Global initiatives (Williams, 2009) need to be identified, evaluated and selected by leaders. This inevitably involves filtering out potential global initiatives that the company should not pursue. Other difficult decisions that leaders need to make in this context include strategic moves to pull out or divest from a host country (as in the Tesla case and also in the Infusion case with its foray into India). Leaders need to capture, process and evaluate entrepreneurial knowledge for these decisions to be effective. Such exit decisions are inevitably based on learning from outcomes of prior venturing decisions and are always guided by headquarters' managers.

Alongside the need to make decisions related to the entrepreneurial posture of the company, leaders need to consider how tangible and intangible assets can be used in new ways. Bartlett and Ghoshal (2003) pointed to the role of top-level managers in the MNE as developers of operating-level entrepreneurs engaged in such groupings and being responsible for linking dispersed knowledge across units. One example relates to the motives and locations for establishing formal R&D subsidiaries around the world – these decisions being made by headquarters as a critical component of centrally-driven international strategy (Frost and Zhou, 2000; Kuemmerle, 1999; Kumar et al., 2009). In the Roq.ad case, the company entered into Poland to develop a 'near-shore' development center mandated to develop the new cross-device user advertising technology. In the case of Infusion's Greenfield in Poland, the company's leadership team was personally involved in the evaluation of alternative locations, as well as setting up the process by which existing competence and knowledge residing in the Toronto office could be transferred to new recruits joining in Poland.

In terms of intangible assets, we see headquarters' managers in this context signaling their support and sponsorship for new ventures (Burgelman, 1983; Garud and Van de Ven, 1992; Zahra and Garvis, 2000). In this context then, leaders face the challenge of how to establish a culture for international venturing (Klein, 2011) and how to use corporate culture to achieve performance with new products in new markets (Naldi et al., 2015). We note how charismatic, visionary and articulate headquarters' managers lead companies in Context A venturing. Elon Musk (Tesla), Julio Bruno (Time Out Group) and Antoine van Veldhuizen and Mark Welling (Expatica) feature in the cases discussed in this book and no doubt thousands of others exist around the world where we find centrally-driven corporate aggressiveness and international venturing using pre-existing resources and capabilities going hand-in-hand. One notable additional characteristic of the leaders mentioned above: they understand the technology. At some point in their careers, they themselves have worked closely with technology and show a willingness to embrace new technology in search of entrepreneurial growth. Through the Context A lens, these leaders, and the groups of managers that work with them in corporate headquarters, act as powerful driving forces for change using assets that are already under the hierarchical control of the firm.

What about the challenges facing other managers in this context, such as middle-ranking and subsidiary managers? One major challenge relates to the role that these managers will be expected to play in supporting Context A venturing. The expectation from headquarters will be that subsidiary managers will co-operate with headquarters and be willing to support venturing decisions made centrally. Such decisions will inevitably have consequences for the way budgets and resources are allocated. Some subsidiary managers may see themselves as 'winners' in this process, others 'losers'. Some may gain resources and have their mandate expanded as a consequence of Context A venturing. Some may see resources and mandates diminish or interesting venturing activities being assigned to competing subsidiaries.

The headquarters also will expect middle-ranking managers and subsidiary managers to align themselves with any changes to the internal corporate culture as directed by headquarters. These managers may need to change their own behavioral routines because of changes espoused by the headquarters as part of its venturing strategy. And they will need to signal to their own direct reports and lower-level employees why any new behavioral routines are needed and how they should be followed. In larger international firms, there will be a vast array of middle-ranking and subsidiary managers, completely outnumbering headquarters' managers. This army of change agents will need to 'buy in' to any new corporate culture and reinforce it on a daily basis.

Some subsidiary managers may adopt such changes with relish, and others might be less forthcoming or accepting. There may even be cultural clashes between aspects of the entrepreneurial culture espoused by headquarters' managers and the national cultural traits in the host country. The headquarters may encourage and push for more decentralized decision-making to the subsidiary as part of its corporate culture (e.g., 3M case), while the host country could be one of high power distance where individuals expect those higher up in the organizational hierarchy to make key decisions. Alternatively, high uncertainty avoidance where individuals seek preference for clear guidance and prescribed actions could clash with the firm's own culture (Hofstede, 1997). Hofstede (1997) reported on dimensions of organizational culture in addition to his work on national culture. Derived from an Institute for Research on Intercultural Cooperation (IRIC) study, Hofstede reported on six dimensions of organizational culture: process oriented vs. results oriented; employee oriented vs. job oriented; parochial vs. professional; open system vs. closed system; loose control vs. tight control; and normative vs. pragmatic. One question in the international firm is whether – and to what extent – a subsidiary manager leaves their nationally-defined cultural values outside of the building when they come into the office in the host country? Do the cultural values of the organization prevail in terms of what is expected with respect to common practices over common values (Hofstede, 1997)? In the case of 3M in Taiwan, we could argue that the Taiwanese managers were able to recognize and utilize the corporation's culture and that this prevailed over the national culture to help them in their pursuit of the local opportunity. There are other cases, however, such as the situation facing Lundbeck in Korea (Beamish and Roberts, 2010) where host country national culture has a big role to play in how a subsidiary manager approaches sales and marketing activity and how this can be at odds with the approach set by regional and global headquarters.

Where there is alignment and co-operation, the headquarters can expect to access newly created entrepreneurial knowledge efficiently and effectively. Subsidiaries will be motivated and able to share knowledge of new opportunities or annotations to headquarters' understanding of what an opportunity is. They will be motivated and able to contribute to discussions on solutions to opportunities, and they will be first in line to tell headquarters' managers of outcomes, good or bad. On the other hand, where subsidiary managers feel put out – or threatened – because of a loss of resource or mandate, or a misalignment in cultural and behavioral expectation, a political arena can ensue (Williams and Lee, 2009b). A political arena is an internal organizational situation characterized by conflict between individuals (Mintzberg, 1985). There has been a stream of literature on micro-politics and subsidiary development in MNEs (Dörrenbächer and Gammelgaard, 2006; Dörrenbächer and Geppert, 2006) highlighting the relationship between internal politics and different types of subsidiary entrepreneurs.

However, one line of reasoning suggests that an internal political arena arising as a consequence of entrepreneurial initiative and change is not necessarily a bad thing (Williams and Lee, 2009b). The logic goes that, by allowing more than one voice to be heard, organizational needs are better served through a political arena than simply relying on authority, ideology and expertise (Mintzberg, 1985). When these existing systems of influence act as sources of resistance to change, politics can be used to promote new power bases and strive to bring about change. In effect, disagreements and a lack of co-operation between subsidiaries and headquarters as a consequence of headquarters-driven internal venturing may not necessarily be detrimental. New entrepreneurial knowledge may surface that helps headquarters to re-think or justify and hone their approaches. This leads into the analysis of the role of subsidiaries and subsidiary managers in international venturing in the MNE, something we will go into in Context B.

Understanding and researching Context A is not without its challenges. First and foremost, it is not always possible to access headquarters' managers (the corporate elites) in order to conduct probing interviews on the topic of how they seek change and rejuvenation of their companies. This is often sensitive information that they do not want to fall into the wrong hands. They are also very busy people who spend a lot of time on the road. Problems of access to the strategic leaders of the MNE (Welch et al., 2002) can make primary data collection in the form of personal face-to-face interviews with those responsible for setting levels of EO in large firms very difficult. Leaders in smaller companies may be more accessible and willing to share information about their strategic approaches. I found this to be the situation when developing the cases on Time Out Group, Infusion, Roq.ad and Expatica for example. However, small companies are likely to be less newsworthy than larger, publicly-listed ones. Established scales for EO in an international setting, however, still can be used when constructing questionnaires on EO adopted by top management teams (Covin and Miller, 2014). Such questionnaires do not only have to be targeted at the C-suite managers themselves. They can even be targeted at middle-ranking and non-headquarters' managers, but who have extensive experience of the firm and its strategy. Middle-ranking managers hold a crucial position in terms of their knowledge of the international firm. They can bridge asymmetry in knowledge between corporate level and geographically-remote operating staff. Nonaka (1988) described this in terms of an ability to combine "strategic macro (context-free) information and hands-on micro (context-specific) information" (Nonaka, 1988: 15).

Researchers and analysts also can use firm-level quantitative secondary data (e.g., R&D intensity ratios, patents) and qualitative secondary data (company reports or news reports on how and where formal mandates were allocated to subsidiaries) and take an historical perspective. Secondary data with a substantive qualitative content can be triangulated with quantitative indicators of EO and this can provide a window on the mindsets and priorities of strategic leaders of large international firms. While they might be extremely busy people and difficult to access for interview, leaders of large international firms are often interviewed by journalists and the business press. These interviews are, fortunately, very widely available on social media platforms these days and can contain important historical information on the strategic thinking and approaches adopted by headquarters' managers in terms of innovation, risk-taking and proactivity.

I used qualitative and quantitative secondary data as part of my PhD to analyze the corporate venturing of six large international companies: IBM, GE and HP in high-technology equipment manufacturing and Abbott, Eli Lilly and Merck and Co. in pharmaceuticals. The results are reported in Williams and Lee (2009c). Benefits of this 'firm behavior' approach to understand centrally-driven venturing include independence of the researcher and source data, the ability to devise coding schemes that can accurately tap into corporate aggressiveness and the ability to capture this over time, thus allowing longitudinal patterns to be assessed (Covin and Lumpkin, 2011; Lyon et al., 2000).

Summary

In Context A we have learnt how:

- there is an imperative for strategic leaders to guide corporate strategy in an international firm with entrepreneurial orientation in mind;
- headquarters' managers have an important role to play in driving global initiatives and evolving the firm's fundamental business model and core technology programs in international firms;
- pre-existing resources and capabilities predominantly under the hierarchical control of the firm can be combined and used in new ways

under the guidance of headquarters' managers during international venturing;

- entrepreneurial knowledge can be concentrated in the minds of a relatively small group of headquarters' managers;
- this context for venturing is present in different types of technology-intensive industries, in firms from different countries and different sizes of international firm, from large (e.g., Tesla), right down to small start-ups (e.g., Roq.ad).

Suggested Additional Cases for Analyzing this Context

Choi, D.Y., Kang, B. and Kiesner, F. (2013) 'Caffébene: Master Brewer of Growth and Global Ambition' (North American Case Research Association, product number: NAC3316).

Kumar, K., Kumar, M. and Alsleben, M. (2009) 'SAP: Establishing a Research Centre in China' (University of Hong Kong, product number: HKU817).

Lawton, T. and Doh, J. (2008) 'The Ascendance of AirAsia: Building a Successful Budget Airline in Asia' (Ivey Publishing, product number: 9B08M054).

Ramakrishna, V. and Zhao, L. (2016) 'CPT: The Constant Hunt for Entrepreneurial Opportunities' (CEIBS – Ivey, product number: 9B16M067).

3

'Context B' – Subsidiary-driven Venturing: Unleashing Peripheral Capabilities

Context B is a domain for venturing behavior in international firms where managers in overseas subsidiaries are the driving force for venturing and where the company's own resources and capabilities are leveraged in order to accomplish the change and rejuvenation sought by those managers. When we look at venturing in international firms in this context we emphasize: (1) a role for overseas subsidiary managers in recognizing, assessing and choosing new strategic options as a response to opportunities that they come across; and (2) the use of pre-existing internal resources and capabilities (some of which may reside in the focal subsidiary, some of which may reside in other units of the firm) in new ways to seize new opportunity. This context arises for the MNE because entrepreneurial competences get dispersed throughout numerous locations around the world as a result of the firm's internationalization.

This context has seen a growing amount of research over the last 30 years. While early research looked at organizational characteristics associated with subsidiary entrepreneurship (Birkinshaw, 1997, 2000), more recent research has put a spotlight on the consequences of subsidiary initiative-taking (Ambos et al., 2010). Reviews of the literature have highlighted the Context B phenomenon as a complex one and scholars have used multiple theoretical angles (Strutzenberger and Ambos, 2014). Inevitably, while some initiatives started in subsidiaries are successful, some are failures. In either case, they can have big ramifications for regional and global units in the company, not just in the subsidiary. Indeed, subsidiary-driven venturing involves the subsidiary exerting its power by creating the basis for new business that eventually can change the strategic focus of the MNE (Verbeke et al., 2007).

The Driving Force: Ambitious and Proactive Subsidiary Managers

It is important to understand why subsidiary managers act in the way they do. Entrepreneurial cognition theory helps here, highlighting individual cognitive factors as determinants of entrepreneurial action (Baron, 1998, 2004; Shook et al., 2003) as well as the situational context in which individuals find themselves (Mitchell et al., 2007). An entrepreneurially-minded individual situated within a foreign subsidiary will be alert to the possibility that opportunities may arise in the subsidiary's distinct environment (Birkinshaw, 2000; Strutzenberger and Ambos, 2014; Williams and Lee, 2011b). Consequently, these individuals are better able to spot opportunities within local environments than headquarters' managers and those located outside of the host country. Such individuals are also better able to notice inefficiencies within the internal organizational system as it pertains to a focal subsidiary, and more likely to be alert to opportunities within the internal environment of the subsidiary.

Being alert to new opportunities in the subsidiary environment is one side of the coin. The other side of the coin is deciding to drive initiative forward. Subsidiary initiative-taking is a process unfolding over time and driven by subsidiary managers with the intention of developing new markets for the subsidiary (Strutzenberger and Ambos, 2014). Any such change process requires proactive involvement by individuals at each stage: transformational leadership; risk-taking behaviors; and having a range of ways to influence others. Hence, research has looked at the behavioral dynamics of overseas MNE subsidiary managers when they make the oftentimes bold decision to chase an opportunity that they perceive as potentially lucrative (De Clercq et al., 2011; Gupta et al., 1999).

Proactivity plays an important role here and has been a consistent theme in the literature. Subsidiary managers will need to win acceptance for their idea, and convince others (especially headquarters' managers) of the need to re-allocate scarce resources to the exploitation of an identified opportunity. This requires internal selling and a complex series of repeated interactions involving subsidiary managers. It requires tenacious behavior on their part (Birkinshaw, 2000; Birkinshaw and Ridderstråle, 1999). Birkinshaw (1997) suggested that proactivity within subsidiaries enables the MNE to reconcile global opportunities with internal capabilities, a role traditionally assumed by the corporate center. De Clercq et al. (2011) investigated how characteristics of entrepreneurial initiatives influence the internal 'selling' of the initiative by corporate entrepreneurs. Entrepreneurs are more likely to undertake intense internal selling when they believe the benefits for the organization are high and where there are extrinsic rewards for initiative-taking (De Clercq et al., 2011). Proactive behaviors are also associated with feedback-seeking. Subsidiary managers engage in a form of self-regulatory behavior through proactivity (Gupta et al., 1999) demonstrating a willingness to learn from negative as well as positive feedback from other units of the MNE.

In Context B then, the emphasis is on ideas for change and renewal within the MNE arising in locations that are dispersed geographically. What is particularly interesting here is that subsidiary managers are driving a process that can allow the MNE to become more competitive, that this process can happen on a continuous basis, but it is one that is rather bottom–up and unpredictable. The discovery and identification of new opportunities takes place in remote locations around the world. But the question of when, and how new opportunities are discovered and identified cannot be foreseen or 'designed' in a deterministic manner.

In this context, subsidiary managers are the key players in assessing the gap between local environment and internal capabilities. These dispersed employees often generate ideas that are borne out of a need to enhance the subsidiary's mandate and develop its role (Delany, 2000; Strutzenberger and Ambos, 2014). They want to get the subsidiary to a more powerful and influential place in the organization. Driving subsidiary initiative in this context involves subsidiary managers articulating their view of the opportunity and ideas about how the MNE may provide a solution to the opportunity, and developing proposals to be submitted to regional and/or global headquarters in a quest for approval and funding. It is inevitable that subsidiary managers will face some form of resistance in this process. They may be confronted by a 'corporate immune system' (Birkinshaw, 2000; Birkinshaw and Ridderstråle, 1999) that acts to stifle, postpone or delay initiatives.

The Resources and Capabilities: Importance of Subsidiary Reputation for Credibility

The emphasis in Context B is on how geographically-dispersed overseas employees influence the allocation of MNE scarce resources by identifying new opportunities and proposing new initiatives that would result in the re-allocation of those scarce resources. Hence, as in Context A, the company's asset base may end up being used in new ways. However, the difference is this asset re-allocation is a result of proactive subsidiary managers. At the outset of an initiative, it is likely that the resources and capabilities that matter are localized in the subsidiary. The subsidiary may have used assets under its control to explore, probe and reflect on how any identified opportunity could be pursued on a larger scale. Assuming good relationships with other subsidiaries, informal channels can be used by the subsidiary in this initial probing and reflecting process. The type of subsidiary initiative that is important in our analysis is one that goes beyond the subsidiary; the type that requires the subsidiary to receive a sanctioning from the headquarters in order to proceed. In other words, the intended result is a new agreement with headquarters on how company assets are allocated. Nohria and Ghoshal (1997) referred to this type as 'local-for-global'. We are less interested in very small-scale initiatives that the subsidiary can solve by itself without any need to call on others. These happen all the time in all organizations. For us, in Context B venturing, assets that are under the hierarchical control of the firm but which are not necessarily controlled by the subsidiary are highly relevant.

In terms of tangible assets, the subsidiary may require financing from the headquarters. Direct finance for new projects where expenses are incurred in the host country is, of course, entirely possible. So too is direct financing for project-related expenses where the subsidiary in the host country acquires new assets from suppliers around the world. These types of project-related expenses need to be financed. For large-scale projects, headquarters' involvement is critical. The headquarters may also be required to sanction a transfer of raw materials, systems and technology from the home country to the host country, or to orchestrate its transfer from other countries where the company has operations. These types of tangible asset transfers and re-allocations are common in subsidiary initiatives. They are one of the main reasons why subsidiary initiatives are carefully scrutinized, can be seen by some managers in the MNE as controversial and why they may ultimately lead to confrontation within the company.

In terms of intangible assets, subsidiaries may require access to the know-how of others across the MNE who can shed light on how to increase the chances that the initiative is a success. Such know-how is likely to be largely tacit in nature and it will therefore be necessary to allow subsidiary managers to interface directly with people around the firm with this know-how. Headquarters' managers can legitimize and encourage this through internal introductions, communications and meetings, and follow-ups (Ghoshal and Bartlett, 1988). It may be that another subsidiary in a far-flung corner of the globe has already pursued a similar or analogous initiative in the past, and their experience will be important. In this sense, headquarters' managers provide an important intangible resource: they legitimize initiative-taking behavior by one subsidiary, while underpinning a culture for lateral communication flows across the organization.

In addition to this, a subsidiary's own reputation for credibility can be very important in determining how a headquarters perceives a new request for funding and investment by the subsidiary. Credibility among economic actors is a crucial intangible resource in the modern information age (Keohane and Nye, 1998). A subsidiary needs to provide accurate and timely information as requested by the headquarters to help establish credibility. Also, information about prior successes in initiative-taking by the subsidiary will matter here (Birkinshaw, 2000; Delany, 2000). If a subsidiary has a reputation for credibility in the eyes of headquarters' managers, gained through positive outcomes in previous initiatives, the progress of a new initiative will be smoother. Proactivity is one way to help establish credibility and an "enhanced image in the eyes of others" (Crant, 2000: 450).

The Nature of Entrepreneurial Knowledge in Context B

The process underpinning dispersed subsidiary-driven venturing can be seen as a 'bottom-up' one, and somewhat unpredictable. Discovery and entrepreneurial knowledge creation take place in remote locations. They have features that cannot be known in advance and they occur at a time also that cannot be known. Internal socialization mechanisms are often used to transfer tacit knowledge between subsidiary entrepreneurs and headquarters' managers. This socialization will convey information about the opportunity and its possible solution, and will enhance credibility in an attempt by the subsidiary to win approval and investment (Birkinshaw, 1997, 2000; Strutzenberger and Ambos, 2014). Context B venturing comes about because of learning asymmetries that exist between managers in different parts of the MNE. Learning asymmetries refer to differences in the ways individuals acquire and transform information (Corbett, 2007).

In Context B, *knowledge of opportunity* arises because of the alertness of subsidiary managers. This knowledge of opportunity forms in the minds of managers in foreign subsidiaries in host countries that are separated from the home country by various forms of distance. Cross-national distance is a multidimensional construct, including not only geographic distance, but cultural, linguistic and institutional distances, among others (Berry et al., 2010). These multiple dimensions of distance make it difficult for headquarters' managers to be directly involved in the subsidiary at the exact point in time in which a subsidiary manager becomes alert to an opportunity for the subsidiary. These distances prevent knowledge of opportunities around the world from immediately and simultaneously being transferred into the minds of headquarters' managers to appear as vividly as they appear in the minds of subsidiary managers. Williams and Kumar (2012) showed that cultural distance has a negative impact on subsidiary initiative diffusion in MNEs: the greater the cultural distance between a home and host country, the less likely the subsidiary in the host country will generate initiatives that win sanctioning and approval by the headquarters for application in other countries. But home country–host country distance does not necessarily matter to whether an alert subsidiary manager recognizes an opportunity as such. By definition, in Context B venturing, headquarters' managers do not necessarily have to be involved at the point in which the creation of awareness of an opportunity occurs.

Similarly, *knowledge of solution* must involve subsidiary managers in a different way – arguably more prominently in Context B compared to Context A. Importantly for Context B, knowledge of solution develops through the proactivity and credible attempts by subsidiary managers to probe, share and annotate their mental models of how opportunities can be exploited. They will inevitably seek input, know-how, and learning from outcomes of previous endeavors in other countries where similar or analogous initiatives have taken place. This will allow the subsidiary to build up a picture of where resources and capabilities lie within the MNE network that could be part of the solution for exploiting the opportunity. If sufficient resources exist in a subsidiary, and if the subsidiary is empowered to allocate local resources to new opportunities as they deem suitable, then knowledge of the solution also will be retained locally. But if potentially accessible and usable assets in other subsidiaries, and/or financial investment and sanctioning from headquarters are required, the subsidiary will be involved in a sharing of knowledge of opportunity and knowledge of solution to the opportunity as it engages with other units.

Finally, the *learning from outcomes* that takes place in Context B is an aspect of entrepreneurial knowledge creation that puts subsidiary managers in the spotlight. Subsidiary managers will be the key players in monitoring performance and managing issues as they arise once resources are allocated to the pursuit of a new subsidiary initiative. These managers should have a high motivation and willingness to learn from outcomes having invested considerable time and effort in internal selling, negotiating the 'corporate immune system', and helping to bring together assets in order to pursue the opportunity. They will seek to avoid any damage to their reputations for credibility and will need to have accurate information on the outcomes of the initiative should headquarters' and other subsidiary managers make enquiries on the status of the work. Subsidiary managers will be closest to activities that form the initiative. They will learn first-hand from participating in the initiative and will be key points of contact for others in the MNE wanting to know the outcomes, including both early outcomes as well as progress at later stages.

Context B: Cases in Point

An interesting feature of the *Time Out Group* case that falls into Context B is the Time Out Market (TOM) initiative. A TOM was a market-style food-hall space set up in a hip and trendy part of a city; a place where customers could enjoy food, drink and cultural experiences. The TOM initiative was not started by headquarters' managers in the home country (the UK). It was started in 2015 in the Mercado da Ribiera in Lisbon, Portugal. It was also an initiative that took the company into a new business area, namely, providing actual experiences for customers rather than reporting on events and experiences or facilitating the purchase of tickets to events and experiences provided by others. Thus the TOM initiative provided a 'bricks and mortar' counter-balance to all that was happening in the company in terms of its digital transformation. It was consistent with CEO Julio Bruno's vision for Time Out in terms of 'clicks and bricks'. The TOM in Lisbon proved to be an instant hit and, on the back of this early success in Lisbon, headquarters' managers drew up plans to set up new TOMs, including Miami in the United States. As the case notes, the Lisbon initiative provided a basis by which headquarters' managers could appreciate the potential scalability of the opportunity. It also allowed the company to create knowledge of the solution – getting the right balance between restaurants, bars, cafés and even art galleries – and learning from outcomes (the Lisbon TOM received 3.1 million visitors in Lisbon in 2016).

In the case of *Infusion Development Corporation*, the company initially started out in the United States, servicing investment banking clients in Lower Manhattan with training and software solutions. The company branched out into Canada to establish a near-shore development center staffed by interns and graduates from University of Waterloo. The Canadian employees, while working on projects for clients in the United States, were also proactive in trying their hand at sales in the Canadian market as well as exploring new opportunities based on emerging technologies. The Canadian office then developed rapidly into a de facto headquarters for the company and subsequent internationalization into the UK and Dubai were all decisions that were taken by the headquarters' managers in Toronto. As the company grew, it tried to maintain the essence of its entrepreneurial culture. Meanwhile, technology development and sales activities happening at subsidiary level in the UK and Dubai all contained elements of entrepreneurial capabilities at the periphery of the organization. For instance, in the UK, the subsidiary managed to sell into retail banking; in Dubai, the company won new contracts in the hospitality industry, something that had not happened in other countries.

In the case of *3M Taiwan*, an overseas subsidiary in Taiwan identified an opportunity for the use of one of the corporation's established technologies, namely hydrocolloid dressing (a sterile wound dressing). This would be a new application that the US-headquartered corporation previously had not exploited. The technology had existed in the company for a while, but had never been marketed for acne treatment. A subsidiary manager in Taiwan had experienced first-hand how beneficial the product was for helping to heal a skin wound he accidently received. A project team explored new options for the technology and realized it had potential for treating acne. The subsidiary lacked knowledge and resources in how to develop this specific technology for application on people's faces. They also lacked knowledge and resources in how to market this type of new product.

The case charts how the subsidiary was able to identify and pursue the opportunity, and how aspects of 3M's corporate culture and formalized processes for new product development allowed the subsidiary to come up with solutions for developing the product itself as well as solutions for the local marketing campaign. In this case we see existing assets (hydrocolloid dressing) being used in new ways. We also see the important role of corporate culture to legitimize and support the subsidiary's proactive efforts to develop and launch the new product. The subsequent launch of the new product was successful and the marketing campaign had an impressive impact. The product later was launched in neighboring countries in East Asia. The upshot of this was a strengthening of the subsidiary's reputation for credibility and learning from outcomes that had impact beyond the host country.

Challenges for Leaders, Managers and Analysts

Perhaps the greatest challenge for strategic leaders in this context is how to make sense of the myriad requests to support new entrepreneurial initiatives springing up around the world. Headquarters' managers continuously need to consider, debate and reconcile multiple requests for new resource allocation from diverse locations. They need to carefully decide which ideas to take forward and which ones to reject or postpone. Furthermore, where headquarters does not have procedures to cope with subsidiary initiative, or has a closed disposition towards them, a confrontational headquarters–subsidiary relationship can occur, although this also can be overcome by proactive behaviors on the part of subsidiary managers (Birkinshaw, 2000).

Upper-level headquarters' management may give subsidiaries support to pursue initiatives. For instance, a subsidiary with a global mandate (what Infusion Poland ultimately became) or one given a formal endowment as a Centre of Excellence (CoE) (such as Xerox in Grenoble and

Palo Alto) will be expected to innovate and create competences in search of competitive advantage for the wider MNE (Cantwell and Mudambi, 2005; Moore, 2001). In the case of Xerox, researchers at Webster in New York had conceived of a two-engine photocopier – an innovation that could be exploited by the company globally. This headquarters' support is not just restricted to innovation and R&D functions. For instance, Gammelgaard and Hobdari (2013) showed that, in the case of Danish brewer Carlsberg, the company deliberately gave subsidiaries "room to maneuver" (Gammelgaard and Hobdari, 2013: 207). While there was a tendency in the industry for newly acquired subsidiaries to lose their decision-making rights, Carlsberg appeared to buck the trend by allowing certain levels of autonomy, particularly in marketing, to reside at subsidiary level.

However, in other situations, a headquarters may not have been able to fully appreciate the entrepreneurial potential of a subsidiary. A subsidiary may, for instance, be part of a dynamic and growing market that the headquarters has not adequately understood. The headquarters may have allowed a subsidiary to become isolated, and unable to fully tap market opportunities or generate new technological innovation because of lack of support from a headquarters and/or inappropriate control mechanisms applied to the subsidiary (Monteiro et al., 2008; Williams and Nones, 2009).

This latter point presents significant challenges for headquarters, particularly as the company grows in size and ends up with a high number of foreign subsidiaries. The question of management control arises: how should the headquarters manage its foreign subsidiaries in order to allow entrepreneurial knowledge to be generated and exploited? Ghoshal and Nohria's (1989) ground-breaking work highlighted how the control mechanism a headquarters uses for a subsidiary needs to be dependent on the resources and capabilities in the subsidiary, along with the degree of complexity in the subsidiary's host country environment. Ghoshal and Nohria presented a typology of international headquarter–subsidiary relationships where the relationship is classified according to two dimensions: environmental complexity; and level of local resources (Ghoshal and Nohria, 1989). The four relationship types were: (1) Hierarchy – high centralization, low formalization and low socialization – useful where environmental complexity and local resource levels are both low; (2) Clans – moderate centralization, low formalization but high socialization – useful where environmental complexity is high but local resource levels are low; (3) Federative – low centralization, high formalization and low socialization – useful where environmental complexity is low but local resource levels are high; and (4) Integrative – low centralization, moderate formalization and high socialization – useful where environmental complexity and local resource levels are both high.

The same authors also provided insight into how the structure of headquarter–subsidiary relations should match the context of the subsidiary – a concept called *differentiated fit* (Nohria and Ghoshal, 1994). The authors complemented the differentiated fit approach with the idea that subsidiaries can be managed by minimizing the degree of divergence of preferences and interests among the members of the organization and showed how this can be achieved through socialization mechanisms. This 'shared values' approach involves a common set of values with respect to goals and enables subsidiaries to use their knowledge "to pursue the interests of the MNE as a whole and not just their partisan interests" (Nohria and Ghoshal, 1994: 494). Shared values legitimize local decision-making without dispensing with any form of centralization or formalization (Ghoshal and Bartlett, 1988; Ghoshal and Nohria, 1989). Ways of actually implementing shared values include rotation and transfer of managers (Edström and Galbraith, 1977), extensive and open communication among the dispersed units of the MNE (Martinez and Jarillo, 1989) and extensive socialization and communication aimed at building trust.

Research has looked at determinants of decentralization of innovative capabilities to overseas subsidiaries. Using a sample of R&D subsidiaries in Austria, Ecker et al. (2013) showed how the nature of the research, the degree of information asymmetry between headquarters and subsidiary, and the extent of interdependencies between the subsidiary and other units of the MNE all influence the headquarters' choice to decentralize decision rights to a foreign subsidiary. This study also showed why it is important to consider how the R&D subsidiary operates under time pressure. Results indicated that, in situations where basic, exploratory research is conducted in the subsidiary, while at the same time having advanced R&D processes in the subsidiary to accelerate R&D performance, the headquarters is less likely to decentralize decision rights fully to the subsidiary. In other words, the decision to decentralize decision rights to an R&D subsidiary is influenced by an interaction between the nature of the R&D work performed and whether advanced R&D processes – such as parallel and 24-hour R&D – are used in the subsidiary. In such time-pressured conditions, headquarters will still need to have some centralized control. In Williams and van Triest's (2009) study on decentralization in MNEs, analysis revealed that with higher levels of uncertainty avoidance in the host country of the subsidiary, the less likely the subsidiary would receive high levels of decision rights from the headquarters. This study points to the role of national host country culture in influencing whether headquarters gives decision rights to subsidiaries.

Overall, this literature on control of subsidiaries speaks to the complexity facing headquarters' managers as they try to find optimal ways of managing their overseas subsidiaries in order to promote, yet control, Context B venturing. A substantial literature on headquarter–subsidiary relationships has evolved here (Kostova et al., 2016; Paterson and Brock, 2002; Young and Tavares, 2004). While some work highlights the importance of having procedures to cope with initiative (such as the new product introduction process 3M used in the case on 3M in Taiwan), others highlight the importance of understanding how to determine appropriate control mechanisms such that the subsidiary does not become so isolated that it fails to provide entrepreneurial knowledge into the organization. McKern and Naman (2003) made an interesting observation in their discussion of how responsibilities are shared between headquarters' and SBU-level managers:

> SBUs vary in the competences and managerial slack they have available for such initiatives, and a challenge for headquarters is to encourage these initiatives, to avoid judging them prematurely, and yet to be ready to disseminate successful innovations quickly to other SBUs. We see its role here as both initiator and facilitator, by encouraging a climate in which experiments in managerial innovation can flourish.
> (McKern and Naman, 2003: 251)

This managerial consideration also has implications for subsidiary managers. In the same way that subsidiary managers can influence headquarters' managers with respect to accepting and promoting subsidiary initiatives, subsidiary managers can influence how the relationship with headquarters evolves. Socialization mechanisms are used to transfer ideas and win approval for investment (Birkinshaw, 2000; Birkinshaw and Ridderstråle, 1999). Without good personal relationships and communications with the headquarters, subsidiary initiatives will suffer (Birkinshaw and Ridderstråle, 1999). However, subsidiary managers face the challenge themselves of defining what constitutes a 'good personal relationship' with a headquarters' manager, how to proactively develop and nurture these relationships, and how to draw on these relationships as a critical relational asset when seeking approval and funding for their own initiatives (Kostova et al., 2016; Paterson and Brock, 2002). To this end, subsidiary managers pursuing their own initiatives will need to be aware of negative outcomes caused by a lack of transparency and inaccurate information passed to headquarters. This can cost the subsidiary as it will end up damaging its reputation for credibility.

One area that subsidiary managers will need to consider to give themselves a prominent position in Context B venturing is to establish human resource management (HRM) practices in the subsidiary that are conducive to entrepreneurial knowledge flows into and out of the subsidiary. In Williams and Lee's (2016) study of Korean subsidiaries based in three European countries, analysis showed how aspects of the organizational high performance work system (HPWS) (as applied to the subsidiary unit rather than the overall MNE) have a critical role to play in determining knowledge in- and out-flows. An organization's HPWS is the collection of organizational practices aimed at encouraging commitment and performance in employees (Evans and Davis, 2005; Pfeffer, 1998; Pfeffer and Veiga, 1999). Subsidiary knowledge in- and out-flows will inevitably contain entrepreneurial knowledge in addition to production knowledge. They will also contain knowledge about the relationships between subsidiary managers and headquarters' managers. Williams and Lee (2016) showed that the way people are managed in foreign subsidiaries determines how well the subsidiary is integrated into the MNE in terms of knowledge in- and out-flows. In particular, empowering practices within the subsidiary amplify the effect of intra-subsidiary socialization on knowledge flows, while formalized HRM practices within the subsidiary amplify the effect of the subsidiary's human capital. Subsidiary managers do not only need to work on influencing headquarters and maintaining good inter-unit relationships around the world, they also need to manage within their own units such that the ebb and flow of entrepreneurial knowledge into and out of the subsidiary is not hindered.

Researching and analyzing Context B has a different set of challenges compared to Context A. First, reliable secondary data on subsidiary initiatives at the overseas subsidiary level is simply not available. International firms do not disclose all of the internal subsidiary requests they process and manage to outside parties! Some of the more high-profile initiatives will be conspicuous to external parties once they have got underway. However, analysts and researchers will not have access to the internal databases and systems used by international firms to capture knowledge about their own Context B initiatives. Furthermore, some subsidiary managers may not want to take part in interviews and/or questionnaire surveys on the topic of subsidiary initiatives without the prior approval of headquarters' managers. Nevertheless, primary data gathering is an accepted approach for studying entrepreneurial dynamics in overseas subsidiaries (Birkinshaw, 2000; Birkinshaw and Ridderstråle, 1999; Ecker et al., 2013). Researchers can reassure informants in subsidiaries by not explicitly seeking to expose details of specific initiatives, concentrating instead on subsidiary manager perceptions of the diffusion of their initiatives within the MNE (see for example Williams and Lee, 2011b).

Given the complex system of factors that can determine the progress of subsidiary initiative and the fact that this is multi-level[1] (including variables at corporate level, subsidiary level, individual manager level, and even the nature of the initiative), researchers also can benefit through the use of exploratory interviews and cases in a phenomenological approach. Such an approach can take into account differences between new and established firms operating in Context B. For example, in the case of 3M Taiwan, the company's well-established new-product introduction system – a formalized control mechanism – contrasts vividly with the challenge faced by Infusion, a much younger and smaller organization at the time and one that was seeking to find the right balance between administration and entrepreneurial spirit. Longitudinal cases can expose the role played by different features of the organizational environment over time; a powerful advantage of the case method given that these organizational features are often co-evolving at the same time as the market-focused venturing activities that they aim to support. We note this co-evolution in the Infusion case and to some extent in the Time Out case with respect to changes in the company's organizational culture.

Summary

In Context B we have learnt how:

- remote subsidiary managers are an important driving force for entrepreneurial rejuvenation in the international firm;

- headquarters' managers have an important role to play in evaluating myriad requests for funding and sanctioning of subsidiary-driven initiatives across multiple markets simultaneously;
- pre-existing resources and capabilities controlled by the firm can be used to underpin subsidiary initiatives, and subsidiaries may need to draw on a wider asset base for larger initiatives that have a wider scope;
- entrepreneurial knowledge can be concentrated in the minds of subsidiary managers, while being dispersed across the cadre of subsidiary managers around the world;
- this form of venturing is present in different industries, different sizes of international firms, and has the potential to occur in all countries in which the international firm has a presence.

Suggested Additional Cases for Analyzing this Context

Beamish, P.W. (2012) 'Firstwell Corporation and the Production Mandate Question' (Ivey Publishing, product number: 9B12M024).

Beamish, P.W. and Roberts, M. (2010) 'Lundbeck Korea: Managing an International Growth Engine' (Ivey Publishing, product number: 9B10M012).

Bidault, F. and Feraud, G. (2010) 'Auchan in Syldavia: Formulating a Strategy for the New Subsidiary' (ESMT, product number: ESMT-309-0091-01).

Lu, L., Beamish, P.W., Bo, J. and Lu, J. (2016) 'EBS in China' (Ivey Publishing, product number: 9B16M215).

Note

1 Williams and Lee (2011b) incorporated variables at corporate level (entrepreneurial strategy), subsidiary unit level (tolerance for local initiative) and individual manager level (subsidiary manager proactivity) in their study of dispersed entrepreneurship in the MNE.

4

'Context C' – Headquarters-driven Venturing: Accessing Strategic External Capabilities

In Context C, we will analyze venturing behavior in international firms at a strategic level, and with a focus on the company's use of external resources and capabilities in order to achieve its venturing goals. In this context, the force for venturing is predominantly headquarters, but rather than relying on assets under the hierarchical control of the firm to pursue venturing, the company seeks out and accesses resources and capabilities outside of the boundaries of the firm. The existence of markets for technology means that a firm does not have to develop all of its own technology (Van Rooij, 2005). The existence of many potential alliance partners means companies can enter into strategic alliances voluntarily, for a plethora of possible reasons, and at more or less any time (Gulati, 1998; Haskell et al., 2016; Inkpen and Tsang, 2005; Wassmer, 2010). This context involves: (1) a role for top managers in recognizing, assessing and choosing new strategic options as a response to competitive challenges (in this respect having some similarity to Context A); but (2) using external assets through inter-organizational collaboration with strategic alliance partners and/or acquisition of new assets in order to seize new international opportunities.

In this view, external collaborators provide critical impetus to the strategic entrepreneurial dynamics of the MNE. While the ingredients of innovation, risk-taking and proactivity may be present in the espoused corporate strategy of the MNE, the realization of venturing across borders will be done in collaboration with partners, or using new external assets brought into the firm through acquisition. Consequently, these external strategic assets provide the key to developing entrepreneurial knowledge.

We see this phenomenon in companies of all sizes. For example, IBM shifted from a predominantly internal focus to using a web of external partners to transform itself into a more innovative and services-oriented organization in the 1990s (Dittrich et al., 2007). A comparable story unfolded with Eli Lilly (Stach, 2006). And a similar type of strategic shift was undertaken between 2006 and 2010 in the Expatica case in this book.

This type of externally-oriented venturing occurs where the means for identifying, evaluating and exploiting opportunities lies outside of the traditional organizational boundary. Various modes for achieving this are possible, including mergers, acquisitions, joint ventures and alliances, venture capital investments and non-equity alliances (Hayward, 2002; Keil, 2002; MacMillan et al., 1986). Furthermore, MNEs increasingly have turned to open innovation: ". . . a paradigm that assumes that firms can and should use external ideas as well as internal ideas, and internal and external paths to market, as the firms look to advance their technology" (Chesbrough, 2006: 1). Research has shown that open innovation activities have become very prominent in MNEs (Mortara et al., 2009; Williams and Vossen, 2014). These activities are characterized by a high degree of co-operation between partners (Billington and Davidson, 2010; Dooley and O'Sullivan, 2007; Gassmann and Enkel, 2004) with MNEs joining forces with different types of partners for different functions (e.g., buyers, suppliers, competitors, universities and research institutes) (Haskell et al., 2016) in an attempt to create value.

The Driving Force: Strategic Leaders Turning to the Outside

Context C relates to the determinants and consequences of *externally-oriented* entrepreneurship as a deliberate component of corporate strategy. Headquarters' managers who are alert to opportunities in the global environment may conclude that the best way of pursuing the opportunities is through externally-oriented venturing modes. A range of modes is possible here and headquarters' managers need to consider the most appropriate given the specific circumstances facing the firm. Headquarters' managers may decide to take equity stakes in other companies (through full ownership acquisitions or partial ownership joint ventures) or undertake non-equity strategic alliances. The important point in our analysis is that, in each of these different types of modes, new opportunities can be identified, developed and exploited (Keil, 2002). The decision made by the top management team on whether and how to pursue externally-oriented venturing requires them to assess the costs and benefits of alternative modes of collaboration, and in particular, the costs and benefits of whether to internalize or externalize knowledge (Rugman and Verbeke, 2003). Strategic collaborative investments can be large-scale, international affairs requiring attention to leveraging and integrating vast amounts of knowledge from partner firms under conditions of uncertainty and competition. However, they also are seen in smaller entrepreneurial firms (Alvarez et al., 2006), as illustrated by the Expatica case in this book.

In driving externally-oriented venturing, headquarters' managers would have concluded that any costs of utilizing external assets for venturing will not outweigh the benefits in terms of achieving the desired change for the organization. For instance, an open innovation strategy represents a risk for MNEs because intellectual property and valuable knowledge about the firm's proprietary technology can potentially leak out to other – often smaller – partner firms. Headquarters' managers will be keen to protect the company's knowledge in order to be able to appropriate value from their innovation strategies. As Hurmelinna-Laukkanen and Ritala (2010: 12) noted: reaping "benefits from positive network externalities, standardization, and collaboration most often requires protection to be used strategically in order to enable safe and controlled knowledge transfer rather than to prevent knowledge flows." Thus, headquarters' managers are not only involved in (a) decisions to identify and select external assets with which to pursue venturing, and (b) choosing the most appropriate mode given the circumstances, they are also involved in managing the collaboration or acquisition such that implementation risks are minimized.

However, it has also been noted in the literature how Context C venturing may involve headquarters' managers actively encouraging an externalization of the company's knowledge. Gassman and Enkel pointed out that to: "co-operate successfully, a give and take of knowledge is necessary, therefore a coupling of the outside-in and inside-out processes is key for success" (Gassmann and Enkel, 2004: 12). In an inside-out process, knowledge flows from the inside of the firm to external actors. An outside-in process, on the other hand, is used to bring outside knowledge and expertise into the firm. A so-called 'coupled process', in turn, is a combination of the two. Thus, in the case of open innovation, the headquarters seeks competitive advantage for the firm by attempting to appropriate value through the 'give and take' of co-operation with partners (Williams and Vossen, 2014).

Headquarters' managers may be tempted to pursue external venturing options because they are associated with short execution times (Roberts and Berry, 1985). Williams and Lee (2011a) cited the example of Millennium Pharmaceuticals' corporate strategy of inter-organizational collaboration within the pharmaceutical industry: "Through a series of ambitious partnerships, the company . . . migrated down the value chain and across product categories" (Champion, 2001: 110). While these benefits may hold, headquarters' managers need to manage the execution of each collaboration. Research has shown this to be equally, if not more, important to outcomes as making decisions about the formation and setting up of collaborations (Dyer et al., 2007). Some international companies, such as Eli Lilly, have even established formal units under headquarters' control in order to manage all aspects of multiple international collaborations (Dhanaraj et al., 2007; Stach, 2006).

The Resources and Capabilities: External Assets Enabling the Company's International Venturing

An international firm may use various 'sourcing' modes to access external resources and capabilities as part of its venturing strategy. These range from non-equity alliances through to low equity stake ventures to fully-owned acquisitions (Van de Vrande et al., 2009). The choice of this governance mode will be determined by how the headquarters' managers view the level of uncertainty surrounding the decision (Van de Vrande et al., 2009). This form of venturing will inevitably make the boundaries of the firm more permeable with respect to knowledge flows (Mortara et al., 2009).

First, accessing external assets to support strategic venturing can involve the international firm establishing and operating collaborative, non-equity partnerships. Eli Lilly do this on a strategic level through their Office of Alliance Management (Stach, 2006) with some impressive results. Collaborating with other firms overseas can act to augment R&D investment as a way of improving international performance (Tomiura, 2007). Recent evidence suggests many MNEs have become more engaged in open innovation strategies in pursuit of new resources and capabilities, particularly headquarters-driven activities in their home countries (Williams and Vossen, 2014). Further examples include Philips and DSM in the Netherlands and Novartis in Switzerland (Chesbrough and Garman, 2009; Tödtling et al., 2011). In all of these cases, the international firm seeks access to new resources and capabilities, including innovative and tacit knowledge, and new ways of using these external assets to exploit opportunities. The firm is seeking to source its venturing capability.

Some thought needs to be given to how the international firm needs to deploy its own assets to ensure a successful innovation sourcing or open innovation strategy. According to Pisano and Verganti (2008: 86): "the new leaders in innovation will be those who can understand *how to design collaboration networks and how to tap their potential*" (emphasis added). Gary Stach at Eli Lilly noted:

> we at Lilly took a hard look at our partnering capabilities. And although we had a solid track record of working with other organizations, we knew we had to do better. So we very consciously researched and discussed how we could consistently create the best opportunities for us and for our partners to meet our goals.
>
> (Stach, 2006: 28)

Similarly, Mortara et al.'s (2009) study of open innovation projects involving MNEs in the UK revealed a mix of tangible and intangible assets needed for open innovation. Specifically, these authors noted how international companies need to develop an accepting culture for open innovation, have procedures and rotation practices aimed at supporting open innovation, use training to prepare employees for open innovation, and incentivize employees to take part. Hence, when we think about resources and capabilities in the context of externally-oriented international venturing, we need to think beyond what assets the firm will source as a result of operating in this context; we also need to consider what assets it needs to deploy for the effort to be worthwhile.

Second, at the other end of the spectrum, Context C venturing can result in the international firm taking advantage of external investment opportunities other than non-equity collaborations, and augmenting the existing asset base through acquisition. In resource-based theory, Penrose (1959) referred to this as a task of 'empire-building' entrepreneurs. Examples include acquiring other firms, investing in joint ventures and taking equity stakes in risky ventures, and even capital purchase of new equipment to give existing production activities new capability (Keil, 2002; Van de Vrande et al., 2009). In the brewing industry, for example, large, well-established international companies such as Carlsberg have sought to grow with acquisition. However, as Gammelgaard and Hobdari (2013) note, despite the size and experience of the acquirer, these transactions are never without risk and can lead to failure, such as the ones that Carlsberg experienced with Tetley and Holsten.

Taking advantage of investment opportunities in this way requires the firm to look away from its existing set of assets, resources and capabilities at where it can invest in pursuit of new opportunities for growth. While an external market for firm ownership makes equity investments possible, an external market for new technology also facilitates Context C venturing. In situations where the 'outside' technology can be used to lower production costs and at the same time is mature and available, this approach will make sense. In the bulk commodities sector of the chemicals industry, for instance, Van Rooij (2005) showed how the existence of markets for technology allowed Dutch-headquartered DSM to acquire breakthrough technology for its fertilizer business in the 1960s. Indeed, the company also had been active during the twentieth century in acquiring complete new plants to serve its fertilizer business around the world.

International firms that are aggressive in Context C will emphasize a greater resource commitment to external opportunities for gaining competitive advantage and growth (Williams and Lee, 2009a). This is an aggressive approach to asset growth that involves the firm applying its own resources in new ways in order to make the entrepreneurial stance in this context viable. Some research goes further and suggests that spin offs and divestments of technology and business units from the focal firm to other firms also should be considered a part of Context C venturing (Keil, 2002). Firms that actively do this also use the fact that external markets exist for businesses and technologies on a global basis. The very existence of these markets allows international firms to adjust asset deployment levels in their venturing endeavors.

The Nature of Entrepreneurial Knowledge in Context C

In Context C, *knowledge of opportunity* happens because the firm has been proactive in seeking out and acquiring new assets (e.g., DSM) and collaborating in networks (e.g., Eli Lilly) with other actors outside of the hierarchical control of the firm (Müller-Seitz, 2012). Knowledge of opportunity arises because of the existence of external markets for technology, know-how and inter-organizational collaboration with alliance partners. The opportunity can reside in an external organization, and, as a consequence of engaging with the external organization through equity or non-equity arrangements, knowledge of the opportunity is created. A separate company that is part of a network through which new opportunities for investment are identified becomes a gatekeeper of opportunities, a way in which a focal company can open doors to as-yet-undiscovered opportunities. Joining forces with a gatekeeper allows the focal company to access a new opportunity space. Finally, an external organization may become an opportunity per se if managers come to view it as a target for acquisition.

This same network of collaborators will also provide the means for developing *knowledge of solution* to opportunity. Collaborating parties bring specialist knowledge to bear on the decision to commit resources to the opportunity and are likely to have prior expertise in both the technology and commercial application of the technology in the market. Headquarters' managers need to access these sources of knowledge and evaluate the opportunity before any investment decision regarding acquisition or participation in new strategic alliances can be made. However, in this networked view, the possibility exists that the solution to the opportunity will involve the firm seeking inputs from other firms that were not involved in the identification of the opportunity. The network's membership may change as a result of this, with new ties being formed as the entrepreneurial process moves from exploration to exploitation. Dittrich et al. (2007) showed how this happened in the case of IBM in the 1990s.

Inkpen and Tsang's (2005) work on social capital and networks provides insight into how knowledge of solution can be achieved in Context C venturing. It is one thing for a network partner to alert our international firm to a new opportunity; it is quite another for them to give us the solution to the opportunity, or for us to expect that they should necessarily be part of the solution. Inkpen and Tsang (2005) highlighted how opportunism in strategic alliances may affect willingness to transfer sensitive knowledge, emphasizing how the development of behavioral trust matters in this respect.

Learning from outcomes is also highly relevant in Context C. While organizational learning can be a motive for external entrepreneurship, there are no guarantees that collaboration will be successful (Inkpen and Tsang, 2005; Lam, 1997). As evidenced by the case of Millennium Pharmaceuticals, large-scale inter-organizational collaboration in pursuit of corporate entrepreneurship and strategic renewal needs to be monitored and interventions may be needed (Champion, 2001). International firms will need to be able to access and process learning of outcomes from Context C venturing promptly and make any interventions necessary. In one sense, IBM demonstrated a strategic willingness to continually adjust its alliance network for innovation on the basis of what it had learnt from venturing with new partners in emerging industries (Dittrich et al., 2007). This learning ultimately allows the optimal balance for Context C venturing and helps ensure that, following the MNE's participation in co-development activities, the created value is appropriately distributed among partners (Ritala and Hurmelinna-Laukkanen, 2009).

In large firms, a centrally-located alliance function can be set up to facilitate the process of entrepreneurial venturing with external partners (Stach, 2006). This function is more likely to be condensed in the set of activities performed by the owner/founders or CEOs of smaller born-global companies. As illustrated in the Expatica case, smaller companies will not have the scale to set up formal administrative units for handling entrepreneurial knowledge in this context. Nevertheless, in firms of all sizes, this function will need to take place in some shape or form to support Context C venturing. It performs a critical role for handling flows of entrepreneurial knowledge between multiple partner firms on an ongoing basis. While formal organizational units and knowledge management systems may have their benefits (Stach, 2006), in some instances, governance structures may be limited due to the socially-embedded nature of knowledge in different cultures around the world (Lam, 1997). To allow entrepreneurial knowledge to flow among international partners in Context C venturing, managers will need to incentivize, prepare and train staff operating at the boundary of the firm to deal with different models of organizational knowledge and overcome any impediments to knowledge transfer that these differences may bring (Lam, 1997; Mortara et al., 2009).

Context C: Cases in Point

In the case of *Expatica.com*, we see an interesting form of Context C venturing take place. Expatica was not large enough – and did not have the deep pockets required – for a large-scale acquisition that it could use for transforming itself into a profitable small business. The company was a small, Dutch born-global company with a clearly defined mission to offer services to expatriates relocating within Europe. However, it was unable to make its business model profitable in multiple markets in the first decade of operation. For most of this initial period the company had support from a government incubator called Twinning. In the early years, the company produced its own content for its website. The changes made at Expatica over a number of years shifted the company towards a partner model. Partners were used not only for news content, but also for events services, a new dating website, as well as for the IT and platform development. This put the company at the center of a network of value-creating actors in different countries. The company was ultimately able to demonstrate financial success in the years after the case was published as a consequence of this headquarters-driven change and strategic shift from internal towards external venturing.

In the case of *Infusion Development Corporation*, we see a strategic shift for the company as its headquarters' managers steered the company towards a global partnership with Microsoft and .NET technology. .NET was Microsoft's open source cross-platform software framework that was part of its expansion into the corporate end of the market. Infusion saw this open source framework as an opportunity for its rapidly growing organization. It had become dependent for revenue on a small group of investment banks, and Infusion viewed a Microsoft partnership as a way of diversifying into new market segments. The effort paid off. Infusion had diversified sufficiently for the global financial crisis and collapse of Lehman Brothers (a key client) to have little impact. Case Exhibit 5 shows the number of employees at year end between 2007 and 2010 to have almost doubled . . . and the sales (in US$) did double! Indeed, the subsequent international expansions into Dubai and London were largely founded on the company's evolving strategic alliance with Microsoft. The opportunities for closing new deals in the hospitality sector in Dubai came about as a consequence of the company's relationships with Microsoft, and the company's team in London became involved in Microsoft's Industry Solutions University (ISU).

In the case of *Xerox*, the company faced a strategic challenge in terms of how to transform away from being a global equipment provider with a limited range of services, including managed print services, towards a customer-centric service provider to global accounts. The goal was to offer a much broader range of advanced knowledge-intensive services. At the forefront of the corporate transformation effort was the company's technological division, Xerox Innovation Group (XIG), headed by Sophie Vandebroek. The key challenge was how the company should innovate in services, and whether it possessed all the resources and capabilities to do this by itself. Analyzing the situation in this case requires an assessment of internal capabilities versus external capabilities residing outside of the boundary of the firm. It also requires work to clarify how such capabilities could underpin the strategic renewal that was required. The company did take some steps to complete the corporate transformation itself. The company had become more customer-centric and had set up user-led innovation teams within strategic clients such as Proctor and Gamble. And it opened a new center in India to make progress on new service delivery. However, the subsequent events reveal that the company ultimately made a major acquisition in its home market (the United States) to strengthen its capabilities in service delivery and allow the transformation to take place. The acquisition was made in 2010 and was of Affiliated Computer Services (ACS), a company with 78,000 employees and $6.6 billion in revenue supporting thousands of large corporations and government agencies.

Challenges for Leaders, Managers and Analysts

The cases illustrate how Context C venturing is present in international firms of all sizes. Smaller firms like Expatica and Infusion are likely to be more reliant on non-equity alliancing than large-scale acquisitions when choosing to pursue this type of externally-oriented venturing. Larger firms have more of a choice. We see Xerox attempting certain initiatives to drive its transformation before embarking on a large strategic acquisition.

And we see IBM using a range of equity and non-equity alliances in order to further its explorative journey into new technological and market domains in the 1990s.

Apart from considerations of sheer size, a range of other challenges face strategic leaders and headquarters' managers when considering Context C venturing. First, headquarters' managers will need to be clear about what assets they think the company needs from external markets in order to progress with their venturing initiatives. Tesla, for instance, needed Panasonic's expertise in lithium-ion rechargeable batteries to help solve issues with driving distances per charge. Assessing the value of external assets inevitably will require headquarters' managers also to have a full and complete picture of the current internal asset base within the boundaries of their firm. This might be relatively straightforward in smaller companies, but as the firm grows in size and becomes more complex and international, maintaining an accurate and up-to-date picture of all entrepreneurial resources and capabilities throughout the organization will be more difficult. Headquarters' managers will be reliant on middle-ranking and regional and divisional managers to keep them informed about what is – and what is not – possible in terms of venturing using the existing internal asset base.

On the flip side of this, headquarters' managers will need to identify partner organizations, many of which may be headquartered in other countries, and assess them for the specific assets that they could contribute to joint initiatives. Selection criteria will need to be clear and related to the function and objective of each initiative (Haskell et al., 2016). Related to this, it is important for headquarters' managers to be ready to end arrangements with strategic partners as and when it becomes necessary to do so. We see this in the case of Tesla when the contract with Lotus Cars to provide the case component for the Roadster expired. Similarly, in the case of IBM, we see ties with innovation partners forming and expiring over the course of the 1990s (Dittrich et al., 2007). These actions on identifying partners and external assets are essential to improve the chances of a successful outcome in Context C, and are likely to involve headquarters' managers utilizing their social capital and influence in different markets (Gulati, 1998; Inkpen and Tsang, 2005).

A second challenge facing headquarters' managers is to answer the question of whether the company needs to engage in coopetition in order to venture with external partners. Coopetition involves firms competing and co-operating at the same time – something still seen as somewhat paradoxical by scholars (Bengtsson and Kock, 2014). This is seen as a more complex form of interaction than either competing or co-operating (Bengtsson and Kock, 2014; Brandenburger and Nalebuff, 2011). Padula and Dagnino (2007) argued that firms can interact based on partly-converging interests. Headquarters' managers will need to assess exactly what these partly-converging interests are and identify whether engaging in venturing with other companies that previously were – or are otherwise seen to be – competitors, constitutes too much of a risk. Following the logic of Brandenburger and Nalebuff's (2011) seminal work, headquarters' managers might need to look at external organizations as 'players in a game of coopetition'. Seeing the external environment in terms of a game may need some to adjust their mindset accordingly. They would need to view and understand the 'value net' of players across the world. Players add value through their roles as customers, suppliers, competitors or complementors (Brandenburger and Nalebuff, 2011) and it would be critical for headquarters' managers to identify and understand the organizations and their roles, and assess whether irrational moves in the game by any of the external organizations would damage the firm.

A third challenge concerns the issue of managing 'openness' (Williams and Vossen, 2014) as it pertains to entrepreneurial knowledge. Williams and Vossen (2014) empirically examined – in the context of MNEs – Laursen and Salter's (2006) assertion of an inverted U-shaped relationship between external knowledge sourcing and innovative performance of firms. Williams and Vossen (2014) specifically looked at this from the point of view of international firms and showed that headquarters' managers considered there to be an optimal point for openness when engaging in open innovation. Too much – and, conversely, too little – openness caused trust and knowledge transfer issues that hindered the innovative performance of the collaboration. These studies argue that it is not simply a question of deciding whether to pursue open innovation. What also matters to headquarters' managers is how much openness to adopt in each co-development relationship, how to protect knowledge assets during the 'give and take' involved in these arrangements (Hurmelinna-Laukkanen and Ritala, 2010), and how to extract value from them. Hurmelinna-Laukkanen and Ritala's (2010) analysis focused on service innovations, pointing out how traditional IP strategies that work in the protection of product technology are less useful and how human resource management, lead time and contracting mechanisms are more useful in offering protection. Headquarters' managers in international firms that pursue strategies of open innovation would need to consider how these mechanisms are used strategically and in ways that achieve as optimal a point for openness as possible and necessary.

MNEs will be concerned not only with exploration within externally-oriented venturing, but also with various considerations relating to exploitation. Larger MNEs are likely to have to manage multiple innovation projects simultaneously, some open, some closed. They will have critical knowledge and resources spread across different innovation projects, which in turn are likely to be spread out across different countries. This means they need to exercise caution. Too high a degree of openness in explorative activities in one project could mean that critical knowledge will leak into external actors. This would have adverse consequences for other projects that are in an exploitation mode. Revealing too much tacit knowledge may offer an opportunity for partners to take advantage of the situation and enter into a learning race. This may be a serious threat for MNEs as their tacit knowledge is utilized in exploitation activities around the world.

A fourth consideration for headquarters' managers concerns how to put formal organization around the process for externally-oriented venturing. This formalization can be useful to underpin knowledge sharing and awareness of different external venturing modes. Keil (2002: 115) pointed out how levels of knowledge and experience among external corporate venturing managers differs and how this knowledge can be concentrated around a narrow range of venturing modes. Organizational units that act to consolidate and enhance knowledge sharing across different modes, as well as different functional areas, can help to alleviate this concern. As Stach (2006) described, Eli Lilly established a dedicated Office of Alliance Management precisely for this purpose. The company's success in the pharmaceutical industry is arguably attributed to the efficiency and effectiveness of this organizational unit. For smaller companies, the function of alliance management may rest more with owner/founders, CEOs and other senior managers in a looser sense. However, the headquarters' managers in these types of firms will need to consider the optimal timing of implementation of formal administration around an alliance strategy (Wassmer, 2010). This will inevitably require an assessment of the pay-back of such an investment. McKern and Naman (2003) used the example of PPG to highlight the importance of headquarters' managers in setting up organizational units to handle key account relations:

> The company's executives believed that there was a need to co-ordinate relationships with ... important customers or suppliers across the divisions. Headquarters had not taken direct responsibility for this role, but had created an inter-SBU team for the task – a use of formalization rather than centralization, which seemed characteristic of PPG.
> (McKern and Naman, 2003: 253)

When we consider the role of subsidiary managers in Context C venturing, we first need to ask whether the subsidiary is affected by – or involved in – the specific external venturing modes selected by the corporate headquarters. A subsidiary may have little or no involvement due to its geographic or functional responsibility. Alternatively, a subsidiary may be required to dedicate resources to assist in the integration of new knowledge and capability (e.g., as a result of a merger or acquisition) or to participate in a new external collaboration (e.g., joint venture or alliance). In either case, the requirement – and request – for subsidiary participation is likely to originate from the headquarters. That said, proactive subsidiary managers may feel inclined to approach headquarters' managers to offer their assistance in working with global collaborators or acquisitions. Indeed, there will be relational benefits for the subsidiary to do so.

With this type of venturing there are likely to be concerns for subsidiary managers. First, subsidiary managers may have to accept the choice of strategic partners handed down to them by headquarters. They may not agree. They may have had different experiences working with the overseas subsidiary of a new strategic alliance partner and their relationships with those overseas subsidiaries (possibly co-residing in the same host country) might not be good ones. Second, subsidiary managers may have to work in the execution phase of a new externally-oriented venturing project with foreign subsidiaries of partner firms or newly acquired firms. Subsidiary managers might not have been involved in any or all of the discussions surrounding the decision to venture with an external firm. But they will be under pressure to accept their role in the execution of new value-creating activities. Third, subsidiary managers will be affected if headquarters' managers' involvement with Context C venturing makes it difficult for new subsidiary initiatives (Context B) to progress. The situation can arise when headquarters' managers are so pre-occupied with large-scale strategic alliance-based venturing or integration of a new acquisition that some subsidiary initiatives get postponed or delayed.

While international venturing research has paid less attention to this context, an important literature has emerged that can be used to frame the phenomenon from a venturing point of view. There are also many cases and anecdotal examples involving headquarters-driven externally-oriented venturing. Researchers can draw on these examples to guide their research questions regarding the antecedents and consequences of venturing in this context. Firm-level secondary data such as R&D intensity ratios, patents and alliance data also can be appropriate for researchers wanting to construct larger samples. Williams and Lee (2009a) collected the cash used in investment activities items from the cash flow statement of US MNEs as a proxy for the level of external aggressiveness adopted. The key assumption here is that headquarters' managers would need to have assessed, debated and agreed these positions before cash was invested (or received through divestment) in any financial year. The indicator therefore represents an overall posture adopted by the headquarters.

In common with Context A research, Context C research can encounter problems of access to the strategic leaders of the MNE (Welch et al., 2002). This makes primary data collection from those responsible for setting levels of entrepreneurial orientation in corporate strategy very difficult to implement. In addition, while hard outcomes of global inter-firm collaboration may be possible to collect through innovative or financial performance indicators, it will be more difficult to truly capture and validate headquarters' learning in this context. Despite this, researchers and analysts should not be put off and could use triangulated techniques, obtaining views of Context C venturing from different sources. This can include the partner or target companies themselves, consultants involved in technology transfer, subsidiary managers affected by Context C venturing and managers involved in administrative units (such as Eli Lilly's Office of Alliance Management) that orchestrate the execution of activity in this context.

Summary

In Context C we have learnt how:

- headquarters' managers in the international firm can seek to adopt a strategic posture for the firm that emphasizes large-scale corporate venturing involving outside organizations and strategic partners;

- this can be an important manifestation of corporate strategy in an international firm, allowing headquarters' managers to access entrepreneurial knowledge across the globe efficiently;
- resources and capabilities predominantly under the hierarchical control of outside organizations (including universities, research labs and partner firms) can be used to underpin international venturing;
- this type of venturing can be seen across industries, countries and different sizes of international firm, from small ones such as Expatica, through to mid-size (e.g., Infusion), to the very large (e.g., Xerox).

Suggested Additional Cases for Analyzing this Context

Adhikari, A. and Deshmukh, R. (2013) 'UTV and Disney: A Strategic Alliance' (Ivey Publishing, product number: 9B10M043).

Dhanaraj, C., Lyles, M. and Lai, Y. (2007) 'Innovation without Walls: Alliance Management at Eli Lilly and Company' (Ivey Publishing, product number: 9B07M015).

Kittilaksanawong, W. and Palecki, C. (2015) 'Renault-Nissan Alliance: Will Further Integration create more Synergies?' (Ivey Publishing, product number: 9B15M097).

Pillittere, D.A. (2009) 'GDR versus Kodak – Bart Film Scanner' (Ivey Publishing, product number: 9B09M059).

5

'Context D' – Subsidiary-driven Venturing: Local Embedding to Drive Change

In Context D, we again view venturing behavior in international firms at a host country level, but with a specific focus on the foreign subsidiary's use of external resources and capabilities in order to pursue venturing. In this context, the subsidiary's managers again come under the spotlight. The assets that are most relevant to venturing are outside of the boundaries of the firm. However, these assets are accessible to the foreign subsidiary because of the subsidiary's embeddedness – or degree of closeness – with external organizations that possess them. This context for venturing arises because of: (1) a role for subsidiary managers in recognizing, assessing and pursuing opportunity through embeddedness of the subsidiary within inter-organizational networks; and (2) the possibility of using external actors in host countries around the world to share knowledge of problems and market needs, as well as resources that may be combined to form potential solutions.

In this context, entrepreneurship becomes dispersed, a phenomenon we discussed in Chapter 3 (Context B). However, dispersed entrepreneurship in the MNE in the form of Context D venturing arises because individuals employed in remote units are closely connected with local actors. A stream of literature has emerged showing how counterparts in host countries can influence MNE subsidiaries in the host country as a result of the subsidiary's embeddedness with them (Andersson and Forsgren, 1996; Andersson et al., 2002). Important for our analysis in this chapter is that a subsidiary's external network can supply useful resources that, when needed by the wider MNE, will put the subsidiary in an influential position when instigating change for the MNE (Andersson and Pahlberg, 1997). These external resources in the host country can also allow the subsidiary to develop a wider scope of functional operations for itself (Pu and Soh, 2017). The interactions between a subsidiary and local actors can vary in intensity, from arm's length one-off interactions, through minor adaptation and modification of products, to larger-scale joint adaptation and modification, through to full-scale joint research efforts (Achcaoucaou et al., 2014).

Of increasing importance in the globalized knowledge-based economy of the twenty-first century is the fact that a subsidiary's external network extends beyond commercial, business organizations such as suppliers, distributors and clients. A literature has examined the inter-linkages between foreign subsidiaries and actors within the national innovation system in host countries. A national innovation system is a "well-articulated network of firms, research centers, universities and think tanks that work together to take advantage of global knowledge, assimilating and adapting it to local needs, thus creating new technology" (World Bank, 2016). Collaboration between universities and industry is widely recognized as a critical component of a national innovation system (Acworth, 2008; Ankrah and Al-Tabbaa, 2015; Etzkowitz, 2010; Freeman, 1995; Galán-Muros and Plewa, 2016). Within these collaborative linkages, MNE subsidiaries are able to engage in the venturing process, seeking out knowledge of opportunity, knowledge of solution to opportunity and learning from outcomes. As Lam (2003) noted in her study of US and Japanese R&D subsidiaries in the UK: "MNEs tap into foreign academic knowledge base and scientific labour through collaborative links with higher education institutions" (Lam, 2003: 673).

The Driving Force: Subsidiary Managers and their Local Embeddedness

In Context D, externally-oriented venturing is pursued in geographically-dispersed locations and at host country level. Subsidiaries engage in entrepreneurial activity through alliances and joint ventures in host markets or regions, such as involvement with science parks and participation with universities and R&D networks (Lam, 2003). Such behavior is likely to require the support of regional and/or global headquarters' managers. It may even be influenced by control mechanisms used by the corporate headquarters (Andersson et al., 2005). In Context D, subsidiary managers in the host country play a much more prominent role in identifying new opportunities that arise as a consequence of their embeddedness with host country actors. They are prominent in finding potential solutions to opportunity and for generating learning from outcomes that can be shared with others around the corporation. However, the level of corporate investment (and risk) to the MNE is not likely to be as high as with the large-scale, long-term strategic alliances driven by headquarters' managers in Context C.

Mu et al. (2007) used a sample of MNE subsidiaries in the USA to explore the influence of local embeddedness on subsidiary learning and innovation. This study showed that the degree of local embeddedness influences the subsidiary's ability to learn from the local environment and innovate. The study also showed how diversity in a subsidiary's management team matters for local innovation: one that comprises people from different backgrounds will have a positive impact on a subsidiary's propensity to innovate (Mu et al., 2007).

Embeddedness involves local linkages in activity-based social exchange relationships (Chen et al., 2004). Research has shown how embeddedness involves adaptation to product and production technology, standard operating procedures and best practice as a result of these external relationships (Andersson et al., 2005). Subsidiary manager embeddedness is a prime determinant of whether a subsidiary will come up with new ideas (Mu et al., 2007) and how the subsidiary will develop in terms of its scope of functional operations (Pu and Soh, 2017). Overseas subsidiaries gain knowledge through dense linkages among co-located entities. Relationships develop and promote learning and innovation through spillovers (Porter, 1998). The subsidiary acts as a key conduit by which knowledge spilling over from clusters of innovation in a particular country is captured and absorbed into the wider MNE (Almeida, 1996; Gilbert et al., 2008). Clusters can also provide resources and networking opportunities that facilitate the internationalization of new ventures (Colovic and Lamotte, 2014).

When the subsidiary is active in this context it can build power and the ability to influence decisions within the MNE. The subsidiary forms learning partnerships with local customers, suppliers and institutions; the local context is seen as more useful and more legitimate as a basis for new knowledge creation by the subsidiary (Tregaskis, 2003). It is this that ultimately allows the subsidiary to make attempts at developing its own charter and competitive capabilities (Tregaskis, 2003). According to Cantwell and Santangelo (1999), it is the subsidiary's local embeddedness that cannot be accessed elsewhere that allows the MNE to "tap local tacit advantages" (Cantwell and Santangelo, 1999: 102), ultimately allowing for "corporate technological renewal" (Cantwell and Santangelo, 1999: 118).

The Resources and Capabilities: A Spotlight on Trust

In Context D venturing, we need to recognize that, while the local host country environment was originally seen primarily as a sales market or as a source of cheap labor, increasingly it is viewed as a source of new knowledge (Almeida, 1996; Dunning, 1994; Kumar et al., 2009; Lam, 2003; Tregaskis, 2003). But where does this knowledge come from? It cannot appear out of thin air! Relationships between subsidiary managers and host country agents underpin the exchange of resources between the subsidiary and local partners. These relationships can take time to develop but are essential as they convey arguably the most critical resource for innovation in MNE subsidiaries, namely tacit and explicit knowledge of new opportunities and ways of exploring and exploiting new opportunities (Williams and Lee, 2011a).

The question of intangible assets that are associated with good relationships between subsidiary managers and local agents then arises, and perhaps foremost here has been the question of trust between subsidiaries and local partners. Williams and Du (2014) examined this issue for the case of MNE subsidiaries based in China. Through a questionnaire survey of 306 subsidiary managers across three Tier-1 cities in China (Beijing, Shanghai and Guangzhou) they showed that while learning from local partners only mattered in Beijing, trust mattered to innovative performance of subsidiaries in all locations. In a further study, Du and Williams (2017) identified 33 cases of innovative projects between MNE subsidiaries and local organizations in China and showed how different components of inter-organizational trust interact with location characteristics in determining innovative outcomes. In particular, the sociological type of trust was more apparent in successful innovative projects with partners in Beijing, while the economic type of trust mattered in Shanghai and Guangzhou. Sociological trust places a greater emphasis on honesty, confidence, benevolence and reliability, while economic trust emphasizes credibility, responsibility and predictability (Seppänen et al., 2007). Trust with local partners, then, is a critical intangible resource for Context D venturing. It is an asset that applies across whole countries even where there is variance in levels of economic development within the country. However, managers will need to pay attention to subtle differences in trust and how these might be used as a resource for enabling Context D venturing in different types of foreign locations.

Andersson et al. (2002) made an important distinction between business and technical embeddedness. While this distinction can be appropriate for analytical reasons, these often go together as subsidiaries use embeddedness to seize new opportunities in host countries. The 3M Taiwan case in this book shows how both of these facets of embeddedness were needed during a new subsidiary initiative in Taiwan. The Infusion Poland case stresses technical embeddedness and the need to identify, penetrate and influence communities that control technical resources and capabilities in host countries. Case Exhibit 2 shows the selection criteria used by the company as it evaluated different locations around the world; note how the company has highlighted the role of 'insiders'. These can be used to develop trust and learning about the innovative assets potentially available to the company. This case also stresses the importance of training new recruits – human capital – from Poland so they become quickly familiar with the global commercial requirements and corporate culture for entrepreneurship. Business and technical embeddedness are often inter-linked in Context D venturing.

Further support for this is found in the national innovation systems literature. Local universities, research labs and incubators have competences in specialized technological areas and actively participate in the entrepreneurial process alongside firms (Etzkowitz et al., 2000). When universities and industrial firms collaborate in R&D, the needs of business and society become incorporated into basic research activity. New ideas can be put into practice in such a way that they are viable for commercialization and actually useful to end-users (Acworth, 2008). Nelson and Winter (1982) described this in terms of an interweaving of basic research and market-focused R&D. Universities, industry and governments coalesce around innovation, their inter-linkages providing a basis for knowledge transfer and joint scientific exploration and commercialization (Etzkowitz, 2010). However, countries are not all equal when it comes to the maturity of national innovation systems. Furthermore, politically-unstable countries are less capable of attracting investment and promoting and nurturing a rich ecology of innovation as represented by what has become known as the Triple Helix model of government–university–industry relations (Leydesdorff and Meyer, 2006). International firms considering investing in politically-unstable countries[1] in order to become embedded with national innovation systems will face challenges in terms of who they can trust to supply resources and capabilities for innovation projects.

The Nature of Entrepreneurial Knowledge in Context D

When we consider Context D venturing, it is the embeddedness of the subsidiary with local actors that becomes the prime mechanism by which knowledge creation occurs for the subsidiary (Andersson et al., 2005). This knowledge is not just limited to production knowledge – i.e., knowledge associated with that which the firm already exploits – it will also relate to entrepreneurial knowledge and the creation of new ideas (Mu et al., 2007). Subsidiaries gain entrepreneurial knowledge through working with local, external actors and being more closely embedded with them through social ties and individual relationships than headquarters' managers can be (Andersson and Forsgren, 1996; Andersson et al., 2002). This enables the transmission of knowledge surrounding specific entrepreneurial initiatives.

Knowledge of opportunity arises through embeddedness of the subsidiary within a local business and technology context (Andersson and Forsgren, 1996; Andersson et al., 2002; George et al., 2002; Pu and Soh, 2017). Local actors in the supply and distribution chains share knowledge of commercial problems that need addressing as well as market needs and trends. Local actors in the technology domain, such as universities, share knowledge that allows subsidiaries to identify and master new technology (George et al., 2002). These represent opportunities for the subsidiary to create value and their embeddedness with local actors heightens their awareness of opportunities. In many cases, embeddedness with multiple host country actors will increase the diversity of knowledge that the subsidiary will be exposed to. Du and Williams (2017), for instance, found evidence of subsidiaries in Beijing benefitting from their closeness to sources of information about new government policy. This could put the subsidiary in an advantageous position through early awareness of policy change and related implications for innovative projects. Other subsidiaries in Du and Williams' (2017) study highlighted inter-linkages with host country industry associations as a source of knowledge of opportunity.

In terms of *knowledge of solution*, external collaborators and other actors in host countries provide important input into alternative ways of exploiting opportunities. Depending on the identity of the actor in question, the particular aspect of knowledge of solution that the actor can provide to the subsidiary will vary. Local universities and incubators, for instance, have entrepreneurial competences and may actively participate in the entrepreneurial process (Etzkowitz et al., 2000; George et al., 2002). Technology transfer from universities to industry inherently includes knowledge of solution and a process of constant learning during the operational phase (Ankrah and Al-Tabbaa, 2015). But their specific contribution to knowledge of solution for any given opportunity is more likely to be technology- and development process-related than marketing or commercially-related. Actors in the supply and distribution chains, meanwhile, also matter. Andersson et al. (2002) noted how the "external network can play a crucial role as a strategic source for such competence development" (Andersson et al., 2002: 991). Interestingly, Andersson et al.'s (2002) study showed how host country business embeddedness stimulates host country technical embeddedness, and it is the latter, not the former that drives subsidiary performance. In other words, closeness with business actors in the host country will set the subsidiary on a path to search for potential solutions to opportunities, and this can end up being in the form of adaptation of product and production technology.

Finally, *learning from outcomes* in Context D has some interesting features that set this context apart from the other three contexts for venturing. Learning from outcomes will not be restricted to the subsidiary. The subsidiary's business and technical embeddedness will mean host country collaborators and partner organizations will quickly learn about how specific opportunities were pursued by the subsidiary, how the subsidiary galvanized resources and capabilities from different sources in pursuit of the opportunity, and what happened next. Indeed, it is even possible that external organizations within the host country become exposed to performance outcomes before the subsidiary's own corporate headquarters! Their closeness will mean they will have an early warning about any adverse performance problems.

Research shows how technology transfer from universities to firms can improve firms' financial performance and even develop the economy through successful spin-out companies (Lockett and Wright, 2005). Entrepreneurial knowledge surrounding specific technology transfer and spin-out companies involving a subsidiary will be readily available to host country actors. That said, research has also showed how headquarters will use control mechanisms, including the number of expatriates deployed to the subsidiary, as a means of exerting direct control to influence the degree of subsidiary local embeddedness (Andersson et al., 2005). Expatriate managers can be used as agents of knowledge transfer (Tsang, 1999) and thereby provide a mechanism by which headquarters gains insight into learning from outcomes associated with Context D venturing. As noted by Horak and Yang (2016), expatriate performance is at least partly made up of their ability to transfer knowledge bi-directionally from home to host country and vice versa. In the case of Tommasi Motorcycles in Japan, expatriate management were unable to become effectively embedded with local dealers and they under-performed in their roles as agents of knowledge transfer and learning for the MNE (Hicks and Lehmberg, 2012). Similarly, Horak and Yang's (2016) case study on Yongo in South Korea puts a spotlight on the importance of long-standing affective ties in the local social context as a determinant of expatriate success.

Context D: Cases in Point

In the case of *Infusion Poland*, the company sought to find a new location to develop strategic assets for the corporation: a new hub that would spearhead .NET development and solutions for clients around the world. The company had had an uncomfortable experience with a previous entry into India, and had subsequently exited India. This experience led them to exercise diligence in scouting new locations. The case shows how the company ended up choosing Krakow in Poland. Previously, other well-known high-technology companies were drawn to Krakow for sourcing technical talent as the city had three reputable universities (Jagiellonian, AGH University of Science and Technology, and Politecknike Krakowska). Multiple visits to Poland allowed the company's managers to understand where local communities of .NET programmers existed and how to penetrate these communities. Through a careful process of increasing embeddedness within these communities, Infusion was able not only to identify talent, but also to set out its own stall, selling itself as a potential employer when candidates also could target companies such as IBM, Motorola and Google. Through ongoing embeddedness within the .NET community in Poland, Infusion was able to select and recruit the best available talent in multiple rounds of recruitment.

In the case of *Time Out Group,* embeddedness of the subsidiary managers in Lisbon enabled the company to develop a unique offering to customers. Embeddedness was needed with multiple types of local actors and was not restricted to those working in knowledge-intensive organizations such as universities and research labs. In this case, the required embeddedness was with architects and shop planners, with restaurateurs and chefs, and with other key stakeholders in the cultural industries, such as arts and events companies. This aspect of the Time Out Case may not have involved exploratory IP development as seen in industries such as pharmaceuticals, high-technology equipment manufacturing and software services. But it was, nevertheless, exploratory. The company had not attempted anything like this before. And there were no similar analogs around the world to compare or learn from. Embeddedness with resource providers with intimate knowledge of local service delivery, culture and tastes was what was important.

In the case of *3M Taiwan,* the embeddedness of the subsidiary in the local host country context played a crucial role in both the identification of the opportunity and the development of knowledge related to the solution to the opportunity as well as subsequent learning from outcomes. When exploring the idea for using the company's hydrocolloid dressing product in new ways in the Taiwanese market, a project team member in the subsidiary recalled a conversation with a local medical instrument retailer. The retailer had told the subsidiary employee that local nurses were the main customers for the existing 3M hydrocolloid dressing rolls. They would cut the rolls into smaller pieces to use on patients' skin blemishes. This was a vital piece of information that galvanized the project, giving it specific focus on a new opportunity for acne treatment. In terms of developing knowledge of solution to the opportunity, the subsidiary gained support from local medical experts, including a dermatologist at Tri-Service General Hospital in Taipei. The dermatologist even reported the findings of the new product's efficacy in a professional medical journal. 3M Taiwan also engaged a local advertising company to assist with innovative commercials on mass rapid transit systems. They also collaborated with local retailers on understanding how to increase the product's visible presence in stores. Finally, 3M Taiwan worked with Internet companies to launch an innovative animation game based on the idea of combating skin blemishes. These different facets of the go-to-market strategy were driven by subsidiary managers in Taiwan, and utilized the resources and capabilities of a range of external and local organizations in order to achieve a successful outcome for the initiative.

Challenges for Leaders, Managers and Analysts

MNE leaders face various challenges when it comes to Context D venturing. On the one hand, the headquarters' role can be seen as relatively passive; the headquarters can only sit and wait and, at some unknowable moment in time, will learn about a new initiative that has risen or progressed in a foreign subsidiary as a consequence of its external embeddedness. In this sense, strategic leaders need to keep on their toes; they need to assess the global potential of new opportunities arising as a result of subsidiary participation in dispersed business networks. And they need to do this on a constant basis. This view resonates with aspects of headquarters' manager roles in Context B.

However, research highlights some important nuances and alternative considerations here. First, when assigning a mandate to a subsidiary to perform a given role, headquarters' managers will be cognizant of the extent to which an external network orientation of the subsidiary is desirable and necessary. It may be the case that the headquarters has established the subsidiary within a cluster of related organizations within a host country for the very purpose of joint R&D and collaboration with local actors (Almeida, 1996; Gilbert et al., 2008; Porter, 1998). In this scenario, it will be expected that the subsidiary develops valuable relationships with local actors in the search for entrepreneurial knowledge. Second, scholars have noted how MNEs need to understand multiple embeddedness as it pertains to foreign subsidiaries (Meyer et al., 2011). Headquarters' managers need to consider how to organize across multiple host locations, while at the same time balancing internal and external embeddedness for each and every subsidiary.

I believe the subsidiary also has a role to play in determining its own balance between internal and external embeddedness (see point below on challenges for subsidiary managers). But at the headquarters' level, a key imperative is to recognize and reconcile two issues: (1) that each and every host country where the MNE has operations will have its own distinct culture, customs and set of actors with the potential to contribute to Context D venturing; while (2) global integration will be needed across the MNE in order to transfer entrepreneurial knowledge between units. Meyer et al. (2011) note how strategic leaders of the MNE need to manage multiple embeddedness. At the firm level, the MNE needs to be able to develop and execute different strategies in different host countries. At the subsidiary level, the right balance between internal and external embeddedness is needed.

Third, given that the dispersion of MNE activities allows the company to generate large amounts of diverse knowledge from different locations (Meyer et al., 2011), the MNE will need to develop mechanisms for co-ordinating and managing this knowledge. Unlike Context C venturing, this knowledge does not necessarily need to be co-ordinated through a central alliance function – as in the case of Eli Lilly (Stach, 2006). But this does not preclude the MNE from using a central alliance function also to manage and co-ordinate important locally-embedded projects and initiatives around the world. In this sense, headquarters' managers would be using a central alliance function to oversee local alliance entrepreneurship. Another way by which co-ordination can take place in Context D is through direct involvement of headquarters' managers, as was the case in Infusion's preparation and set-up of its Greenfield subsidiary in Poland.

Fourth, some subsidiaries may belong to regions or geographic subsystems (Porter, 1998) where the entrepreneurial process is encouraged, while others may not. Du and Williams' (2017) study of different types of relationships between subsidiaries and local partners in China highlights the imperative for headquarters to choose locations not only that will support the desired mandate of the subsidiary, but also to select and train subsidiary managers that have the people skills to develop the appropriate types of relationship given the nature of the location.

Challenges for subsidiary managers in Context D venturing are numerous. First and foremost, the subsidiary will need to assess the impact of increasing levels of embeddedness in the host country on its overall level of isolation. Achcaoucaou et al.'s (2014) case studies of the effects of external and internal embeddedness of subsidiaries showed that increasing external embeddedness at the expense of internal embeddedness with other units of the MNE can lead to isolation of the subsidiary. This is consistent with Williams and Nones (2009) finding that, without internal rotation and training, isolation of R&D subsidiaries can occur. This is, arguably, counter-productive from a venturing perspective; it defeats the point of setting up a subsidiary to perform R&D for the whole MNE in the first place! Achcaoucaou et al.'s (2014) point is an important consideration for subsidiary managers pursuing Context D venturing. It brings attention to a key danger of subsidiary 'over-embeddedness' in host countries in pursuit of entrepreneurial knowledge.

Second, and building on this point, subsidiary managers will need to find the right balance between internal and external embeddedness. Achcaoucaou et al.'s (2014) case studies reveal that too much internal embeddedness at the expense of external embeddedness in the host country can have an effect on how the mandate of the subsidiary evolves. In this situation, the subsidiary will evolve towards a competence-exploiting mandate, potentially dampening the entrepreneurial potential of the subsidiary. This balancing act between internal and external embeddedness has been referred to in terms of 'dual-embeddedness' of a subsidiary (Morgan and Kristensen, 2006; Nell et al., 2015; Pu and Soh, 2017).

Third, external embeddedness of foreign subsidiaries will necessitate bi-directional knowledge flows with actors in the external environment. The subsidiary must be receptive to knowledge in-flows and willing and capable of knowledge out-flows. Echoing the point made in our discussion on Context B, in Context D the subsidiary will also need to think about using HRM practices in the subsidiary that support entrepreneurial knowledge flows into and out of the subsidiary. Following Williams and Lee's (2016) study of Korean subsidiaries based in three European countries, the subsidiary's own use of a high performance work system (HPWS) will play a crucial role. As Lam (2003: 680) noted: "When learning is central to the missions of overseas R&D units, firms' strategies for developing a global human resource system and gaining access to local scientific personnel becomes crucial." Encouraging commitment and performance in employees (Evans and Davis, 2005; Pfeffer,

1998; Pfeffer and Veiga, 1999) will matter to how those employees become engaged in local, inter-organizational social networks.

Some of the challenges facing analysts and researchers of international venturing in Context D are similar to those in Context B. For example, there are no validated, publicly-available secondary databases that a researcher of Context D venturing can access and utilize across MNEs and countries. It would be wonderful if this was the case but researchers have to work within the boundaries of reality! There are numerous constructs in Context D that researchers are interested in. These include the level of internal and external embeddedness of a subsidiary, the extent to which different types of local actors in host countries influence adaptation and modification of MNE products and services as offered by subsidiaries, the degree to which a particular relationship in a host country constitutes opportunity, the way in which trust is used in different locations. And within these, the constructs can be decomposed further. For instance, Du and Williams (2017) looked at different types of trust between overseas subsidiaries in China and local actors. Andersson and Forsgren (1996) operationalized embeddedness through the notion of adaptation for the subsidiary through relations with different types of external actors (i.e., customer/supplier/other). Lam (2003) captured, amongst other variables, aspects of the human resource strategy adopted by the subsidiary. While these are all types of constructs that are impossible to access as reliable secondary data sources across firms and countries, using primary data opens up many possibilities.

Developing effective research designs based on primary data collection plays a much more important role here. There are also practicality and cost considerations for researchers in this context that will differ to the other contexts. Researchers and analysts need to be able to visit host countries in order to obtain primary data. They will not only need to gain access to managers within subsidiaries, but also they will need to consider whether they need to access different types of external actors as well. In doing so, researchers will be able to use the primary data through interviews, questionnaires and observational techniques to understand both sides of the external embeddedness coin: the view from the subsidiary, as well as the view from the external actors. Another approach is to use exploratory cases. Achcaoucaou et al.'s (2014) study demonstrates the usefulness of cases in this context, in particular, studies using multiple longitudinal cases. Given the path-dependent nature of subsidiary embeddedness, and the fact that control mechanisms used by headquarters to integrate and manage a subsidiary can change over time (Andersson et al., 2005; Ecker et al., 2013), longitudinal case studies have the advantage of being able to tap into factors that determine increases and decreases in subsidiary embeddedness and the impacts these changes have on venturing outcomes.

Researchers need to weigh up the costs of research projects based on primary data collection and longitudinal case analysis in this context. A decision will need to be taken with respect to research design: whether to stay in one host country and collect primary data from a number of subsidiaries located in that country on questions related to external embeddedness (Achcaoucaou et al., 2014; Du and Williams, 2017), or whether to focus on one MNE and trace its different subsidiary investments around the world using primary data on Context D venturing for each of them. The former approach has more appeal for reasons of practicality, cost and convenience. However, the interplay of multiple embeddedness and entrepreneurial knowledge dynamics in Context D venturing could be explored more fruitfully using the latter approach. Some researchers have adopted research designs somewhere in the middle of these and compared subsidiary embeddedness phenomena across host countries (e.g., Finland and China in the case of Andersson et al., 2005).

Summary

In Context D we have learnt how:

- remote subsidiary managers can pursue entrepreneurial subsidiary initiatives as a consequence of their embeddedness in local host country networks;
- headquarters' managers will need to understand this embeddedness and network orientation of subsidiaries in order to fully evaluate knowledge of opportunity and knowledge of solution emanating from embedded subsidiaries;
- externally-embedded resources and capabilities not under the hierarchical control of a subsidiary can be used by the subsidiary to advance its entrepreneurial activities;
- entrepreneurial knowledge developed by subsidiary managers around the world has an externally-embedded component that headquarters' managers may find difficult to access and evaluate;

- this form of venturing happens in many different industries, different sizes of international firms (note: Tesla in Singapore vs. Infusion in Poland), and can occur in any country in which subsidiary managers develop business networks with local actors.

Suggested Additional Cases for Analyzing this Context

Comas, M and Sagebien, J. (2010) 'Wal-Mart Puerto Rico: Promoting Development through a Public-Private Partnership' (Ivey Publishing, product number: 9B10M024).

Hicks, J. and Lehmberg, D. (2012) 'Collision Course: Selling European High Performance Motorcycles in Japan' (Ivey Publishing, product number: 9B12M025).

Kanter, R.M. and Scannell, J. (1999) 'IBM Ireland: Reinventing Education Crosses the Atlantic' (Harvard Business School, product number: 300034).

Moller Larsen, M. and Pedersen, T. (2012) 'Nokia: From In-House to Joint R&D' (Ivey Publishing, product number: 9B11M114).

Note

1 A cursory examination of the World Economic Forum's Global Competitiveness Report shows that the African countries such as South Africa, Kenya, Rwanda and Uganda rank equal to or higher than certain EU countries (including Italy and Poland) in terms of university–industry collaboration in R&D (Global Competitiveness Report, 2015). The balance of power with respect to the location of national technological competence has changed, and will continue to change.

6

'Across the Contexts' – Strategic Integration and Leading the Firm in International Venturing

In this chapter we bring together the main threads from the previous four chapters (i.e., the four contexts) and discuss the reality of venturing in international firms in an integrative, cross-contextual way. The foregoing discussion of the four contexts shows how there can be a multiplicity of driving forces behind innovation, risk-taking and proactivity in international firms. It also shows how a wide range of resources and capabilities underpin the venturing process and that these differ across contexts. Furthermore, as the cases illustrate, this broad range of potential driving forces and assets determine how venturing unfolds over time. It is then necessary to understand the driving forces and assets in a dynamic sense. More precisely, it is necessary to appreciate how entrepreneurial knowledge moves, often seamlessly, between entrepreneurial contexts in international firms through interfaces that often are not formally defined. I argue that harnessing this dynamic process is a strategic imperative for the leadership of MNEs that want to pursue international venturing. Leadership challenges as discussed in this chapter take on a completely new meaning when we consider venturing in international firms in an holistic, cross-contextual way.

This holistic view is important for various reasons. First, it is *unrealistic* to expect a firm to operate exclusively in one context. Even smaller firms can be active in multiple contexts. This is illustrated by cases such as Infusion and Expatica in this book. Second, firms inevitably *shift* their strategic emphasis over time in terms of how they venture within and across contexts. These shifts are often in response to environmental changes and performance outcomes, and will differ from firm to firm due to the path-dependent nature of a firm's decision-making. Third, firms are able to *transport knowledge* gained by venturing in one context for application in other contexts. I argue this knowledge transportation capability is a fundamental determinant of performance in the modern MNE, vitally important for technology-intensive MNEs. It is a unique feature of an MNE that distinguishes this type of organizational form from other types (such as purely domestic firms and public sector organizations). Each of the individual contexts and their corresponding academic literatures set out in the previous chapters are but building blocks for an holistic view of venturing in international firms; a view that covers all angles.

This chapter will discuss implications for such an holistic, cross-contextual view. It will analyze corresponding challenges for the leadership of the MNE. There are also implications for researchers and analysts (and students!) that this perspective raises and these are discussed.

Cross-Contextualization of Initiatives: Cases in Point

In the case of *Time Out Group*, a subsidiary initiative originating in a host country became a strategic thrust for the company to be considered for deployment in a wide range of other countries around the world. What we are referring to here is the Time Out Market (TOM) initiative. This was originally started by managers on the ground in Lisbon, Portugal. Time Out only had a minority stake in the initiative until a point in time shortly before the IPO in June 2016 when the company took full ownership and control. After experiencing exceptional operating performance from the initiative, many others around the world became alert to what was going on with TOM and expressed an interest in replicating it in their own countries. Headquarters' managers soon realized that the opportunity could be scalable and become one of the foundation stones for corporate rejuvenation. Following a period of review and careful reflection, headquarters' managers looked towards Miami (United States) and London (UK) as possible next locations for wholly-owned and operated TOMs. In essence the initiative started out as a part–Context D and part-Context C one. It was a Context D initiative in the sense that it was driven by subsidiary managers in Portugal and the key knowledge of opportunity, knowledge of solution to opportunity and learning from outcomes, came through these managers working with local chefs, restaurateurs and store designers. It had elements of a Context C initiative as the initial majority partner in the venture was Oakley Capital, a UK-based private equity investor. The initiative become an important and highly conspicuous Context A initiative as knowledge of the solution and learning from outcomes promulgated through to headquarters' managers, including CEO Julio Bruno. Indeed, as part of the IPO of the company in June 2016, £20 million of the £59 million in net IPO proceeds were ear-marked for roll out of TOMs, including geographical expansion into other countries.

In the case of *3M Taiwan*, knowledge of a new opportunity to use hydrocolloid dressing to treat acne in the Taiwanese market arose through internal discussions and interactions involving subsidiary managers in the host country. The corporate culture and management control systems were supportive of experimentation and risk-taking at the periphery of the organization and were highly pertinent to the decision made by subsidiary managers to devote resources and time to exploring the opportunity. However, the eventual solution to the opportunity involved a range of locally-embedded actors in the host country, including dermatologists, market research and advertising agencies, and retail outlets. The initiative started out as a Context B (subsidiary-driven) initiative, and then progressed into a Context D (locally-embedded) one where knowledge of solution and learning from outcomes were shared with a variety of local actors.

In the case of *Xerox*, the company wanted to move from 'products to services'. The company had sought options to achieve a new level of customer-centricity within its innovation divisions. This would enable it to offer more advanced services – arguably consultancy-like ones – on top of its existing managed print services (MPS) and traditional technology and product range. Headquarters' managers were clear on the strategic direction but were challenged by the question of how to achieve the desired customer-centricity and broader set of global capabilities to offer advanced B2B services to global clients with complex information-processing requirements. A number of corporate-driven initiatives were started, including innovation councils with key clients in the home market, and opening a new offshore center (the Xerox Research Centre – XRCI) in Chennai,

India. Ultimately, though, the company achieved its goal through a strategic acquisition of Affiliated Computer Services (ACS), a services company itself with 78,000 employees and clients in more than 100 countries. In this case, the initiative started out in Context A; headquarters' managers had spotted the opportunity as a consequence of shifts in the business landscape. They had also embarked on some resource deployments and centrally-driven initiative-taking; evidence of their stance on knowledge of solution to opportunity. Inevitably they would have gained critical learning from outcomes of these initiatives within a short period after embarking on them. However, with the ACS acquisition, we see clear evidence of a shift into Context C venturing. The strategic capabilities required to fulfill the vision were found outside of the hierarchical control of the organization and, through the acquisition, were brought into and within the boundaries of the firm.

Implications of Having a Multiplicity of Driving Forces

The cases illustrate how each context allows for opportunities to be identified, valued and captured by the MNE. But they also show how the MNE may engage in any or all of the four contexts for entrepreneurship at any point in time. An MNE's participation in one entrepreneurial context does not necessarily preclude it from participating in another. Furthermore, as any given initiative develops and evolves, its 'center of gravity' can move from one context to another. Most international firms experience this phenomenon and it is not just restricted to the cases in this book. Microsoft, for instance, is globally recognized for introducing new computer software to global markets that was developed centrally and internally as part of its headquarters-driven corporate strategy (Context A). In addition, Microsoft has built an international network of R&D subsidiaries that are embedded with universities and research networks in the countries in which they are located (Context D). Microsoft also has developed strategic global alliances (Context C). Initiatives that companies like Microsoft take part in, can – and will – move around the contexts as different driving forces from the different contexts exert influence on them.

The discussions in the previous chapters show how driving forces vary by context. Headquarters' managers play a key role in Context A, subsidiary managers in Context B, strategic alliance partners in Context C, and local actors in Context D. This multiplicity of driving forces has a number of implications for the MNE. First, the likelihood that 'someone, somewhere' will decide to embark on an entrepreneurial initiative that has ramifications for the MNE is greater when we take an holistic view. The chance is ever-present that a new opportunity will be identified in one of the contexts and an initiative to pursue the opportunity will start. While any given manager in the MNE (regardless of whether a headquarters or subsidiary manager) could be fully allocated to day-to-day tasks and/or work on previously sanctioned initiatives, any other manager operating in another context could be forming new initiatives that eventually could have impact on the first manager. This heightens the level of uncertainty surrounding MNE entrepreneurial initiatives as they pertain to managerial tasks in the MNE. The point in time of the genesis of an entrepreneurial initiative is difficult to predict, as is its ultimate impact.

Second, the task of determining where assets can be identified and accessed to support an initiative necessitates a consideration for the various forms of driving force. As in the cases mentioned in the previous section, the paths that initiatives take across contexts occur because driving forces seek out resources and capabilities to fully exploit opportunity. Different driving forces will have control over different types of resources, including both intangible and tangible resources. The identity of the driving force is likely to play a big role in determining which assets are sought in order to progress any given initiative.

Third, the fact that there is a wide array of driving forces for entrepreneurial initiatives in the MNE means any impact from outcomes will not be uniformly distributed. Benefits of Context A venturing will be distributed by those driving centrally-driven and internally-resourced initiatives. An example is how Tesla used its learning from Singapore, as well as learning from the home country, when deciding how to enter China. The headquarters' learning proved to be a beneficial asset as the company succeeded in its entry into China, while previously it had pulled out of Singapore after less than a year. Benefits of Context B venturing may be limited – at least initially – to the host country in which the subsidiary initiative was created and energized. An example is 3M Taiwan's initiative for acne dressing, where the benefits were initially only felt in Taiwan, followed later by some other East Asian countries.

The Need for Entrepreneurial Knowledge Co-ordination Across Contexts

Raising the prospect of cross-contextual analysis means we need to examine the issue of co-ordination of entrepreneurial knowledge between contexts. This issue broadly translates into the following question: How can MNEs know whether entrepreneurial knowledge that forms in a given context *might* be useful in other contexts? Also: How can entrepreneurial knowledge be transported between contexts such that the MNE maximizes the potential of its entrepreneurial capabilities to the full?

I argue the answer to both of these questions lies in the concept of entrepreneurial knowledge co-ordination. I define this as the sharing of entrepreneurial knowledge from one context to another such that entrepreneurial activity in the receiving context becomes augmented and upgraded. In this definition we explicitly recognize that entrepreneurial knowledge may arise in a given context without necessarily being accessible to individuals from other contexts. Without entrepreneurial knowledge co-ordination between contexts, entrepreneurial knowledge will remain constrained to distinct contexts within the MNE.

Social networks play a major role in facilitating knowledge flows in international companies, and will therefore also be central to any transportation of knowledge between entrepreneurial contexts. According to social network theory, organizations are social systems comprised of numerous individuals inter-linked through various forms of relationships (Burt, 1997; Granovetter, 1983; Nahapiet and Ghoshal, 1998; Tsai and Ghoshal, 1998; Wasserman and Faust, 1994). Structural ties and relational trust provide inducement for individuals to share and receive knowledge (Nahapiet and Ghoshal, 1998). Motivational disposition to share and receive knowledge is also important in this respect (Gupta and Govindarajan, 2000; Minbaeva et al., 2003), as well as the need for information corridors and channels to convey entrepreneurial knowledge (Shane and Venkataraman, 2000).

Building on social network reasoning, there are two important facilitating conditions for entrepreneurial knowledge co-ordination at the interface between contexts: (1) a degree of openness in the interfaces themselves (Lee and Williams (2007) referred to this as "boundary porosity"); and (2) an ability of individuals operating at these inter-contextual interfaces to assimilate and translate entrepreneurial knowledge from other contexts, i.e., an absorptive capacity (Cohen and Levinthal, 1990).

Boundary porosity in the MNE refers to "the ease with which members are identified, selected and recruited into a community" (Lee and Williams, 2007: 509). In the current analysis, we can think of an entrepreneurial community as the group of people surrounding and working on an entrepreneurial initiative in an MNE in a given context[1]. Where boundary porosity is high, individuals who would otherwise be discouraged from participating in venturing activity are encouraged to spend time and engage with entrepreneurial endeavor within the context. Boundary porosity is beneficial for entrepreneurial communities to develop across traditional boundaries because it enables the development of new structural connections and weak ties (i.e., new acquaintances outside of an individual's close group of contacts and friends) (Granovetter, 1983), as well as developing the relational dimension of social capital (Nahapiet and Ghoshal, 1998). Having 'porous boundaries' between different entrepreneurial contexts within an MNE will allow entrepreneurial knowledge to flow such that knowledge generated in one context can be evaluated by those working in another context. Furthermore, while disseminative capacity will encourage individuals to share entrepreneurial knowledge across contexts, absorptive capacity is needed to enable individuals to make sense of entrepreneurial knowledge arising in other contexts. Disseminative capacity in the MNE relates to the willingness and capability to share knowledge with others (Minbaeva and Michailova, 2004). Absorptive capacity is concerned with receiving, internalizing and utilizing that knowledge (Cohen and Levinthal, 1990; Minbaeva et al., 2003). Boundary porosity lies in the middle: it enables individuals in one context to make use of the disseminative capacity in other contexts to access entrepreneurial knowledge from those contexts. Absorptive capacity then enables recipients of entrepreneurial knowledge to evaluate its usefulness, assimilate it and apply it appropriately.

A Strategic Challenge for the Venturing Workforce

The multiplicity of driving forces for venturing, and the need for effective entrepreneurial knowledge co-ordination, have implications for the employee base within international firms that become involved in venturing. Let's call this set of people the *Venturing Workforce*. To be a member of the firm's Venturing Workforce an employee will have to spend a tangible part of their work time on activities that will create entrepreneurial knowledge. Some employees want to be corporate entrepreneurs; they wish to be involved in venturing activities. Others may be assigned venturing roles; it is part of their formal role description. Hopefully, for many in the Venturing Workforce, the formal role assignment and the self-identification and willingness to do the role will go hand-in-hand.

The discussion in this book so far has shown that it is possible for any employee to become a driver of change within the international firm. It was a former part-time receptionist that triggered Infusion's move from Canada into London. It was a nurse on a camping trip with a subsidiary manager in Taiwan that helped in the identification of a new opportunity for hydrocolloid dressing at 3M. And it was a Polish technical team outside of the boundaries of the company that made Roq.ad aware of its potential as the engine of technology development for the Berlin-based company. These examples even suggest we should view the Venturing Workforce as it pertains to a specific international firm as including certain employees of that firm's global and local partners. After-all, our framework does include drivers and assets both internal and external to the firm!

So, how can this workforce make a contribution to the venturing strategy of a focal MNE? Our analysis suggests that the contribution of the Venturing Workforce should not be isolated to just one of the contexts. The Venturing Workforce has a critical role to play in allowing strategic integration of venturing effort across contexts for any given MNE. The broad literature on social networks (Burt, 1997; Granovetter, 1983; Nahapiet and Ghoshal, 1998; Tsai and Ghoshal, 1998), embeddedness (Andersson et al., 2002; Garcia-Pont et al., 2009), boundary spanning (Tushman, 1977) and knowledge transfer in the MNE (Gupta and Govindarajan, 2000; Minbaeva et al., 2003) is useful in understanding how this strategic integration works. The Venturing Workforce is spread out across contexts. Members of the Venturing Workforce continually operate at the interfaces between contexts. It is at these interfaces that entrepreneurial knowledge co-ordination is needed. Strategic integration of venturing across contexts happens when the Venturing Workforce takes action to share entrepreneurial knowledge across contexts in line with strategic objectives of the firm.

Furthermore, the roles that will be most useful to entrepreneurial knowledge co-ordination will depend on the specific interface and the contexts concerned. Williams and Lee (2011a) argued that there will be role differentiation in this respect. In other words, it is necessary to understand 'what matters most' at the different interfaces. So, for Contexts A and C, the key interface will be between the MNE's top management team and reciprocal managers within strategic international partners. There will be a need for high interdependence between these sets of managers for entrepreneurial knowledge to flow in a timely and accurate manner. In other words, if they become highly dependent on each other, they will meet often, work together on a collective goal, share their views of opportunities in global markets frequently, and express opinions to each other about where priorities will lie (Barrick et al., 2007). This happened in the case of Expatica. For Contexts B and D, the key interface is between subsidiary managers and host country network partners. Embeddedness matters here: a close, meaningful social interaction with actors in the local environment will allow the subsidiary to access dispersed sources of knowledge (Andersson and Forsgren, 1996; Andersson et al., 2002; Pu and Soh, 2017). This was present in the case of the Time Out Market in Lisbon. For Contexts A and B, the key interface will be between the MNE's top management team and subsidiary managers. Establishing empowerment between headquarters' managers and subsidiary managers will lead to effective co-ordination of entrepreneurial knowledge between these contexts. Research has demonstrated a positive link between empowerment and the propensity to engage in knowledge sharing (Srivastava et al., 2006; Williams and Lee, 2016). Subsidiary managers that are empowered will be more pre-disposed to relating entrepreneurial knowledge to headquarters' managers. We see this in the 3M Taiwan case, for instance. And for Contexts C and D, the key interface will be between strategic international partner top management teams and host country network partners. Ideally, the MNE will be involved in brokering interactions between managers of the MNE's strategic international partners on the one hand, and host country networks on the other (Billington and Davidson, 2010). Billington and Davidson (2010: 2) defined knowledge brokering in terms of: "a systematic approach to seeking external ideas from people in a variety of industries, disciplines, and contexts and then of combining the resulting lessons in new ways." If the MNE is not present during these interactions, it risks losing its view (and grip) on how entrepreneurial knowledge develops between particular constellations of actors in its global network. We see signs of this in the Infusion Poland case, where top-level managers were intricately involved in the setting up of a new Greenfield using embeddedness with local engineers for human capital and a strategic alliance with Microsoft for technology. Hence:

Venturing Workforce implication #1: The ability of the international firm to structure itself with roles within its Venturing Workforce that facilitate entrepreneurial knowledge co-ordination at the interfaces between entrepreneurial contexts will act as a source of competitive advantage for the firm.

Consequently, the strategic challenge for the Venturing Workforce is not just about managing 'an' entrepreneurial process, or 'a' change and renewal project, and doing this over and over again in a fairly predictable way. Instead, the challenge is one of tolerance for the notion that there will always be a multiplicity of driving forces for venturing from numerous geographically-dispersed locations. And, that there will always be a need to co-ordinate entrepreneurial knowledge at the interfaces between contexts.

If people are managed in such a way that they are able to deal with these facts of life, the international firm will be able to unlock its enormous potential as a global venturing machine. The arguments we have put forward and cases we reviewed suggest that the way people are managed will be critical to how they tolerate new drivers and how they respond to interface demands. Important for management policy is that tolerating multiplicity in driving forces, and allowing entrepreneurial knowledge to be shared, will mean an array of focal points for venturing can form. These each can grow and provide value to the MNE in all of its contexts. Multiple layers of entrepreneurial initiatives in different contexts will be able to run concurrently. At any point in time, some initiatives are at an early stage, some at a later stage. Some are rigidly located in a given context. Others will have moved – or will be about to move – between contexts and end up having a broader (or narrower) impact.

Managing the Venturing Workforce such that it tolerates multiplicity and encourages entrepreneurial knowledge co-ordination will help the international firm cope with the complexity that arises through venturing across contexts. The multiple concurrent initiatives at various stages and the moving of focal points between contexts happen together. In the meantime, managers set roles for employees, manage the workforce through ongoing formal and informal appraisals, implement work systems that cater for time spent on venturing activities as well as time spent on regular production activities, and monitor performance of staff according to their tolerance for multiplicity and ability to co-ordinate entrepreneurial knowledge.

In the case of 3M Taiwan, the organization's well-established culture of decentralization and experimentation played a big role in determining how a new driving force for venturing was tolerated, and how entrepreneurial knowledge was shared between local internal and external contexts. In the case of Infusion Poland, a well-designed process for recruitment and integration of new staff in Poland that involved structured training and cultural indoctrination in Toronto acted to open the minds of established staff to new possibilities as well as to educate and motivate new Polish staff. In the Time Out Group case, the CEO's introduction of new types of meetings in different locations acted to share entrepreneurial knowledge and made a wide range of employees aware of new driving forces for change. Hence:

Venturing Workforce implication #2: The ability of the international firm to use its organizational culture and people processes to facilitate sharing of entrepreneurial knowledge across contexts will act as a source of competitive advantage for the firm.

The Challenge for Strategic Leaders: Dynamic Resource Adjustment in Pursuit of Entrepreneurial Knowledge

Leaders of MNEs need to access knowledge of opportunities, knowledge of solutions, and learning from outcomes within each of the four contexts. There is a need to direct this knowledge to the decision-making body in the organization with the authority to allocate and re-allocate resources strategically, i.e., the top management team. Each case discussed in this book required a decision to be reached regarding whether – and how – to pursue a specific opportunity. While certain decision rights can be decentralized to subsidiaries to make local decisions regarding local resources, ultimately it is the top management team that decides which of the four entrepreneurial contexts to emphasize. Venturing in international firms is not just concerned with decisions related to individual opportunities, it is also about how to emphasize whole contexts as domains for uncovering and pursuing opportunities over time. This in itself represents a series of path-dependent strategic decisions[2] that subsidiaries and external partners at global and local levels may attempt to influence.

The dynamic capabilities view is useful for understanding how strategic leaders reinforce entrepreneurial knowledge co-ordination in the MNE and how they make ongoing adjustments to the distribution of assets within and across the contexts. In this view, all types of firms, including MNEs, need to destroy existing resources and build new ones in order to sustain competitive advantage (Eisenhardt and Martin, 2000; Zahra et al., 2006). This is especially the case in knowledge-intensive and dynamic markets where competitive advantage cannot be sustained through a single, static set of resource allocations (Brown and Eisenhardt, 1997; Eisenhardt, 1989b; Zahra et al., 2006). Zahra et al. (2006) defined dynamic capabilities as: "the abilities to reconfigure a firm's resources and routines in the manner envisaged and deemed appropriate by its principal decision-maker(s)" (Zahra et al., 2006: 918). Organizational changes are made as a result of newly identified opportunities, or to neutralize newly emerging threats (Barney, 1991). Internal technology, organization and processes are adapted accordingly (Teece et al., 1997). Such changes aim to provide a mechanism by which resources can respond "sooner, more astutely, or more fortuitously than the competition," enabling "managers to compete by creating a series of temporary advantages" (Eisenhardt and Martin, 2000: 1117).

I argue three fundamental processes are at play here, processes that happen on an ongoing basis and involve strategic leaders. If, for whatever reason, any or all of these processes are impeded, the potential of the MNE as a global venturing machine will be hindered.

First, there is a process by which knowledge is channeled out of each of the entrepreneurial contexts and received/internalized by members of the top management team. I refer to this as *entrepreneurial knowledge channeling*. Second, there is a process by which the entrepreneurial knowledge that is received by top-level managers is evaluated and by which certain initiatives are selected for continued investment and emphasis while others are postponed or rejected. I refer to this as *initiative filtering*. Third, there is the tricky issue of how the top management team can guide the strategic allocation of resources as a consequence of the previous two processes. I refer to this as *adjusting entrepreneurial resource allocations*. A schematic for this process is shown in Figure 6.1.

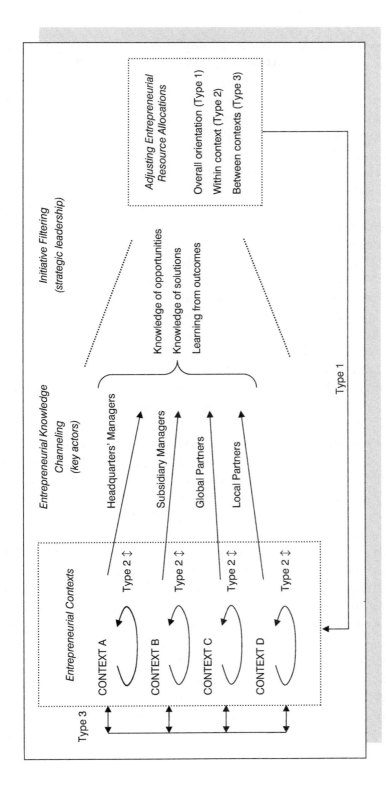

Figure 6.1 Venturing within the international firm

Entrepreneurial knowledge channeling. Without this, the top management team will remain unaware of the discovery and potential of entrepreneurial opportunity within each context. In each context, the knowledge that will inform the decision to proceed with, or reject, a given opportunity will include financial performance (Alvarez and Busenitz, 2001; Shane and Venkataraman, 2000), innovative potential (Kirzner, 1973; Schumpeter, 1934), capability development potential (Teece and Pisano, 1994) and stakeholder impact (Sen and Bhattacharya, 2001). Shane and Venkataraman (2000) referred to the need for information corridors in this respect. The essence of the challenge faced by the top management team is the problem that prior information required to make a decision to commit to a new opportunity is not widely available across a population (Hayek, 1945). In a large MNE such as Xerox or 3M, it is impossible for a top management team to receive entrepreneurial knowledge directly from all employees and all partner–organization employees at the same time. Hence, key drivers of knowledge flows within each context become crucial; they act as conduits by which knowledge of opportunities, solutions and outcomes will flow. Knowledge in this sense may be formally articulated or may be unarticulated and tacit (Polanyi, 1966). Important is that the top management team, as the strategic resource-allocating authority within the MNE, is able to access entrepreneurial knowledge from each context on an ongoing basis.

The knowledge-based view of the MNE suggests knowledge channeling to be a complex and heterogeneous capability. Not only is it complex because of its multidimensional content (financial information, innovative potential, capability development information, stakeholder impact), it is also socially-complex. Much of this knowledge is held in tacit form, and, given the problem of articulating and sharing tacit knowledge (Polanyi, 1966), incentives must be in place within the MNE to motivate actors to facilitate knowledge flows between contexts. As discussed above, boundary porosity will help here, as will absorptive capacity on the receiving side, namely among the top management team. Various forms of distance between foreign subsidiaries and partner organizations on the one hand, and headquarters' managers on the other, will hinder knowledge flows (Berry et al., 2010; Williams and Kumar, 2012). Psychic distance incorporates aspects of both cultural difference, and business difference (economic, legal and political, business practices, market structure and language differences) (Evans and Mavondo, 2002). As these distances increase, so does knowledge stickiness (Jensen and

Szulanski, 2004). Motivational disposition to share and receive knowledge is therefore important in this respect (Gupta and Govindarajan, 2000; Minbaeva et al., 2003); subsidiary managers and partner managers will need to feel motivated that there is a benefit for them to share entrepreneurial knowledge with headquarters' managers.

Social networks also play a role in facilitating knowledge flows such that opportunities are recognized (Ardichvili et al., 2003). As socially-complex resources, these networks may be hard to imitate (Alvarez and Busenitz, 2001). The capability to channel entrepreneurial knowledge out of distinct entrepreneurial contexts is unlikely to be homogeneous across MNEs. Hence:

Strategic leadership implication #1: The strategic leadership capability in establishing and maintaining an organizational environment conducive to channeling entrepreneurial knowledge from multiple contexts to the top management team will act as a source of competitive advantage for the international firm.

Initiative filtering. Based on knowledge gleaned from the entrepreneurial contexts, a top management team in the MNE can evaluate and select the most promising opportunities and initiatives for continued resource allocation. It is also able to make decisions about which contexts should be emphasized for ongoing resource allocation (and by the same token which ones should be de-emphasized). This type of evaluation and selection activity has been highlighted as critical in facilitating the progress of ideas into tangible initiatives that exploit opportunities and create long-term value for the firm (Ardichvili et al., 2003; Birkinshaw, 2000; Low, 2001; Shane and Venkataraman, 2000). Many large international companies have implemented Stage-Gate® or similar formalized processes for handling requests for innovation within the firm (Cooper, 2008; Cooper et al., 2002). While this is a formalized way of managing the process of innovation "from idea to launch," as Cooper et al. (2002) pointed out, this should not be seen as a rigid or linear process. At each stage of the process, senior managers have an opportunity to assess all aspects of the business case for the idea and to make a decision about whether to proceed with it to a next stage. The precise number of stages, and how they are used, can vary from firm to firm. Importantly, formalized mechanisms like this can help top management teams in larger international companies to gain a running overview of all of the innovation projects in the pipeline. The process creates management reports and insights for the top management team to make subsequent resource allocation decisions. We see an example of this in the 3M Taiwan case in this book.

Nevertheless, opinion on what constitutes a successful evaluation may vary among members of the top management team (Lee and Venkataraman, 2006). Cognitive differences and dissimilarities in personal characteristics such as age, education, tenure and experience are likely to exist between top-management team members (Lévesque and Minniti, 2006; Wiersema and Bantel, 1992). To this end, the characteristics of the top management team will matter to whether the company will deploy scarce resources to opportunities with uncertain outcomes in the different entrepreneurial contexts. Research has emerged in recent years examining characteristics of the top management team in relation to corporate entrepreneurship and venturing (Srivastava and Lee, 2005). As noted by Guth and Ginsberg (1990), strategic leaders have a direct influence on levels of corporate entrepreneurship in large firms; their characteristics, beliefs and visions determining whether, and how, entrepreneurship is pursued.

Cognition theory highlights individual cognitive factors as determinants of entrepreneurial action (Baron, 1998, 2004). An entrepreneur is someone with an increased propensity to adopt certain types of thinking (counterfactual thinking, regret affect infusion, self-serving bias, planning fallacy and self-justification) and who thrives in an environment characterized by features such as information overload, high uncertainty, high novelty, strong emotions, high time pressure and fatigue (Baron, 1998). Baron (2004) argued that cognitive bias plays a role in the decision to act in an entrepreneurial way; individual perceptual processes such as object and pattern recognition, and opportunity recognition, play a role in the successful discovery of opportunities. Such biases are not just important to untapped opportunities faced by individual entrepreneurs operating in the wider economy. They also will be present when members of top management teams in international firms are confronted with entrepreneurial knowledge emanating from the contexts. So, for instance, a tendency to be over-optimistic (Alvarez, 2007) or characteristics such as personal ego, or a strong desire to be seen as a courageous leader (Hines, 2004) may all combine to reinforce continued support for a failing initiative.

The ability, therefore, to simply identify opportunities from the entrepreneurial contexts and to channel knowledge about these to the top management team is only one part of the equation. What is also needed is an ability of the top management team to understand, evaluate and sort through diverse entrepreneurial knowledge from the contexts. Let us refer to this as 'initiative filtering'. The desired outcome of initiative filtering is a shared conclusion among the top management team of the potential contribution of new opportunities – and initiatives to exploit them – to the long-term competitive advantage of the firm. This can be considered a capability that, due to differences in both contexts and cognitive and perceptual biases of top management teams, will be heterogeneous across international firms. In other words, some international firms will be better at this than others. Hence:

Strategic leadership implication #2: The capability on the part of the strategic leaders of the firm to filter initiatives from multiple entrepreneurial contexts will act as a source of competitive advantage for the international firm.

Adjusting entrepreneurial resource allocations. Following initiative filtering, a top management team needs to decide *how* to utilize resources strategically in order to make the most of the copious and diverse entrepreneurial knowledge emanating from the contexts. I refer to this as a process of 'adjusting entrepreneurial resource allocations' and it applies both within – and across – contexts. There are three prominent ways in which this can work: (1) by changing the overall entrepreneurial orientation (EO) of the MNE; (2) by adjusting resource allocations within a specific context or contexts; and (3) by facilitating resource transfer between contexts.

First, the strategic emphasis placed on entrepreneurship by a firm can be assessed in terms of its stance on the passive–aggressive continuum. In other words, the firm can intentionally and deliberately adopt an overall stance on what its relative aggressiveness, or EO will be. According to Fombrun and Ginsberg (1990: 298): "aggressiveness involves: (1) the *depth* of the resource commitment, and (2) the *riskiness* associated with resource allocations designed to achieve innovation and improve market share." Any decision to be 'aggressive' rather than 'passive' is a critical component of strategy, as set by a top management team (Covin, 1991; Dess and Lumpkin, 2005; Hitt et al., 2001; Knight, 1997). Thus the degree of resource allocation to the superset of all four entrepreneurial contexts is a key decision that needs to be made by the top management team. I refer to this with the arrow labeled 'Type 1' in Figure 6.1.

This stance is strongly linked to the overall level of innovativeness espoused in corporate strategy and will ultimately be reflected in the corporate culture of the firm (Covin, 1991; Dess et al., 2003; Dimitratos and Plakoyiannaki, 2003; Fombrun and Ginsberg, 1990).

By taking an overall aggressive stance, the firm can expect to generate higher volumes of entrepreneurial knowledge compared to the situation in which it takes a passive stance. Its EO will encourage employees around the world to be alert to new opportunities, experiment in new ways, and share insights on how challenges may be solved, irrespective of context. Type 1 adjustment will not specify any specific context for entrepreneurial knowledge generation. But it will legitimize entrepreneurial behaviors among employees at all levels and locations.

Second, the MNE may pursue within-context adjustment. Here, the top management team shows its hand in terms of which context or contexts matter. Re-allocating resources within a specific context can mean devoting more resources to venturing within a given context. It can also mean taking resources away from venturing within a given context. This type of resource allocation adjustment allows the top management team to balance their overall posture across contexts. Perhaps they conclude the firm needs to emphasize externally-oriented venturing at a global and local level. In this case, more resources will be needed to handle the venturing process in Contexts C and D. Perhaps the top management team considers a complete decentralization of venturing is needed given the nature of competitive threats and other industry factors. In this case, Contexts B and D will be emphasized for resource allocation accordingly. This type of resource adjustment process is denoted by the set of arrows labeled 'Type 2' in Figure 6.1.

For instance, resources currently deployed on one entrepreneurial initiative with an internally-focused context may be re-deployed to a new emerging opportunity within that same context. This would be the case, for example, where managers who have helped establish a particular subsidiary as a global center of excellence (Moore, 2001) in one functional area or country are re-deployed to assist another subsidiary to develop as a global center of excellence in another area or country. In this instance, the managers are still working on establishing centers of excellence around the world, they are just doing this in different functional areas or countries. Similarly, if managers are involved in assessing the nature of innovation clusters in one country in order to decide whether – and how – to deploy assets to any of those clusters, and then later are re-deployed to doing the same task, but in other clusters in other countries, then they are still operating in the same context (in this instance, Context D).

Third, the MNE may pursue between-context adjustment. This is where a top management team makes a deliberate attempt to shift resources between entrepreneurial contexts. I label this as arrows 'Type 3' in Figure 6.1. In this form of resource allocation adjustment, a top management team shifts the emphasis between internal, external, headquarters-driven and subsidiary-driven orientations not just by increasing or decreasing them within context (Type 2), but by explicitly moving them between contexts. This transfer of resources for venturing is particularly salient when the focal point of the opportunity itself has transferred across entrepreneurial contexts. For instance, an opportunity identified in a single MNE subsidiary may move from Context B to Context A if the top management team decides to sanction investment for exploiting the opportunity across multiple markets. This happened in the case of Time Out Group's Time Out Market. If the same opportunity required collaborating with a strategic partner on an international basis, the opportunity and its solution for exploitation would then move into Context C. The point is that the solution for exploitation and generating additional entrepreneurial knowledge also requires resources in other contexts.

This demonstrates how the concept of EO takes on a different meaning for an MNE compared to a purely domestic firm. It does not just relate to the one-dimensional passive–aggressive continuum; in the case of an MNE it is a multidimensional construct that can be considered as a relative emphasis across a two-dimensional (internal–external, headquarters-driven–subsidiary-driven) space.

Unfortunately, barriers to implementing resource allocation adjustments inevitably will arise. Prahalad and Doz (1981) described how headquarters' initiatives may lead to resistance and resentment from subsidiaries and a subsequent lack of progress. Birkinshaw (2000) showed how headquarters' managers can have a predisposition to resisting initiatives originating in subsidiaries. Bartlett and Ghoshal (1989) identified the unique administrative heritage of the MNE as a potential constraint on strategic renewal and change. Clearly, barriers that prevent the efficient re-allocation of resources within and between contexts, will result in the MNE not being able to fully (if at all) seize newly discovered opportunities. On the other hand, MNEs that are able to control their own organizations (as well as exerting some influence over alliance partners – Müller-Seitz (2012)) such that resources can be re-allocated efficiently within and across contexts, will be more likely to succeed than those that cannot. Instilling shared values (Nohria and Ghoshal, 1994), a strong culture (Deal and Kennedy, 1982) and allowing organizational goals to be internalized (Eisenhardt, 1985) are possible ways by which barriers can be overcome. These are mechanisms aimed at establishing normative integration across the firm. These types of firm characteristics are socially-complex and not easily imitated or substituted by competitors. Hence:

Strategic leadership implication #3: The strategic leadership capability in implementing effective resource adjustments towards (Type 1), within (Type 2) and between (Type 3) entrepreneurial contexts will act as a source of competitive advantage for the international firm.

Uncontrolled Networks are Chaos: Venturing in International Firms Requires Guided Heterarchy

As discussed in the Introduction, the heterarchical view – dating back to the 1980s – has been put forward as a suitable archetype for portraying innovative and entrepreneurial dynamics in MNEs. The main characteristics of a heterarchical MNE include many centers of different kinds, a strategic role for foreign subsidiaries, a wide range of governance modes, integration primarily by normative means, coalitions with other firms, radical problem orientation, holographic organization (basic values and strategy shared widely), a 'firm as a brain' model of action, and action programs for seeking and generating firm-specific advantages (Hedlund and Rolander, 1990). Heterarchy allows for autonomy of work units, with authority emerging laterally (Stark, 1999). Autonomy provides a basis for subsidiary embeddedness in internal and external networks and subsequent learning and capability development (Young and Tavares, 2004). In essence, heterarchy displaces static organizational forms with flexibility and subsidiary co-participation becomes crucial for competitive advantage (Morgan and Whitley, 2003).

Despite this portrayal of the archetype and the benefits of heterarchy for rejuvenation and change in MNEs, the analysis we have made in this book provides only some support for heterarchical thinking. The situations in the cases of 3M in Taiwan, Time Out in Portugal and Expatica in Belgium show the importance of giving autonomy to staff in host countries. The case of Infusion in Poland shows how global mandates can be given to subsidiaries in emerging economies. The case of Roq.ad highlights how near-shored operations can be used as part of the company's radical problem-solving efforts. However, heterarchy only provides one part of any solution for the control of venturing in international firms.

We also see a big emphasis on the importance of hierarchy and headquarters' managers and their role in influencing the control systems around technology development and venturing activities. This supports recent interest and emphasis on the role of MNE headquarters (Ambos and Mahnke, 2010; Ciabuschi et al., 2011; Egelhoff, 2010), and even suggests that it is dangerous to espouse heterarchy without strategic oversight and attention. Hierarchy still matters, and we see this in small, medium-sized and large international firms. In Roq.ad, Expatica and Infusion, as one might expect, the strategic leaders played a crucial role in deciding which technologies to invest in, which international opportunities to pursue and how to pursue them. They were personally involved. In mid-size cases of Time Out Group and Infusion, CEOs were instrumental in setting the conditions for venturing in the different contexts. They also were personally and directly involved in the 'hiring and firing' that often goes hand-in-hand with adjusting resource deployment within and across contexts, as well as in efforts to make changes to the organizational culture and how the culture took effect across different locations. In larger cases, such as Tesla and Xerox, top management teams were engaged with the strategically critical decisions of exiting and entering new markets (Tesla), as well as engaging in strategic acquisitions for the long term (Xerox).

So, while heterarchy offers a useful way of understanding organizational features of international companies that are conducive to international venturing, leadership, involvement and guidance from the top still matter. Left unchecked, heterarchy could even be a dangerous solution that could result in the company being unable to co-ordinate its venturing efforts across contexts in a deliberate, effective and efficient manner.

Implications for Researchers and Careers

Oftentimes, when researchers have looked at entrepreneurial dynamics in international firms, despite elaborate research designs, inclusion of countless control variables, and sophisticated statistical techniques, the variance explained is still quite low. In my own work, for instance, I have found 'adjusted R-squareds' of up to 55 percent (Williams, 2009), 49 percent (Williams and Lee, 2011b) and 65 percent (Williams and Du, 2014). Many times they are much lower. Research designs using larger samples never fully explain the dependent variable.

So what explains the missing variance in the phenomenon we have been discussing in this book? One thought that might be explored in future work is that the missing variance in international venturing studies involving MNEs comes from entrepreneurial knowledge mulling about in other contexts. Few of the research articles in Chapters 2 to 5 spanned contexts. Most – including my own – were limited to analysis of a specific phenomenon in one context. If research designs based in a given context were able to capture the existence and impact of entrepreneurial knowledge in other contexts they might go some way to increasing the accuracy of models and the precision of our interpretation. The reason for this is that entrepreneurial knowledge in other contexts will influence a dependent variable in a given context because of the activities of the Venturing Workforce as well as the resource allocations made by the leadership team. Controlling for the interfaces between contexts as well as the strategic leadership's ongoing entrepreneurial resource-allocation adjustments between and across contexts will go some way to account for how entrepreneurial knowledge in one context will influence the venturing process in other contexts.

Another approach for researchers is to adopt more holistic research designs that incorporate all four contexts. Such holistic research design not only would need to address issues of operationalization, validity and reliability within *each* entrepreneurial context but also the integration and synthesis of findings *across* contexts. The challenges for researchers and analysts in each context were touched on in the previous chapters. In short, Contexts A and C may suffer from problems of access to the strategic leaders of the MNE (Welch et al., 2002) (although this may depend on the size and type of MNE), making secondary data more practical than primary data. Contexts B and D present problems for researchers wishing to develop constructs and measurement techniques that tap into dynamic social networks and interdependencies between actors in lots of different countries around the world. Researchers may face issues validating perceptional data in these contexts while secondary indicators are likely to be difficult to access and justify in Contexts B and D.

It is a tall order to expect unified research on strategic integration of venturing in international firms that addresses all of these sorts of issues. However, I believe a fresh approach to examining the phenomenon holistically will yield ever more interesting results, improve on variance explained and open the theorist's eyes to new possibilities. Holistic research will also resonate with strategic leaders of international firms and have normative implications that are relevant to strategy-in-practice, as opposed to units of analysis that are isolated in time and space.

Holistic case studies that capture activities across contexts as well as case studies on specific initiatives whose focal points move around the contexts over time will be useful. New ways of looking at how case research can be deployed could also be productive. Results from case research can be used to challenge existing theory and generate new theory. Teaching cases, such as those reproduced in this book may also be beneficial even if used as part of a broader program of investigation. It may be possible to publish, distribute and discuss the content of teaching cases on the holistic nature of venturing in international firms before academic case-based research is even past the first round of review!

I believe the analysis put forward in this book raises lots of new research questions. If you have got this far, you also may have jotted down a few new questions yourself. Here are five of my own thoughts on new lines of research.

First, what is the nature of the relationship between cross-contextual venturing and digital transformation in international firms? In most of the cases in this book we find digital transformation and technological developments underpinning digital transformation to be central themes. This was very prominent in the Time Out case, where £25 million was ear-marked for investment in e-commerce offerings and technology as a result of the IPO. It was also prominent in the Expatica case as the company continually upgraded its web-based interface over time and sought to establish reach. Eventually, in 2013, Expatica launched a new campaign using the domain-name www.reachexpats.com to target potential clients and make them aware of the company's breadth of offerings. We also saw novel ways of using e-commerce to market the acne dressing products launched by 3M in Taiwan. Likewise, in Tesla we see the use of the Internet in allowing customers to select and order vehicles using Tesla's online design studio. At Roq.ad, we see a company growing around cutting-edge technology to help all sorts of organizations market to consumers in a cross-device world.

Research is limited on the relationships between venturing in international firms and how those firms seek and use digital transformation in innovative, risk-taking and proactive ways in order to win in their industries. Furthermore, the literature on digital transformation may itself become obsolete as the phenomenon rapidly changes. For instance, Andal-Ancion et al. (2003) commented that: "Books and airline tickets sell readily over the Internet whereas automobiles and high fashion clothing do not" (Andal-Ancion et al., 2003: 34). As the Tesla case shows, selling models have changed dramatically in the last decade and will continue to do so. Berman (2012) highlights the role of digital technologies in reshaping customer propositions as well as transforming companies' operations. Indeed, changes in how the Internet is used is influenced by "People everywhere" (Berman, 2012: 16). We should expect that international venturing by MNEs has a big role to play in terms of how other MNEs can harness and utilize digital transformation. Cases such as Roq.ad, Infusion and Xerox all show how commonplace digital transformation has become for MNEs offering B2B services to other MNEs. We should expect venturing in the different contexts to provide entrepreneurial knowledge that will assist MNEs in their digital transformation offerings as well as in how they digitally transform themselves.

Second, what is the relationship between the internationalization process of the firm and its cross-contextual venturing? There is a vast literature on the process firms go through when they internationalize. Johanson and Vahlne's (1977) model of the internationalization process, along with their 2009 revised model are both highly cited, but may be challenged or extended by a cross-contextual view of international venturing. The 1977 model saw the process as one of increasing incremental commitments (gradual commitments) to foreign markets as psychic distance is overcome through learning and experience in those markets. The 2009 model emphasized networks, the importance of not being an 'outsider' to business networks when going abroad, and the role of learning from a web of partners through trusting relationships (Forsgren, 2016; Johanson and Vahlne, 2009). The cross-contextual view of venturing may add to the debate around these models and what they mean for theory development (Forsgren, 2016) as well as for practice.

In addition, real-life cases, such as those presented in this book, can be used to explore how these models fit within a cross-contextual view. For instance, it could be argued that Infusion followed the logic of Johanson and Vahlne's (1977) model when they entered Canada for the first time in a Context A mode. This example had low distance in terms of culture, geography, time zone and language. Incremental commitments to Canada ensued that eventually resulted in the Canadian subsidiary becoming the global headquarters. However, the company's emerging relationship with Microsoft (Context C) brought the company into new networks in other countries, opening up new opportunities in London and Dubai. And their entry into Poland was based on meticulous planning and on-the-ground networking in Poland, bringing in logic from Contexts C and D. These later years, and the shift into Contexts C and D have more of a Johanson and Vahlne (2009) flavor. Hence, one potential research question here is to look at different models of the internationalization process and examine how they are influenced by the characteristics of the different contexts for venturing in international firms.

Third, what are the implications of a cross-contextual view of venturing in international firms for the eclectic (or OLI) paradigm? Dunning's highly influential OLI theory (Dunning, 1981, 1988, 2000) integrated logic on how ownership ('O'), location ('L') and internalization ('I') advantages will influence the pattern of international production and investments made by MNEs abroad. 'O' logic was essentially based on resource-based theory, emphasizing firm-specific advantages and sources of competitiveness that a firm can bring to foreign markets. 'L' logic draws from economic geography and emphasizes features of specific locations in which the MNE is (or will be) investing as potential sources of advantage. 'I' draws from internalization theory and transaction-cost logic to assess the extent to which the boundary of the firm (internalized vs. externalized) presents an advantage. It would be interesting to explore these three strands of the eclectic theory in light of a cross-contextual view of venturing. On the surface of it, 'I' logic might be appraised with respect to the differences between Contexts A and B on the one hand, and Contexts C and D on the other. However, as we have developed the logic in this book, we have seen that 'O' advantages might be present in all four contexts, and that the capabilities of the Venturing Workforce and the strategic leaders of the company in their resource allocation process may also constitute 'O' advantages. While none of the four contexts say anything about specific 'L' advantages (i.e., in specific countries or types of countries), we expect that diversity in the number of countries in which an MNE has a presence to influence its stock of entrepreneurial knowledge, as well as the co-ordination costs of sharing and utilizing entrepreneurial knowledge. A larger number of countries with employees and assets could mean a larger amount of entrepreneurial knowledge emanating from Contexts B and D, for instance. Research work could progress these types of thoughts and develop implications of cross-contextual venturing for the eclectic paradigm. It may even pose new questions about the continued relevance of OLI.

Fourth, what does cross-contextual venturing mean for emerging market MNEs and firms operating in non-traditional economies (Kostova et al., 2016), i.e., ones that are catching up, politically unstable and/or full of institutional voids? Some firms start their international venturing from a place of relative disadvantage, being headquartered in a catch-up economy and possibly surrounded by institutions that lack the ability to support market transactions in effective and efficient ways. Other firms may seek to venture into such host countries and develop entrepreneurial knowledge as a consequence of their assets in those countries (Du and Williams, 2017; Pu and Soh, 2017). In the first scenario, recent research looks at the outward foreign direct investment (OFDI) of MNEs from emerging countries, focusing on factors such as the role of host country institutions and the motives for internationalization (Lamotte and Colovic, 2015; Ning and Sutherland, 2012). Buckley et al. (2007) examined the determinants – in terms of motives – of Chinese OFDI, developing arguments for a special theory of internationalization for firms internationalizing from such countries. The role of the government at national and local levels, different types of business groups, social customs and *guanxi* and other such 'country-specific' factors mean researchers need to be ready to challenge established theory and frameworks derived from data in Western or advanced nations. The way in which the four contexts for venturing in international firms are characterized and the way they interface and are managed are themes that could be examined in future research in emerging country settings.

In the second scenario, i.e., for MNEs in developed countries seeking to enter less-developed and/or politically-unstable countries, the framework presented in this book may need to be further developed. This could include, for instance, assets that matter in each context that help the MNE deal with uncertainty, and other mechanisms that allow the MNE to develop entrepreneurial knowledge from such countries as a consequence of venturing in each of the contexts.

Fifth, how does our appreciation of ethical concerns and corporate social responsibility (CSR) considerations in MNEs change in light of a cross-contextual analysis of international venturing? MNEs – especially larger MNEs – play a huge role in dealing with ethical and CSR issues as they yield their influence around the world. They may be seen as part of the problem, but also as part of the solution (Kolk and van Tulder, 2010). Cross-contextual venturing in MNEs may be a way of dealing with both the MNE as 'problem' as well as the MNE as 'solution' in ethical and CSR issues. Taking the latter first, the process of identifying solutions to ethical challenges and committing resources to those solutions could be seen as an entrepreneurial process and one that will create entrepreneurial knowledge. The leadership team of the MNE will need to decide which context or contexts are the ones where it would like to see the development of entrepreneurial knowledge related to solving ethical and CSR issues. Regarding the former point on 'the MNE as part of the problem', entrepreneurial knowledge co-ordination between contexts and tight coupling within the Venturing Workforce could be ways by which the MNE becomes self-aware of its own failings, as well as finding ways to deal with any failings. Future research could examine ethics, CSR and sustainable development in MNEs using the ideas of cross-contextual venturing.

For students about to embark on a career in international firms or those that are studying but already have started their careers, the cases and central ideas put forward in this book have some important implications. Of course, the following points are not exhaustive, and will, to a large extent, be determined by the nature of the firm, its industry setting, and the characteristics of the individual concerned. So please bear these in mind when considering implications in any given situation.

First, any role you take in an international firm may give you the opportunity to engage in venturing initiatives. You may find yourself operating in any of the four contexts and identifying new opportunities in that context. You may find yourself involved in the creation of knowledge about how to pursue the opportunity, i.e., what the solution to the opportunity should be. And you may find yourself involved in the learning from outcomes that inevitably occur as resources are deployed on new projects in practice. You may be engaged in initiatives in host countries, such as the TOM initiative in Portugal for Time Out Group or the hydrocolloid dressing initiative for 3M in Taiwan. Alternatively, you may work in the headquarters of the firm, either as an owner-founder, a member of the top management team, or a close advisor to the top team. Here you may influence critical decisions about where and how to venture, as we see in the examples of Elon Musk at Tesla, Alim Somani and Sheldon Fernandez at Infusion or Richy Ugwu and Carsten Frien in the Roq.ad case. Your aptitude and ability in contributing to the stock of entrepreneurial knowledge in the company may determine outcomes, not only for your employer, but also for your career.

Second, you may adopt a role, either within the company's Venturing Workforce, or as part of the top management team, where you co-ordinate entrepreneurial knowledge across contexts and contribute to the ongoing allocative task of directing resources towards venturing efforts. These are real roles, not just theoretical implications for cross-contextual venturing, although they may be subsumed within existing job titles and established positions within the company's hierarchy. I would encourage you to be alert to how much time you find yourself spending on tasks that not only generate entrepreneurial knowledge, but also co-ordinate it across contexts. Similarly, be self-aware of how your role influences the ongoing strategic allocation of resources within and between contexts. This awareness is important if you are to communicate to other stakeholders on how you have contributed – and will continue to contribute – to the company's overall strategic venturing. This is important as you demonstrate your value to your current or future employer and it may help open up new career possibilities for you. In other words, blow your own trumpet!

Third, you can use venturing in international firms as a way of being geographically mobile and pursuing an interesting and stimulating career in different countries. We only live once! Headquarters' managers in the Infusion case ended up being relocated to London and Dubai. At Expatica and Time Out, the leaders spent a lot of time 'on the road', establishing and following up on venturing initiatives. Venturing is a way by which employees at all levels of the firm can relocate on a more permanent basis, or enjoy the world through extensive travel. This may not suit everyone. And those that do not want to travel through venturing initiatives do not have to. But those that want to see the world can use the international firm as a vehicle to do this. And to do this while working on projects that are innovative, risky and involve high levels of proactivity and competitive aggressiveness . . . well, what more could you want as material for dinner party conversations once you retire?

Fourth, while there are many advantages of being a part of the Venturing Workforce in an international firm, there are likely also to be disadvantages. Advantages include the fact that, for some, venturing is fun, and work should be fun! There also are career benefits as firms realize how important it is for their overall competitiveness to have employees who can generate and co-ordinate entrepreneurial knowledge as well as employees who can allocate resources in entrepreneurial contexts effectively. Insightful firms will put a premium on employees who do this well; rewards will be high. And we have already made the point about venturing and individual mobility, and that venturing in an international firm can take on a new meaning at an individual level.

However, there are potential disadvantages that you might want to consider. These include what might happen if risky initiatives that you are involved in continually fail? If the organization is not utilizing its learning from outcomes to guide new initiatives, questions might be raised about the ability of individuals and groups in terms of their entrepreneurial knowledge co-ordination. Too much failure might produce a wealth of learning, but hit the bottom line. This could force the firm to assess whether it needs to devote less resource to overall venturing (Type 1 adjustment in Figure 6.1). And even if there is a moderate level of success with venturing in an international firm, those involved in continual and multiple initiatives across many contexts may suffer stress due to being stretched in the pursuit of too many new opportunities. If this occurs, discussions with human–resource management functions might be needed to find ways for the organization to support individuals. We can think about the professional services layer that Infusion introduced into its organization here. Also, the case of the office of alliance management at Eli Lilly shows how an organizational system can be used as a solution to cope with the seemingly complex array of entrepreneurial ventures and the large volumes of knowledge that this then generates.

As you plan your career path and make decisions about which employers to target, selecting companies where you might 'fit' in terms of venturing can be useful. By engaging with them in informal discussions and at formal interviews, you have the opportunity to learn about their venturing cultures and approaches, not only about their 'business as usual'. It will be worthwhile to ask questions about how they support different types of venturing internationally and what career opportunities there might be for you to become involved, as well as the rewards and incentives that are on offer. Doing your homework in this way, and placing venturing at center-stage as you talk with prospective employers or new units within your current employer, will help you decide if the role on offer is suitable for you.

Summary

In this chapter we have learnt how:

- there is an imperative for international firms to co-ordinate entrepreneurial knowledge across and between the various contexts where this knowledge is created;
- different mechanisms, including specific roles, organizational culture and processes can be used for co-ordinating entrepreneurial knowledge across and between contexts;
- as a consequence of this co-ordination, the focal point of an entrepreneurial initiative can move around contexts over time;
- entrepreneurial initiatives in one context can trigger new initiatives in other contexts at any time;
- every international firm has a Venturing Workforce that is responsible for creating entrepreneurial knowledge and transporting this knowledge within and across contexts;
- strategic leaders of international firms will be faced with the continual issue of trade-off in where they put emphasis for entrepreneurial venturing;
- the success of a venturing strategy will largely be determined by the international firm's use of appropriate organizational mechanisms for co-ordination of entrepreneurial knowledge as well as using entrepreneurial knowledge to make resource allocation decisions within and across contexts;
- there are copious opportunities for researchers and analysts to progress the central ideas put forward in this book; the 'narrowly-focused' research found in the academic community has only touched the surface as far as venturing in international firms is concerned.

Suggested Additional Cases for Analyzing Strategic Integration Across Contexts

Bartlett, C.A. and McLean, A. (2003) 'Genzyme's Gaucher Initiative: Global Risk and Responsibility' (Harvard Business School, product number: 303048).

Compeau, D. and Mark, K. (2010) 'IBM Canada Ltd.: Implementing Global Strategy' (Ivey Publishing, product number: 9B10E008).

Kim, J.K., Lee, A., Monaghan, S. and Mudambi, R. (2016) 'FotoNation: Leveraging International Knowledge Connectivity' (Ivey Publishing, product number: 9B16M021).

Kumar, K. and Kumar, M. (2009) 'Gold Peak Electronics: R&D Globalization from East to West' (University of Hong Kong, product number: HKU857).

Maurer, C.C. and Mark, K. (2010) 'L'Oreal S.A.: Rolling Out the Global Diversity Strategy' (Ivey Publishing, product number: 9B10C026).

Weil, M., Meister, D. and Reddin, C.P. (2017) 'Geosoft Inc.: Leading Across Cultures' (Ivey Publishing, product number: 9B17M064).

Williams, C. and Mark, K. (2014) 'Shelby Division in 2012' (Ivey Publishing, product number: 9B14M126).

Wong, K.K-K. (2016) 'Hasselblad: A New Chapter for the Swedish Camera Manufacturer' (Ivey Publishing, product number: 9B16A017).

Notes

1 According to Lee and Williams (2007: 517), it is:

> the attachment of individuals to entrepreneurial initiative supports the proposition of community in multinational corporate entrepreneurship, and that knowledge creation and transfer between community-networked participants enables dispersed entrepreneurship to prosper … This also implies that better performance could be achieved by those parts of the MNC that tolerate entrepreneurial communities and that learning and innovation that emanate from such communities spreads internationally through heterarchy. Thus our theoretical framework supports and extends the heterarchical view of the MNC, and explains the underlying behavioural and organizational dynamics of dispersed entrepreneurship in the MNC.

2 See for instance Asahi's leadership profiles and its readiness to internationalize in Williams et al. (2013).

7

Summary and Conclusion

Challenge the Orthodoxy

A number of ideas have been presented in this book. The central one is that it is possible to frame the phenomenon of venturing in international firms in terms of four analytical contexts. These contexts are defined by the driving force for entrepreneurial initiatives and the control of assets that are used to pursue those initiatives. We have seen that quite distinct sets of academic literatures help us understand what goes on in each of these contexts. These different bodies of literature arguably are a reflection of the interests of the researchers involved, the times and places in which they interacted with international firms to get data, and trends in the academic world in terms of 'hot topics' in their respective areas. However, the case stories of international firms of all shapes and sizes that pursue innovation, take risks, and are proactive in their strategy, tell us that narrow analyses of entrepreneurial phenomena across borders are limited and blinkered. The fragmented orthodoxy that has emerged lacks a full explanation of the reality of what goes on in international firms as they continuously flex their muscles in a world of seemingly unending opportunity.

Having said that, the approach taken in this book has been to argue that there are some common variables in these different contexts. These variables allow the contexts to be compared and contrasted and then for a higher-level view of cross-context integration and leadership to be discussed. The knowledge-based view that we have taken has allowed us to come up with a definition of entrepreneurial knowledge, to argue that this is distinct to production knowledge and to study how entrepreneurial knowledge is related to the contexts in which international venturing occurs. We have seen how entrepreneurial knowledge differs across the contexts and how it is important for international firms to be aware of – and leverage – its entrepreneurial knowledge as a dynamic asset.

Furthermore, we have seen how the contexts can be analyzed both individually (Chapters 2 to 5) and holistically (Chapter 6). Through this holistic approach we can fully appreciate firms' venturing in international markets. This appreciation comes when we consider the issue of strategic integration across contexts, and the implications for the Venturing Workforce, as well as for the strategic leadership of the firm. In sum, it is important to use integrative analysis and thinking when we analyze the reality of venturing in international firms. As we touched on in the previous chapter, integrative analysis raises new implications for researchers and analysts as well as for managers in international firms.

Move Forward

These implications may open up new lines of enquiry and provide managers new ways of looking at strategic problems facing their employers. They may also provide food for thought to consultants grappling with strategic issues for global clients. While not all of the possible managerial issues and imperatives are covered in this book, hopefully some main ones are! I believe there are opportunities to continue the current analysis by linking cross-contextualization of international venturing with themes in international business such as the role of digital transformation, process of internationalization, the relevance of the eclectic paradigm, the dynamics of strategy when international firms enter – or come out of – emerging economies and politically-risky countries, and for ethics and CSR. International venturing has an important role to play in how we view these types of phenomenon and researchers may be able to find ways in which the venturing strategies of international firms can cater for – or integrate with – these types of topics. Future research will show whether this is truly the case and whether cross-contextual international venturing is a platform for all of these different types of behaviors exhibited by international firms.

I have chosen eight of my own teaching cases to illustrate the central arguments in this book. I focused on eight cases of technology-intensive companies, companies in which technology development and imperatives of internationalization collide on a daily basis. You may be able to read and analyze these cases in different ways from the take on them made here. I would certainly encourage this as such cases often portray complex situations and a wide set of cross-enterprise issues and possible decision outcomes. As you think through these cases and discuss them in group settings, I would encourage you to bring in your insights and learnings from other environments, including your own experience in industry. This will help in the learning of others and spark discussion that will add to your own learning. It also should be acknowledged that this set of eight cases on technology-intensive companies is only a tiny drop in the ocean. There are likely to be tens-of-thousands of published teaching cases and real-world examples in international firms that can be used to analyze and discuss the cross-contextual view put forward here. I also would encourage you to draw on real-world insights from these cases to discuss and develop your own perspective on venturing in international firms. In the opening of this book, I mentioned my former colleague, Richard Reed, and his journey in a converted Land Rover Defender from London to Sydney with his friend, Dwyer Rooney. The final point I would like to make picks up on one of Richard's comments. As he noted: *"You can read or watch the adventures of others, but discovering with your own eyes, drawing your own conclusions from your own experience is priceless."*

Why should any international firm leave it up to others to break all the new ground? The possibilities across the contexts are large and potentially unlimited. Somewhere, somehow, there will be a way for all international firms to venture into new territory, learning and growing as they do. Choosing not to do this is a cost not worth considering. Choosing to do it strategically necessitates the company 'discovering with its own eyes'. If each of the entrepreneurial contexts is a separate lens, the international firm will be able to see clearly when all the lenses are lined up. Its adventures in international markets will then stand a better chance of being successful because it has the benefit of being able to see clearly.

Case List (arranged by size)

Fewer than 100 employees:

- **Expatica.com:** Williams, C. and van Herwaarden, J. (2011) 'The challenges of international entrepreneurship at Expatica.com', *Ivey Publishing* (product ID: 9B11M085).
- **Roq.ad:** Williams, C. and Shafique, U. (2016) 'Roq.ad and the ad-tech industry', *Ivey Publishing* (product ID: 9B16M069).

Between 100 and 1,000 employees:

- **Time Out Group:** Williams, C. and Shafique, U. (2017) 'Time Out: A new global strategy to bring back profit', *Ivey Publishing* (product ID: 9B17M063).
- **Infusion Development Corporation:**
  - ☐ **Canada:** Williams, C. and Davis, M. (2011) 'International entrepreneurship at Infusion', *Ivey Publishing* (product ID: 9B11M014).
  - ☐ **Poland:** Williams, C., Van Eerde, W. and Thé, D. (2012) 'Infusion's Greenfield subsidiary in Poland', *Ivey Publishing* (product ID: 9B12M076).

Greater than 1,000 employees:

- **Tesla:** Williams, C., Shafique, U., Kayssi, A., Zhao, W., Barczyk, A. and Gluszynski, L. (2015) 'Tesla: Internationalization from Singapore to China', *Ivey Publishing* (product ID: 9B15M074).
- **3M Taiwan:** Williams, C. and Liaw, E. (2011) '3M Taiwan: Product innovation in the subsidiary', *Ivey Publishing* (product ID: 9B11M101).
- **Xerox:** Ramasastry Chandrasekhar and Williams, C. (2014) 'Xerox Innovation Group – from products to services', *Ivey Publishing* (product ID: 9B14M034).

The following table shows how these may be used by instructors in class.

TABLE 7.1 Suggestion for thematic emphasis when analysing the cases

Case	Context A: headquarters-driven initiatives – internal	Context B: subsidiary-driven initiatives – internal	Context C: headquarters-driven initiatives – external	Context D: subsidiary-driven venturing through external embeddedness
Expatica.com	**	**	***	
Roq.ad	***		**	
Time Out Group	***	***		**
Infusion (Canada)	**	**	***	*
Infusion (Poland)	*	*	*	***
Tesla	***			*
3M (Taiwan)	*	***		**
Xerox	***		***	

*** = suggested main focus; ** = strong thematic overlap; * = some overlap.

APPENDIX: CASES OF VENTURING IN INTERNATIONAL FIRMS

⚜IVEY | Publishing

9B11M085

THE CHALLENGES OF INTERNATIONAL ENTREPRENEURSHIP AT EXPATICA.COM

Christopher Williams and Judith van Herwaarden wrote this case to provide material for class discussion. The authors do not intend to illustrate either effective or ineffective handling of a managerial situation. The authors may have disguised certain names and other identifying information to protect confidentiality.

This publication may not be transmitted, photocopied, digitized, or otherwise reproduced in any form or by any means without the permission of the copyright holder. Reproduction of this material is not covered under authorization by any reproduction rights organization. To order copies or request permission to reproduce materials, contact Ivey Publishing, Ivey Business School, Western University, London, Ontario, Canada, N6G 0N1; (t) 519.661.3208; (e) cases@ivey.ca; www.iveycases.com.

Copyright © 2011, Richard Ivey School of Business Foundation   Version: 2017-05-25

In April 2011, the management team at Expatica Communications B.V. was reviewing the progress of the company and the opportunities for future growth. The management team had to take stock: the external environment was rapidly changing and threats from competitors were on the rise. Expatica was founded 11 years earlier to provide English-language information and news to the expatriate community in Europe, delivering its services primarily over the Internet. One of the central issues Expatica faced was how to make its core business model effective across multiple markets. Recent launches of the online platform in new countries were not as successful as hoped and the performance of traditional 'bricks and mortar' offerings was also mixed. The company had made tremendous progress over the years but needed to re-evaluate its position and decide which new opportunities for growth, if any, should be pursued. Key questions facing the management team were: (1) Should the company continue to internationalize into new markets? If so, how? Should they pull out of any existing markets? (2) What product development strategy should they adopt going forward? Should they make line extensions to existing products? What kinds of radical innovations could be appropriate? Was Expatica fulfilling the needs of its target audience and was the profile of this audience changing? Was the focus audience the right audience for advertisers? (3) What organizational decisions should be made to underpin future international strategy?

BACKGROUND

Expatica was a 'born global'[1] firm established in the Netherlands with the aim of providing information and services to expatriates (expats) living abroad. The company was founded in 1999 with the help of funds provided by a government incubator (called Twinning) and had a business model based on the revenues of online advertising. The users of the website were expats and the original offering was high quality local and international news delivered in English, for free. The story of how one of the founding members of the company was inspired to start the venture was well known in the company and the expat community.[2]

---

1 *A company establishing international operations at or near their founding.*
2 *Canadian expatriate Bram Lebo had been waiting at the tram stop for more than half an hour and there was still no sign of a tram. In fact, the stop was ominously empty that Monday morning in 1999 and the only other people waiting seemed to be foreigners like him. If only Lebo had known that public transport workers were on strike that day, he might have realized that a bicycle was the best way to arrive at his destination; however, since his Dutch was not sufficient for understanding local radio or newspapers, he was unaware of the strike.*

Appendix: Cases

By 2011, the main Expatica website was live in 11 countries (see Exhibit 1). There were eight online offering areas: jobs, housing, listings, community, ask the expert, classifieds, forum and dating (see Exhibit 2). The online dating product was launched in 130 countries simultaneously in 2010. The income generated by online advertising contributed 90 per cent of Expatica's total income. In addition to its online products Expatica offered events, of which the "i am not a tourist" Expat Fair was by far the most popular and expensive. Other events included education fairs, human resources seminars and social events (see Exhibit 3). Expatica also offered a "survival guide" for expats, which was published in countries in which the "i am not a tourist" Expat Fair was held. The Fair had been shown to increase survival guide sales.

In 2006, Antoine van Veldhuizen and Mark Welling, two of the Dutch entrepreneurs involved in the original venture that became Expatica, were presented with an opportunity to acquire the majority of the company's shares and take control of the firm. They saw great potential in Expatica and aspired to set a new course for the company based on their understanding of the opportunities created by emerging technologies and the changing needs of internationals living abroad.

ESTABLISHING A PLATFORM FOR NEW INITIATIVES (2006–2007)

Having the majority of priority shares meant that van Veldhuizen and Welling could implement changes in the organization. Previously, the company had been organized with a central editorial desk and management team. News editorials and journalism had been bespoke and in-house and advertising space had been managed/sold centrally. Van Veldhuizen and Welling began to initiate a number of changes with the aim of reducing costs and bringing new sources of revenue to the company.

They began implementing these changes within the management team, reducing its size from six people to three. Van Veldhuizen and Welling reorganized the editorial team responsible for news, giving staff greater autonomy to write and publish articles, thus reducing dependence on a central editorial desk. The sales team was also reorganized. Expatica moved from five full-time sales representatives to two and started using agencies on a franchise basis to sell advertising space on its website.

By the end of 2007, Expatica was working with a sales agency in France. In Spain, Expatica had an employee who was more of a designer than a sales representative: as a part of the new regime, he received payment on a commission basis rather than a fixed salary. Expatica became increasingly engaged with local partners on a franchise basis for selling and reduced its dependency on the in-house sales team. Overall, the number of full-time employees was reduced from 25 to 10.

Van Veldhuizen and Welling set about transforming the company's administration systems and making the work environment even more entrepreneurial. They changed the company's bank to one with more suitable terms and conditions for their purposes. Many changes were made in order to increase employee communication: the company moved from downtown Amsterdam into a new building in Haarlem, west of Amsterdam. The original building was very large and housed a variety of companies. At the new site in Haarlem, Expatica found an office with a central open area, which encouraged staff and visitors to interact; this enabled coordination and communication between different functions.

There was a large shift in strategy and execution which affected all areas of the business. The annual "i am not a tourist" Expat Fair held every October in Amsterdam had been a success from its inception. Expatica increased its activity in the area of events such as wine-tasting and speed-dating (see Exhibit 4). These events were more like parties and were profitable. Previously, the events were managed in-house. As part of its new strategy, Expatica began to outsource event management to a specialist agency, with the exception of the fair, reducing operational involvement for the events. The company's main input for events became one of conceiving the theme and checking the quality of the execution.

Van Veldhuizen and Welling also began a new project to renovate the company's website — Expatica's key interface with its users. The new site included a more accurate mechanism for measuring hits (impressions) on the site's pages, new tools for users to engage in forums and discussions about different aspects of life in their adopted countries, an improved classified advertisement section, improved housing, job and dating sites and upgraded information for expats (see Exhibit 3). The upgrade was a major step forward for Expatica and central to van Veldhuizen and Welling's plans for the site, which was a distinction between fact-based information services and other services that helped expats socialize and integrate. Inevitably, there were delays with the site upgrade. The main developer had been a one-man company based in Poland. He knew the technology well and provided good value; how-ever, the developer had already indicated his intention to move into new areas in the future and this exposure was a major concern for van Veldhuizen and Welling. They needed to test and launch the new site before the developer moved on and they also needed to find a new partner for the site's maintenance and future development. They started the search for such a partner, focusing on companies in Eastern Europe and India: Dutch developers were too expensive. Van Veldhuizen and Welling finally found and contracted two developers in Bulgaria through a company called Bianor. Van Veldhuizen and Welling were generally satisfied with the new developers, although they faced a quality-cost struggle on some requests since Expatica was Bianor's smallest client.

With the reduction of in-house editorial and bespoke journalism for The Netherlands, Belgium, Germany, Spain and France, van Veldhuizen and Welling needed to address the question of how to continue to pro-duce quality local news stories in English in order to attract users. There was no point in becoming a leaner organization if users were going to desert the website because of a lack of local news. Following input from the user community, van Veldhuizen and Welling realized it was still necessary to provide quality local news in English; the solution was to use external providers for news stories. Contracts were set up to source articles that were already translated into English from organiza-tions with news-generating capabilities: these ranged from radio stations to newspapers and varied across countries. This arrangement gave Expatica increased flexibility; van Veldhuizen and Welling identified a range of sources in each country and were able to negotiate advanta-geous deals for quality content for their online publishing on a country-by-country basis.

NEW INITIATIVES IN A TURBULENT ENVIRONMENT (2008–2010)

As Expatica entered 2008, the management team faced a serious prob-lem: the sub-prime mortgage scandal in the United States had triggered a global recession. Many global financial institutions were being forced to merge, declare bankruptcy or request financial aid from their respect-ive governments. Some commentators were saying that the global economy was close to a collapse: it was the worst financial crisis since the Great Depression of the 1930s. As van Veldhuizen and Welling sat in their Haarlem office, they pondered the consequences of this crisis.

Expat movement around Europe decreased significantly, which caused concerns about decreased site traffic. Corporate advertising also decreased and competition for advertising budget became fierce.

However, despite this threat, the new Expatica seemed to have enough traction and flexibility to weather the storm. Costs were under control and there was little exposure to the credit markets. User impressions on the website were actually increasing, which was important for maintaining advertising revenue. The crisis led to some expats in managerial positions being sent home from their overseas assignments or losing their jobs entirely; however, there were still enough expats to target and the services offered by Expatica had become increasingly beneficial to this segment.

Van Veldhuizen and Welling conducted a market segmentation exercise in order to understand the challenges that expats (and, in some cases, their spouses and/or families) faced during foreign assignments. Obtaining more information on Expatica's users and categorizing them also helped van Veldhuizen and Welling in attracting more advertisers and subsequently increasing revenues. In conducting this exercise, the management team acknowledged that not all expats followed the same route: some settled in faster than others and some remained for significant lengths of time while others did not. The exercise defined a four-phase pattern that most expats experienced while living abroad; orientation, settling in, living in and moving on (see Exhibit 4).

Even though the number of new expats moving to Europe and around Europe was down, Expatica focused on understanding the needs of the remaining user community, increasing this attention through more forums and surveys, as well as feedback. Major enhancements to two of the company's online products were made: "Expat Voices," which allowed expats to write about their experiences in their adopted countries and have their work published on Expatica, and "Ask the Expert," a publication encouraging users to submit questions on a variety of themes such as finance, health care and relocation. These products enabled readers to become more involved in the site but they initially required active marketing to gain sufficient interaction. Readers were not as willing to participate in site dialogue as had been imagined.

Offering this categorized user community to advertisers showed van Veldhuizen and Welling that clients were mostly interested in expats in the first two phases of the expat lifecycle; in these phases, the expat had to make the majority of the critical decisions involved in starting life abroad (i.e., insurance, banking, schooling, and housing). This knowledge shifted the management team's focus and led to another revision of the website's content. Although van Veldhuizen and Welling were reluctant to ignore expats after they moved into the third phase, the site became more focused on serving expats in the first two phases in order to attract advertising opportunities. This was not entirely welcomed by the site's editorial staff, as they found it more interesting to write for expats living in their adopted country instead of writing purely informative and factual 'reference' articles.

Expatica increasingly supported local initiatives, giving their agents in other countries autonomy to experiment with new ideas. Paul Morris at Expatica Belgium, for example, piloted an idea for a light-hearted editorial reflecting on the country's news stories.

Van Veldhuizen and Welling worked not only on the website's usability, but also on the accuracy of the information reported. Expatica continued to look for partners to provide new sources for local information: sources that were reliable and useful to their user base. Van Veldhuizen and Welling made sure they were never locked into any one supplier. This increased emphasis on content partners, however, meant that the editorial team was primarily selecting stories from live RSS feeds instead of writing them. Expatica placed an increasing focus on quality of information from its suppliers in light of the information overload that was present on the Internet. Working with specialized content publishers enabled Expatica to deliver trustworthy information to their users; this was reflected in the company's mission and vision statements, revised in 2009 (see Exhibit 5). The previous mission statement (to be "Europe's number one helping hand for the international community") had been less specific on the issue of quality of information.

During 2009, van Veldhuizen and Welling's previous successful franchise structure began to crack. The management team received an increasing amount of complaints from clients, as well as complaints from agents claiming that the products were selling for a price too low to generate any meaningful returns. At the end of 2009, financial results were down and few local agents were still carrying Expatica. With regret, van Veldhuizen and Welling decided to re-centralize operations to their Haarlem office. With the exception of the Bulgarian web developer, all Expatica countries were once again served from one location.

In addition to the disappointing results of the franchise sales agents, foreign partners hosting the "i am not a tourist" Expat Fair were unable to make a profit from the event. This was in contrast with the huge success of the fair in the Netherlands. A partner in France, where the fair was held in 2007 for the third and last time, insisted that the location had to be the Louvre. As a result, proceeds were too low to cover the enormous location costs. In Belgium, Expatica found a very eager partner, who set out to give the "i am not a tourist" fair its own spin. Unfortunately, these changes were not enough to persuade a sufficient number of expats in Belgium to attend. The management team decided to terminate the event in Belgium in 2010. The success of the Dutch event had proven to be difficult to replicate elsewhere.

Even though these results were unfortunate, van Veldhuizen and Welling strongly believed that the "i am not a tourist" Expat Fair had great potential internationally. They found that advertising sales from the Expatica survival guide were much higher in countries where the fair was held. In 2010, they hosted the fair in Madrid, which was a success. They were considering re-launching the event in France, albeit in a more affordable location. As events were generally profitable for the company, the management team pondered other event opportunities. This resulted in a partnership for a human resources (HR) seminar in 2010. In addition, wine-tasting and speed-dating events grew in size and frequency.

As van Veldhuizen and Welling witnessed the great success of competitor online dating products, they decided to transform Expatica's dating offering, eventually re-launching the product with a new partner (World Dating) in 2008. In 2010, Expatica separated its dating section from its overall website, and developed a new dating format with World Dating. This format and design could easily be adapted to fit any country. As a result, Expatica Dating was launched in 130 countries simultaneously in 2010. As van Veldhuizen commented: "It is logical, as the product only needs to be designed and manufactured once and afterwards can be applied to as many countries as you wish. So why not?"

Van Veldhuizen and Welling deemed the online dating industry to be a lucrative opportunity that could reduce the dependence on online advertising revenue. They were especially attracted by the mix of revenues a dating site could render; users pay for a membership and organizations pay for advertising space. Another appealing aspect of a separated launch of the dating product was the ability to offer 'occasionalization' to advertising clients by being able to repeat passive advertising exposure to one user on different occasions.

By 2011, the Expatica dating site had 85,000 members, 15,000 of which were in the Netherlands. Van Veldhuizen and Welling were most surprised by the success of Expatica Dating in the United Arab Emirates. They pondered whether they should launch their regular Expatica website there as well. In 2010, van Veldhuizen and Welling launched the Expatica website in Moscow at the instigation of a client request. In 2011, Expatica also opened in Portugal, which seemed a logical choice after Spain and South Africa — ventures also instigated by client requests. Unfortunately, none of these new sites were able to generate a sufficient amount of page views and this triggered a management discussion on how to market to potential users in these locations.

FRESH CHALLENGES AND OPPORTUNITIES

With a business model dependent on online advertisers for 90 per cent of their revenue, Expatica was highly sensitive to the shrinking of advertising budgets. This was most pronounced during the 2008–09 global economic recession but continued into 2011 as well. Furthermore, van Veldhuizen and Welling saw an increase in the number of competitor expat websites (especially in new markets) and lead generation tools. Expatica was unable to secure a viable number of users in newly entered countries. In addition, the sales force struggled with clients' perception of product value for those outside of the housing and jobs categories. Van Veldhuizen and Welling found themselves in a precarious situation again — a situation that demanded entrepreneurial skill and creativity to ensure future success.

Expatica had been an ever-changing organization, shifting from centralization to a franchise model and back again. In 2011, there was a serious stagnation in revenue growth, leading management to downsize personnel from about 17 full-time employees to 12. Reducing the costs of operations allowed van Veldhuizen and Welling to invest in usability improvements of the website with the hope of substantially growing revenue; however, because the website had been live for almost 10 years, alterations were cumbersome. In addition to ongoing usability improvements, the management team felt pressure to focus the website's content on expats in the first two phases of the expat lifecycle (see Exhibit 4). With regards to the 'living in' phase, Expatica launched a social media platform in 2011 in order to enable expats living in their adopted country to socialize and interact with other local expats.

Van Veldhuizen and Welling also recognized the need to offer their advertising clients 'occasionalized' repeated advertising exposure, which they offered through Expatica Dating; however, other possibilities were being considered as well, such as partnerships with other expat websites. In this partnership model, Expatica would be a sales and customer service partner for organizations who were deficient in this area. This would allow van Veldhuizen and Welling to sell advertising space on the partner's website to their clients as well. Van Veldhuizen and Welling developed a vision of an "expat vertical" in which a network of at least five to eight partner websites would achieve around 10 million page views. This idea could enable Expatica to gather enormous amounts of data on their users and segment specific target groups (e.g. men, 30-40 years). Another possibility, which van Veldhuizen set out to explore in 2011, was real-time bidding: an online auction of advertising space tracking users from website to website. This would allow Expatica to expose their users to the advertisement on yet another occasion.

Despite the opportunities in online advertising at this time, van Veldhuizen and Welling recognized the danger of their business model's heavy dependence on advertising income. They began exploring the idea of an "expat card" — a loyalty card on which daily purchases would accumulate to earn a discount that could be applied to partner websites (e.g. housing or job sites). Other possibilities revolved around the value of the data collected by the company on labour mobility, launching a jobsite for international vacancies and business-to-business events.

The idea for Expatica originated in 1999, when one of the company's founders, expat Bram Lebo, was left waiting for a tram that failed to arrive due to a strike he was unaware of since local news was not available in English. By 2009, Expatica's mission had become one of providing "a high quality news, information and community platform for people living and moving abroad." However, in early 2011, Expatica failed to report on a public transport strike in the Netherlands, leaving many expats in a frustrating situation identical to the one Lebo had faced.

In April 2011, the management team was reviewing the progress of the company and the opportunities for future growth. Key questions facing them were: (1) Should the company continue to internationalize into new markets? If so, how? Should they pull out of any existing markets? (2) What product development strategy should they adopt going forward? Should they make line extensions to existing products? What kinds of innovations could be appropriate? Was the profile of the target audience changing? Was Expatica fulfilling its target audience's needs and was this focus audience the right audience for advertisers? (3) What organizational decisions should be made to support future international strategy?

Appendix: Cases

Exhibit 1

INTERNATIONALIZATION HISTORY

YEAR	COUNTRY	NOTES
2000–2002	The Netherlands Belgium, France, Germany	Company launch period
2003–2006	Spain	2006: van Veldhuizen and Welling take ownership of the company
2007–2009	Switzerland, United Kingdom	
2010	Russia (Moscow only), Luxembourg	Client request
2011	Portugal South Africa	Geographically chosen Client request

Source: Interviews

Exhibit 2

OVERVIEW OF ONLINE PRODUCTS

Offering	Description	2007	2008	2010	2011	Ideas being considered
Expatica website	Overall website	Launched in Switzerland (CH)		Launched in Russia (RU)	Launched in Portugal (P) and South Africa (SA)	Idea to launch in countries "Expatica Dating" is most successful
Jobs	Jobsite publishing vacancies by live RSS feed selection	New job search product in the Netherlands (NL) and Belgium (BE)		Added RSS feed of job portals outside BE & NL		Exploring possibilities of separate worldwide expat jobsite
Housing	Housing site publishing houses for sale or for rent by live RSS feed selection	New housing product in NL and BE		Added RSS Feed of housing portals outside BE & NL		
Listings	Listings overview of key listings for expats during phase 1 & 2				Four Bulgarian interns used for upgrade	Limit categories to 'Survival Guide' type of categories. Drive micro payments module

Appendix: Cases

Exhibit 2 *Continued*

Offering	Description	2007	2008	2010	2011	Ideas being considered
Community	Social platform for expats to connect, discuss, share				Launch of a completely renewed social media platform	Idea to launch specific platforms, e.g., for jobseekers or house hunters
Ask the Expert	Interactive tool linking clients and users					
Classifieds	Classifieds		Replacement with partner product		New product release from partner	
Forum	Platform for blogs, posts and comments				Integration within community product	Creating a social engine
Dating	Dating site for expats		Re-launch with partner (World Dating)	Separated from Expatica website; launched in 130 countries	Search engine optimization	Active marketing by intern team

Source: Interviews and company documents

Exhibit 3

OVERVIEW OF 'BRICKS AND MORTAR' PRODUCTS

Offering	Description	2007	2008	2009	2010	2011	Ideas being considered
Expat Survival Guide (print)	Annual guide for expats providing need-to-know information	Updated print editions NL, BE and FR (quit DE and ES)	Terminated in France			NL, BE, FR (reintro-duction)	Adding CH, Spain (ES)
"i am not a tourist" Expat Fair	Event for internationals	4th edition NL & 3rd edition Paris	5th edition NL	6th edition NL & 1st and 2nd edition BE	7th edition NL & 3rd edition BE & 1st edition Madrid	8th edition NL & 2nd edition Madrid	Exploring possibili-ties to return to Paris and to launch Barcelona
Education Fair	Themed fair on education and personal devel-opment in the Netherlands - in combination with guide					1st edition	Launch dedicated website as well

Appendix: Cases

Exhibit 3 *Continued*

Offering	Description	2007	2008	2009	2010	2011	Ideas being considered
Expat of the year award	Award in categories such as service providers, individual expats & employers (NL only)				1st edition	2nd edition	Leverage in national press
HR Seminar	Training seminar for HR, service providers in NL	Organized by Expatica in NL, BE	Moved to partner model (with Lexlumen)		1st edition		Leverage in national press
Social events	Dinner mixers, speed-dating & other social events (only in NL)	Organized by Expatica in NL, BE	Moved to partner model (with individuals)				Adding client events to the mix

Source: Interviews and company documents.

Exhibit 4

THE EXPAT LIFECYCLE

Phase	Description
Orientation	Becoming familiar with a new country for the first time (typically 0-12 months before move)
Settling in	Getting connected with basic support infrastructure and services (0-12 months after move)
Living in	Becoming more deeply embedded in the local culture and society (duration of stay)
Moving on	Planning exit from the country (0-12 months before departure)

Source: Interviews and company documents.

Exhibit 5

COMPANY MISSION AND VISION STATEMENTS

	Statement
Mission	Expatica provides a high quality news, information and community platform for people living or moving abroad.
Vision	In a market of increasing international labour mobility and increasing information overload on the Internet, Expatica wants to help its users feel secure by providing a trustworthy and complete information platform.

Source: Internal company documentation

IVEY | Publishing

9B16M069

ROQ.AD AND THE AD-TECH INDUSTRY

Christopher Williams and Umair Shafique wrote this case solely to provide material for class discussion. The authors do not intend to illustrate either effective or ineffective handling of a managerial situation. The authors may have disguised certain names and other identifying information to protect confidentiality.

This publication may not be transmitted, photocopied, digitized, or otherwise reproduced in any form or by any means without the permission of the copyright holder. Reproduction of this material is not covered under authorization by any reproduction rights organization. To order copies or request permission to reproduce materials, contact Ivey Publishing, Ivey Business School, Western University, London, Ontario, Canada, N6G 0N1; (t) 519.661.3208; (e) cases@ivey.ca; www.iveycases.com.

Copyright © 2016, Richard Ivey School of Business Foundation   Version: 2017-09-28

By August 2015, Berlin-based ad-tech venture Roq.ad GmbH (Roq.ad) had grown from a chance encounter in 2014 between co-founders Richy Ugwu and Carsten Frien to become a revenue generating operation with a total of 18 full-time employees in Germany and Poland. As Ugwu and Frien reflected on the busy year, they were confronted by a strategic challenge. How could they successfully transform the company from its initial mobile advertising agency model to become Europe's number one provider of cross-device user recognition technology?

BACKGROUND AND COMPANY INCEPTION

Roq.ad was formed in 2014 by Richy Ugwu and Carsten Frien in Berlin, Germany. Frien had been working in the ad-tech industry for 15 years and had previously founded and run a company called Madvertise Media, specializing in advertising broadcasted on mobile phones. Through his work in the ad-tech industry, Frien sensed that there would be a growing need for technology with cross-device advertising capabilities and felt that the time was right to look for a co-founder to set up a new venture to develop such technology.

Ugwu had been working in the consulting industry for three years. He had been assigned to projects in Berlin, Paris, and Beijing, and specialized in advising clients on digital strategy in the advertising space. His clients had included Robert Bosch in Germany, Coca-Cola in Paris, and Volkswagen in China. Ugwu also saw a growing need for cross-device advertising while working with such clients, helping them develop their digital strategies. Having spent time in consulting, Ugwu was now keen to pursue a new career challenge. He felt that the time was right to become involved in an entrepreneurial venture in a niche segment.

After Frien and Ugwu met, they soon established common ground and set about starting a new venture to develop technology that would support cross-device advertising. Two other co-founders joined shortly after — Daniel Kramer from Stuttgart but living in Berlin, and Bartek Bogacki, originally from Poland and still living in Poznan, Poland. Kramer was recruited through a mutual contact in Berlin; Bogacki contacted the company after seeing a job advertisement posted by the company. Prior to Roq.ad, Bogacki had put together a technical team of four people in Poznan that had developed technology for what was called a demand side platform (DSP). Roq.ad's job advertisement alerted Bogacki to the existence and location of Roq.ad, where he saw a potential fit. In the latter part of 2014, Roq.ad's new team continued with technology development in Poznan, while the team in Berlin raised capital.

Frien and Ugwu identified two options for financing. The first was to seek venture capital (VC) that would be used to build the business, with a secondary aim of selling the business at some future time. The second option was to use an agency model. In this model, the company would provide a service running advertising campaigns for clients. The revenue generated through these campaigns would be used to finance the technology development for cross-device advertising. The intention would be to move away from the agency model once the technology was mature enough to provide a sustainable income for the company.

Frien and Ugwu chose not to seek VC; instead, they set about running an agency model. As Ugwu noted, "This not only meant we would give up less share and control of the business, [but] we would also have our first clients and good relationships with them for when the user-matching technology was ready."

Appendix: Cases

THE ADVERTISING TECHNOLOGY INDUSTRY

Advertising technology (ad-tech) refers to all technologies, software, and services that are used for delivering, displaying, controlling, and targeting digital ads, and, therefore, making online advertising more automatic and methodical. Digital advertising was initially a two-party model involving a marketer selling directly to a client. Soon, though, an agency model emerged, in which advertising agencies acted as a middleman to connect the marketer to the client. By 2015, the ad-tech ecosystem had become more complex, consisting of advertisers, media agencies, agency trading desks, DSPs, ad exchanges, ad networks, supply-side platforms, publishers, media owners, and pure-play ad-tech companies.

The roots of the ad-tech industry can be traced back about 20 years to October 27, 1994, when an AT&T digital ad was displayed as a web banner ad on *Hot Wired*.[1] Other companies, including MCI, Volvo, Club Med, 1-800-Collect, and Zima, soon realized the potential of such digital ads in attracting customers. Between 1995 and 2000, four leaders in ad-tech emerged: DoubleClick, Engage, Right Media Group, and 24/7 Real Media.[2]

The years 2001–2003 were dominated by the dot-com bust, during which three of the four leaders in ad-tech struggled. They were valued at US$2[3] to $9 million, whereas DoubleClick was valued at $450 million. Following the dot-com bust, DoubleClick and 24/7 Real Media emerged as the winners, along with, ValueClick Media and Right Media. However, competition in the ad-tech companies was heating up and other competitors were emerging, crowding the industry.[4]

Between 2004 and 2007, the industry consolidated with intense mergers and acquisitions (M&A) activity. Over a relatively short period of time in 2007, four major acquisitions took place: Microsoft acquired aQuantive for $6 billion,[5] Google acquired DoubleClick for $3 billion,[6] Yahoo acquired Right Media for $680 million,[7] and WPP acquired 24/7 Real Media for $649 million.[8]

Between 2008 and 2014, the ad-tech industry flourished. Both industry conglomerates and start-ups tried either to build full-stack platforms (i.e., platforms that provided all tools or services for all advertising related needs of a client) or focus on a few niches. This led to a congested and fragmented market with over two thousand ad-tech companies,

140

Appendix: Cases

including several start-ups and around 15 conglomerates. Nevertheless, some industry consolidation did take place through M&A, with data showing that, compared to 2012, M&A deal volumes in 2013 were substantially increased in North America, but fell in Europe and the Asia-Pacific region. Industry consolidation continued into 2014, especially in the United States, with the bigger companies acquiring the small start-ups.[9]

One reason for such consolidation was that the industry giants and established participants recognized the huge opportunity in online, programmatic, and mobile advertising. They also recognized that small ad-tech companies were the innovators in the industry, capable of achieving real technological breakthroughs. In addition to industry consolidation, several ad-tech companies went public in 2014; however, the initial public offerings (IPOs) were weak and the stocks were volatile.

Although the years leading up to 2015 saw high investor confidence in the industry, 2015 itself was a rocky year. IPO showings were weak and companies that went public in 2014 experienced volatile stock values. Investor confidence was low over concerns that the ad-tech industry was not viable in the long-term.[10] There were few IPOs, VC funding dried up,[11] there were several layoff announcements,[12] and the overall value of public ad-tech company stocks was down 12 per cent in the first quarter.[13] Even Facebook was not pursuing ad-tech development as actively as it had before.[14]

Nevertheless, some investors believed that this was just a phase, and that while the ad-tech industry might go in and out of favour over time, it had long-term value and would soon recover.[15] Interestingly, although there was a lack of VC funding, M&A activity in 2015 continued to remain high.[16]

Despite the ups and downs of the ad-tech industry, there was no doubt that, if companies played it right, there were huge opportunities to seize. An eMarketer report estimated that in 2016, global mobile ad spending would be over $100 billion, making it the biggest digital ad market. The increase would be nearly 400 per cent of spending in 2003.[17] Further, global mobile ad spending was expected to double from 2016 to 2019. All top five countries for mobile ad spending (i.e., the United States, China, the United Kingdom, Japan, and Germany) were expected to experience an increase in mobile ad spending.[18]

Data from 2008 to 2015 tracking daily time spent per media platform showed that the time spent on digital media devices (including mobiles and tablets) had been going up, while time spent on radio, television, and print was going down.[19] Data on media platform consumption share for the three top media platforms showed that consumption share was increasing for digital mobile devices but decreasing for radio and television. However, in 2015, television and digital desktops and laptops still enjoyed a 36 per cent and 20 per cent share respectively, compared with a 24 per cent consumption share for digital mobile devices.[20] It was also reported that nearly 60 per cent of people in the United States used multiple platforms, opening up the possibility of advertising or tracking users across platforms.[21]

In 2015, Google and Facebook were considered the leaders in ad-tech, holding 41 per cent of the global digital ad market. Oracle, Adobe, and Salesforce had also entered the fray by acquiring smaller companies.[22] Given that the ad-tech space had become crowded, the lack of differentiation meant that new entrants spent a lot on sales, marketing, events sponsorship, and thought leadership,[23] rather than on developing technology that differentiated them from X. To have a competitive edge in the industry, new entrants needed to either develop full-stack ad-tech platforms, such as Google and Facebook had and WPP would in the near future, or have a niche, tech-specific proposition.[24] One such niche was cross-device advertising.

CROSS-DEVICE ADVERTISING: UTILIZING CROSS-DEVICE USER RECOGNITION TECHNOLOGY

Consumers were not limited to spending most of their time on one device. They switched devices as required by task; therefore, ads needed to be delivered across devices, platforms, and media to the same user. The era of mobile ads was replaced by cross-device advertising.[25] The underlying "cross-device user-recognition technology" was used to identify (and track) whether it was the same user or household that accessed the various devices (e.g., mobiles, tablets, and laptops). This would, in turn, enable a marketer to target the user across devices and deliver an ad in a personalized manner.

The concept of cross-device user recognition could be traced back to U.S.-headquartered start-ups Drawbridge and Tapad (see Exhibit 1). These companies were early participants in this ad-tech niche. Both of these companies were privately held, backed by major VC firms. They worked with several technology partners, and offered tools and services for cross-device advertising that made the companies stand out from the competition. Aside from Drawbridge and Tapad, Google and Facebook had an advantage in the cross-device advertising space. Users accessed Gmail and Google+, YouTube, and Facebook across their devices, and their user identifying information could link a user across the devices.

A white paper by Forrester Consulting released in July 2014, detailed the opportunity in cross-device advertising in the United States. Based on data from 1,500 U.S. digitally connected consumers, it was reported that over 70 per cent of the consumers used at least three devices. Laptop consumption was at 82 per cent and smartphone usage was not far behind (71–78 per cent). Nearly 50 per cent of connected consumers used tablets and 33 per cent used Internet-connected televisions. The study also found that connected customers used digital touch points across the "path-to-purchase," over 30 per cent used multiple devices along this path, and no one device dominated as the initial access point, with consumers switching devices along the way. Device switching was influenced by user experience and convenience. For example, 51 per cent of device switchers transferred due to a better user experience. Finally, consumers expected brand consistency and personalization across devices.[26]

Start-up hubs in Europe included locations such as London, Paris, and Moscow. However, Berlin was considered a hotbed of technology and the ad-tech capital of Europe. Berlin had a particularly fast-growing ad-tech cluster for mobile start-ups because it offered resources ad-tech start-ups needed to thrive.[27] Data from Gruenden, an advisory agency for new businesses in Germany, indicated that a start-up was founded every 20 minutes in Berlin.[28] The city attracted the best talent as a result of a good quality of life, a comparatively lower cost of living than in other European tech hubs, and a city image as a "place to be." Overhead costs were low, financing was available through VCs and industry giants,[29] and Berlin was a more affordable place to live than London.[30]

In addition to Berlin, Poland had a growing ad-tech scene.[31] The wealth of tech talent combined with the opportunity for cost-effective operations meant that Poland was fast becoming a prime location for tech companies.[32] Polish developers had become so familiar with new technologies that new start-ups were originating from Poland, rather than Poland just serving as an outsourcing or development house for richer countries. This start-up activity in Poland meant that investment money followed, mainly through European Union (EU) programs.[33] In addition to the growing outside investments, local governments were also starting to support new businesses.[34]

Although the cross-device advertising market held promise, it was not without its challenges. Firstly, it was still a challenge to precisely link a customer across all of the devices, and the methods used were not completely accurate. Both Tapad and Drawbridge had recently partnered with other technology companies to further develop their own technology.[35] For instance, Tapad had partnered with Oracle to improve their probabilistic and deterministic technologies, while Drawbridge's partnership with Foursquare gave Drawbridge access to a huge reserve of data from Foursquare, among other benefits.

A second issue, which was particularly troublesome in the EU, was that of privacy. Some techniques for identifying and tracking users across devices violated privacy laws in the EU, which did not allow for the capture and unauthorized use of personally identifiable information. These particularly stringent privacy laws in the EU meant that companies needed to develop technology and policies regionally to abide by region-specific privacy laws.[36] Ad-tech competitors and EU regulators had already raised concerns about whether Google was breaking privacy laws.[37] Further, because the barriers to enter the ad-tech industry were low, particularly in the United States, this market was expected to become crowded quickly, increasing the possibility that clones would offer the same or similar solutions. According to the founder of Drawbridge, market leadership was "defined by scale, accuracy, traction as measured by integrations and adoption, and an application stack that proves the value."[38] Companies that wanted to stand out needed to focus on scale, accuracy, and depth of data around their cross-device user technology, as well as how the data could be used beyond advertising applications.[39]

TRANSITIONING ROQ.AD FROM AGENCY TO AD-TECH LEADER

Pursuing the agency model meant that Roq.ad devoted the early part of 2015 to selling what were called "cost-per-install" (CPI) campaigns. For this model, Roq.ad linked prospective partners and clients. Clients would be effectively buying space on mobile devices, publishing their advertising content in applications loaded onto Internet-enabled devices.

However, partners that already had a presence on mobile devices were needed. This meant that they already had an application loaded onto a device and could demonstrate that the application was a source of robust traffic. A deterministic traffic source was a large, well-known, established application or mobile website that had a login or registration area, and was used by millions of people every day. In CPI campaigns, Roq.ad's goal was to identify and recruit partners and clients, retaining a portion of the client's advertising spend. Roq.ad survived the first six months by relying exclusively on revenue from these CPI campaigns. Clients included Axel Springer, Condé Nast, Immo Scout24, and Payback.

Roq.ad established longer-term agreements with various technology partners in areas such as mobile audience targeting. Partners included AppNexus, eXelate, Turn, and Adsquare. These partners were used to help run the campaigns. Some campaigns were desktop-based; others were on mobile devices. Partners were seen as part of a long-term strategy involving ongoing relationships, used for multiple rather than single campaigns. That said, decisions about which partners to use for each campaign were made on a campaign-by-campaign basis. As of October 2015, there were 25 clients and multiple campaigns had been run per client. Some campaigns were global, but the vast majority of campaigns were in Germany, Austria, and Switzerland. Roq.ad was not profitable in its first year of operations, but was expecting to break even by 2017.

As 2015 proceeded and revenues were generated from the agency model, increased investment and focus were placed on new technology development. The core technology would enable cross-device unique user recognition, or "user matching." This technology, based on software that was coded in a mix of object-oriented and Java™-based languages such as Apache Hadoop, Spark, Python, and Scala, was able to identify when more than one Internet-enabled device was used by the same person in a certain time-frame. The technology could not identify the person; rather, it generated a link between Internet Protocol (IP) addresses — which were device-unique — where it found matched usage patterns.

There were two established techniques for achieving these matches, both standard in the industry and available for competitor use. The first technique was based on probabilistic data; the second was based on deterministic data.

With probabilistic data, the algorithm could not determine who was an end user. The company needed data about searches made by individuals using Internet search engines and company website search engines, on a range of devices. The data was provided at an aggregate level. Individuals were not identified by name or identifying codes, email addresses, or logins. Indeed, the company would never receive email addresses or login information. The technique did, however, allow an estimate to be made within a given probability that two or more devices were likely to have been used by the same person. This estimate would then be used to send dedicated advertising campaigns to those devices.

By August 2015, Roq.ad had signed integration agreements with two media companies. The integration agreement involved the client organization using a Roq.ad tracking pixel (sometimes known as a "tag") in the client's website tracking manager software. The pixel was a tracking mechanism that placed a cookie on a user's device, which tracked the user's browsing behaviour. This allowed Roq.ad to collect data on the user's visits to one of the client's websites. Roq.ad did not pay for the right to do this, but instead, provided the client with analytics and reports of user habits. In turn, Roq.ad captured data on IP addresses and browser use. This data could then be used to customize advertising campaigns. The general rule of thumb for this technique was, "the more data, the better."

Setting up integration agreements was time-consuming and required a great deal of Ugwu and Frien's attention. Ugwu noted, "It has taken us up to seven months to set up these integration agreements. So we feel we can only do one country at a time right now."

The second technique, based on deterministic data, took email addresses linked to devices in a hashed (anonymized) format to produce what was known as a "training set," which could be used to train a probabilistic algorithm. This, in turn, matched devices in a world of unknown users. The probabilistic algorithm matched the devices over time by recognizing usage and behavioural patterns and applying a variety of heuristics. The company needed a minimum of 20,000 user–device data points in the "training set" for this technique to be useful. An ideal number would be closer to 5 million. Ugwu commented, "If we had 10 million Euros to spend right now, I am sure we would spend a good third of it on buying some deterministic data."

COMPETITION, POLAND, AND STRATEGIC POSITIONING

While competitors such as Drawbridge and Tapad operated in this industry niche, they were mainly based in the United States, selling to the U.S. market. The U.S. market represented the largest single advertising market in the world, and Frien and Ugwu felt that these competitors would be focusing on the U.S. market for the foreseeable future. There was a perception in the company that the U.S.-focused companies would encounter problems entering the EU because of the need to work with data protection laws that were stricter in the EU than in the United States.

Roq.ad had decided early on not to acquire any small ad-tech companies. The company was also determined not to diversify too quickly, and, instead, to focus on the core technology development for user-matching within the ad-tech space.

STATUS AND DECISION POINT

By August 2015, Roq.ad had twelve employees in Berlin and six in Poznan. In addition to the German employees, there were five others: two Russian, one Icelander, one Portuguese, and one French. The technology development team was in Poznan, and had made acceptable progress. However, the company had not sourced any deterministic data, which was seen as a major outstanding issue. Funding for development still came primarily from running agency campaigns, and this was taking time and attention from the top management team. They had also found that it had taken considerable time to find integration partners. They needed to be careful. They could spend many years running as an agency company while competition, from places including the United States, could enter the market with a technology and data advantage.

How could Ugwu and Frien successfully transform the company from its advertising agency model to become Europe's top provider of cross-device user recognition technology? How could they use an international strategy, leveraging Poland and potentially other locations, to execute this transition successfully?

Appendix: Cases

EXHIBIT 1: PROFILE OF U.S.-BASED LEADERS IN CROSS-DEVICE USER RECOGNITION TECHNOLOGY

Company	Drawbridge	Tapad
Headquarters	San Mateo, United States	New York City, United States
Other locations	Austin, Chicago, Dallas, Detroit, London, Los Angeles, and New York	Atlanta, Chicago, Dallas, Detroit, Los Angeles, Miami, and San Francisco
Areas served	Global (focus on United States)	Global (focus on United States)
Launch year	2011 (Technology created in 2010)	2010
Type of company	Privately held Venture capital funded	Privately held Venture capital funded
Cross-device user recognition technology	Probabilistic graphic model	Deterministic data used to verify findings of probabilistic data
Accuracy of predictiveness	97.3%	91.2%
Key output/ product	Connected Consumer Graph, which shows consumer behaviour, including the probability that it is the same user across devices	Patent-pending Tapad Device Graph, which shows consumer behaviour, including the probability that it is the same user across devices
Stance on privacy	Uses anonymized data	Technology not reliant on personally identifiable information

Appendix: Cases

EXHIBIT 1: *Continued*

Company	Drawbridge	Tapad
Partners	66 partners including Adobe, AOL, Oracle, DoubleClick, Forbes, FourSquare, Google, MasterCard, Twitter, Nielsen, and Yahoo Partners include those involved in ad serving validation, tag management, analytics and measurement, and private marketplaces	Beintoo, NinthDecimal, Apsalar, Medialets, Adometry, Digital Advertising Alliance, Ghostery, Mobile Marketing Association, IABM, and Networking Advertising Initiative

Sources: Company Website, Drawbridge, www.drawbridge.com, accessed November 8, 2015; *Media Kit: Reach Consumers across Devices in Innovative Ways* (San Mateo, CA: Drawbridge, June 2015), accessed November 8, 2015, https://gallery.mailchimp.com/dd5380a49beb13eb00838c7e2/files/Drawbridge_MediaKit_Jun2015_1_.pdf; *Cross-Device Consumer Graph: Enabling Brands to Have Seamless Conversations with Consumers across Devices* (San Mateo, CA: Drawbridge, n.d.), accessed November 8, 2015, https://gallery.mailchimp.com/dd5380a49beb13eb00838c7e2/files/White_Paper_4_24_14_FINAL.pdf; Company Website, Tapad, accessed November 8, 2015; Ilya Pozin, "5 Innovative Ad Tech Companies You Should Know About," *Forbes*, August 25, 2015, accessed November 8, 2015, www.forbes.com/sites/ilyapozin/2015/08/25/5-innovative-ad-tech-companies-you-should-know-about.

Appendix: Cases

ENDNOTES

1 Ryan. Singel, "Oct. 27, 1994: Web Gives Birth to Banner Ads," *Wired*, October 27, 2010, accessed November 8, 2015, www.wired.com/2010/10/1027hotwired-banner-ads; F. D'Angelo, "Happy Birthday, Digital Advertising," October 26, 2009, accessed November 8, 2015, http://adage.com/article/digitalnext/happy-birthday-digital-advertising/13964.
2 "A Brief History of (Ad Tech) Time," YouTube video, 12:02, posted by "AppNexus," November 11, 2014, accessed November 8, 2015, www.youtube.com/watch?v=GGDI3c-2ikg.
3 All currency amounts are in US$ unless otherwise specified.
4 "A Brief History of (Ad Tech) Time," op.cit.
5 Michael Arrington, "Microsoft Pay $6 Billion for aQuantive: Massive Ad Network Consolidation Is Occurring," TechCrunch, May 18, 2007, accessed November 8, 2015, http://techcrunch.com/2007/05/18/microsoft-pays-6-billion-for-aquantive.
6 Michael Arrington, "Breaking: Google Spends $3.1 Billion to Acquire DoubleClick," TechCrunch, April 13, 2007, accessed November 8, 2015, http://techcrunch.com/2007/04/13/google-spends-31-billion-for-doubleclick.
7 Abbey Klaassen, "Yahoo to Acquire Right Media for $680 Million," AdAge, April 30, 2007, accessed November 8, 2015, http://adage.com/article/digital/yahoo-acquire-media-680-million/116440.
8 WPP, "WPP Has Agreed to Acquire 24/7 Real Media for $11.7 Per Share," press release, May 17, 2007, accessed November 8, 2015, www.wpp.com/wpp/investor/financialnews/2007/may/17/wpp-has-agreed-to-acquire-real.
9 Donté Ledbetter, "Why the Ad Tech Industry Is Consolidating Like Crazy," Venture Beat, April 13, 2015, accessed November 8, 2015, www.venturebeat.com/2015/04/13/why-the-ad-tech-industry-is-consolidating-like-crazy.
10 Lara O'Reilly, "The Ad Tech Sector Looks an Awful Lot Like a Bubble That Just Popped," Business Insider, May 12, 2015, accessed November 8, 2015, www.businessinsider.com/the-ad-tech-bubble-2015-5.
11 Mike Shields, "Ad Tech Firms Find Venture Capita Funding Is Running Dry," *Wall Street Journal*, June 10, 2015, accessed November 8, 2015, http://blogs.wsj.com/cmo/2015/06/10/ad-tech-firms-find-venture-capital-funding-is-running-dry.
12 Lara O'Reilly, "Beleaguered Ad-Tech Company Rocket Fuel Announces It Is Cutting 11% of Its Workforce as It Seeks to Reduce Costs by $30 Million," Business Insider, April 23, 2015, accessed November 8, 2015, www.businessinsider.com/rocket-fuel-layoffs-2015-4; Lara O'Reilly, "At the Start of the Year, Ad-Tech Company Fiksu Was on a Hiring Spree and Preparing to Go Public — Now It Has Scrapped Its IPO Plans and Is Cutting 10 per Cent of Its Workforce," Business Insider, April 1, 2015, accessed November 8, 2015, www.businessinsider.com/fiksu-scraps-ipo-plans-and-announces-layoffs-2015-4.
13 Jack Marshall, "Ad Tech Stocks Keep Falling in First Quarter," *Wall Street Journal*, March 31, 2015, accessed November 8, 2015, http://blogs.wsj.com/cmo/2015/03/31/ad-tech-stocks-keep-falling-in-first-quarter.
14 Jim Edwards, "The Billion-Dollar Facebook Business That Never Happened," Business Insider, March 6, 2015, accessed November 8, 2015, www.businessinsider.com/the-history-of-facebooks-fbx-ad-exchange-2015-3.
15 David Pakman, "Why AdTech Is Back (It Never Left)," Venrock, October 30, 2013, accessed November 8, 2015, www.venrock.com/why-adtech-is-back-it-never-left.
16 Tyler Loechner, "M&A Deals in Ad Tech Continue to Rise," MediaPost, April 28, 2015, accessed November 8, 2015, www.mediapost.com/publications/article/248581/ma-deals-in-ad-tech-continue-to-rise.html.

Appendix: Cases

17 Kassem Hashem, "Mobile Ad Spend to Top $100 Billion Worldwide in 2016, 51% of Digital Market," September 2, 2015, accessed November 8, 2015, https://www.linkedin.com/pulse/mobile-ad-spend-top-100-billion-worldwide-2016-51-digital-hashem.

18 Ibid.

19 David Pakman, "May I Have Your Attention, Please?" Venrock, August 10, 2015, accessed November 8, 2015, www.venrock.com/may-i-have-your-attention-please.

20 Ibid.

21 Criteo, "Cross-Device Advertising: How to Navigate Mobile Marketing's Next Big Opportunity" (AdAge, September 2014), accessed November 8, 2015, www.criteo.com/media/1036/cross-device-advertising-criteo-sep-2014.pdf.

22 Lara O'Reilly, "The Ad Tech Sector Looks an Awful Lot Like a Bubble That Just Popped," op. cit.

23 Lara O'Reilly, "This 20-Year Veteran of the Ad Tech Industry Explains Why It's in Such Trouble Now," Business Insider, August 19, 2015, accessed November 8, 2015, www.businessinsider.com/sovrn-raises-10-million-ceo-walter-knapp-interview-2015-8.

24 Lara O'Reilly, "The Ad Tech Sector Looks an Awful Lot Like a Bubble That Just Popped," op. cit.

25 Kamakshi Sivaramakrishnan, "The Commoditization of Ad Tech — How The Cross-Device Landscape is Going to Get Worse Before It Gets Better," Medium (blog), September 22, 2015, accessed November 8, 2015, https://medium.com/drawbridge-inc/the-commoditization-of-ad-tech-how-the-198a40aa9e62.

26 Forrester Consulting, *The New Path-To-Purchase* (New York: Tapad, July 2014), accessed November 8, 2015, www.tapad.com/wp-content/uploads/2015/10/Tapad-The-New-Path-To-Purchase.pdf.

27 Steve O'Hear, "Ad Square Locates $4.3M Funding to Serve Ads Based on Location and Context Without Being Too Creepy," TechCrunch, October 28, 2014, accessed November 8, 2015, http://techcrunch.com/2014/10/28/adsquare; Gili Tidhar, "5 Reasons Why Berlin Is Europe's Ad Tech Capital," Tune (blog), September 24, 2015, accessed November 8, 2015, www.tune.com/blog/5-reasons-why-berlin-is-europes-ad-tech-capital.

28 "The Start up Game," Morillas (blog: NG), November 14, 2014, accessed November 8, 2015, www.morillas.com/en/blog-en/the-start-up-game; "One Born Every 20 Minutes — Berlin Is the City of Start-Ups," July 21, 2015, http://talkbusiness-magazine.co.uk/2015/07/21/one-born-every-20-minutes-berlin-is-the-city-of-startups, accessed November 8, 2015.

29 "One Born Every 20 Minutes — Berlin Is the City of Startups," Talk Business, July 21, 2015, accessed November 8, 2015, http://talkbusinessmagazine.co.uk/2015/07/21/one-born-every-20-minutes-berlin-is-the-city-of-startups; "Berlin Start-Up Scene and Germany Keeps Talent Busy," Talent, July 30, 2015, accessed November 8, 2015, www.talentinternational.com/berlin-start-up-scene-and-germany-keeps-talent-busy.

30 "One Born Every 20 Minutes — Berlin Is the City of Start-Ups," op.cit.

31 Adform, "Adform, Europe's Leading Ad Tech Partner, Opens New Office in Poland to Support the Growing Demand for Real Time Bidding," press release, May 27, 2014, accessed November 8, 2015, http://blog.adform.com/press-releases/adform,-europe's-leading-ad-tech-partner,-opens-new-office-in-poland-to-support-the-growing-demand-for-real-time-bidding.

32 Alison Coleman, "How Poland's Globally Outsourced Tech Talent Became Native Entrepreneurs," *Forbes*, October 24, 2014, accessed November 8, 2015, www.forbes.com/sites/alisoncoleman/2014/10/24/how-polands-globally-outsourced-tech-talent-became-native-entrepreneurs.

Appendix: Cases

33 Ibid.
34 Ibid.
35 Allison Schiff, "Oracle Partners With Tapad — Because Probabilistic vs. Deterministic Data Isn't An and/or Sort of Thing," Ad Exchanger, October 15, 2015, accessed November 8, 2015, http://adexchanger.com/data-exchanges/oracle-partner-with-tapad-because-probabilistic-vs-deterministic-data-isnt-an-andor-sort-of-thing; Kia Kokalitcheva, "This Ad Tech Company Is Boosting Its Image by Partnering With Foursquare," *Fortune*, June 4, 2015, accessed November 8, 2015, http://fortune.com/2015/06/04/drawbridge-foursquare-partnership.
36 Richard Beaumont, "Cross Device Tracking Getting Regulator Attention," OptAnon (blog), May 18, 2015, accessed November 8, 2015, www.cookielaw.org/blog/2015/5/18/cross-device-tracking-getting-regulator-attention.
37 Liz Rowley, "What Germany's Tight-Laced Privacy Mandate Means for Ad Tech Players," Ad Exchanger, October 13, 2014, accessed November 8, 2015, http://adexchanger.com/data-exchanges/what-germanys-tight-laced-privacy-mandate-means-for-ad-tech-players.
38 Kamakshi Sivaramakrishnan, op. cit.
39 Kia Kokalitcheva, "This Ad Tech Company Is Boosting Its Image by Partnering with Foursquare," *Fortune*, June 4, 2015, accessed November 8, 2015, http://fortune.com/2015/06/04/drawbridge-foursquare-partnership.

IVEY | Publishing

9B17M063

TIME OUT: A NEW GLOBAL STRATEGY TO BRING BACK PROFIT

Christopher Williams and Umair Shafique wrote this case solely to provide material for class discussion. The authors do not intend to illustrate either effective or ineffective handling of a managerial situation. The authors may have disguised certain names and other identifying information to protect confidentiality.

This publication may not be transmitted, photocopied, digitized, or otherwise reproduced in any form or by any means without the permission of the copyright holder. Reproduction of this material is not covered under authorization by any reproduction rights organization. To order copies or request permission to reproduce materials, contact Ivey Publishing, Ivey Business School, Western University, London, Ontario, Canada, N6G 0N1; (t) 519.661.3208; (e) cases@ivey.ca; www.iveycases.com.

Copyright © 2017, Richard Ivey School of Business Foundation   Version: 2017-09-28

Julio Bruno, chief executive officer (CEO) of United Kingdom-based Time Out Group PLC (Time Out), had been busy since overseeing the company's initial public offering (IPO) in June 2016. From his office in the heart of London's West End, Bruno, 51, reflected on this recent success. The IPO, which had been achieved in an eye-catching two and a half months, had raised much-needed capital for investment and growth, and all eyes were now on Bruno.

Before the IPO, the company had reported adjusted earnings before interest, tax, depreciation, and amortization (EBITDA) losses of £5.5 million[1] in 2014 and £12.4 million in 2015. Revenues had been flat in traditional areas of print advertising and circulation, and they were falling slightly in international licensing. However, there was momentum in new market areas: digital advertising and e-commerce revenue had grown 19 per cent, to £11.7 million, between 2014 and 2015. In addition,

---

1 £ = GBP = British pound sterling; all currency amounts are in £ unless otherwise specified; £1 = US$1.33 on June 30, 2016.

the company had recently launched a physical Time Out Market in Lisbon, Portugal, and this had seen revenue growth of 67 per cent, from £1.2 million to £2.0 million, between 2014 and 2015.

Now, with £59 million in proceeds from the IPO to invest, Bruno needed to decide how he should lead the newly public company back to profitability. How should he balance foreign direct investment in physical Time Out Markets around the world with investments in digital transformation and the company's global online presence?

TIME OUT GROUP: BACKGROUND

Time Out began as a print publication created by student Tony Elliott with £70 during a summer break from Keele University in 1968. The first two issues were folded-down posters that Elliott distributed himself on the streets of London. By its third issue, the publication had become an A5-sized saddle-stitched magazine. Time Out's contents included information about the events Elliott considered to be the best among those happening in London during the late 1960s. Bands such as the Animals, the Who, the Beatles, the Kinks and the Rolling Stones were in their prime, and London was seen as the epicentre of all things "hip and fashionable." As well as cultural content and listings about events, the magazine also had articles on the issues of the day. The magazine, which evolved into a weekly in April 1971, became an enduring and iconic brand with both a print and online presence.

Elliott internationalized the business in two stages—first, introducing a Time Out publishing operation in Paris in 1989–1991, and then launching Time Out New York in the United States in 1995. The company's first website was launched in the late 1990s, before the peak of the dot-com boom, and the Time Out brand continued to internationalize its presence principally through the Internet. By 2013, the company had set up websites for locations as diverse as São Paulo, Brazil, and Tokyo, Japan. By 2016, the company was present in 108 cities across 39 countries, had a global monthly audience reach of 156 million, and was generating over 1 billion page views per year. The vast majority of Time Out's publications and websites were in English, but by 2016, the company had websites in 11 other languages for 16 other locations (see Exhibit 1). Time Out also had multiple strategic partnerships with web-based service providers, including Uber Technologies Inc., Viator Inc., Broadway. com, Booking.com, and TicketNetwork Inc.

Appendix: Cases

In 2010, after looking for a new investor for Time Out for nearly a decade, Elliott sold 50 per cent of the company to Oakley Capital Limited and retained 50 per cent himself. The company was valued at £20 million, and Elliot intended to use the capital to accelerate its online and digital expansion. This came at a difficult time for the company, which had experienced pre-tax losses of £1.3 million in 2007 and £3 million in 2008, and declining sales in printed circulation. The weekly London edition, which had reportedly peaked at 105,000 copies in the late 1990s, was at around 60,000 per week by 2010.[2] By 2013, Elliott had sold more of his stake and retained a small minority holding.

Due to the growth of the Internet and consumers' preference for web-based content, the Time Out print magazine became a free publication in London (in 2012), in New York and Chicago (in 2015), and in Los Angeles and Miami (in 2016). Launching free magazines across key cities was part of Time Out's unique approach to print distribution, which it used to grow its brand, audience, engagement, and reach. This approach also provided increasing value to advertisers, who could connect through new creative opportunities across the brand's global print, digital, mobile, and event platforms. By 2016, the printed Time Out magazines had a total weekly circulation reach of approximately 600,000 in the company's owned and operated territories, and approximately 260,000 in those territories where it carried on business through international licensing agreements. By 2016, there were 39 magazines available—seven through owned and operated businesses and 32 through international licensing agreements. The company had also offered printed Time Out city guides, but these were discontinued in 2015, and outsourced to another publisher for a few select cities.

Time Out became active in staging live events, putting on over 400 curated events in London and New York every year. These included "Silent Disco" events at the Natural History Museum and the Shard in London, and "Battle of the Burger" contests, sponsored by Amstel in New York[3] and by Guinness in Chicago. In 2016, the group also ran a number of global campaigns, including the Time Out Love City Awards, an annual campaign that ran in seven cities worldwide: London, Lisbon, New York, Chicago, Los Angeles, Tokyo, and Paris. The campaign

---

2 "Oakley Capital Takes 50% Stake in Time Out," *The Financial Times*, accessed November 18, 2016, https://www.ft.com/content/24cd8294-f8c7-11df-b550-00144 feab49a.

3 Ibid.

155

Appendix: Cases

encouraged customers to vote for their favourite local businesses such as attractions, coffee shops, bars, shops, and restaurants.

The company was the recipient of four Professional Publishers Association (PPA) awards between 2010 and 2014: the International Magazine Brand of the Year in 2010 and 2011, and the International Consumer Media Brand of the Year in 2013 and 2014.[4] In awarding Time Out the International Consumer Media Brand of the Year award in 2014, the PPA judges noted, "The sheer scale of launches across multiple territories and platforms made it hard to look anywhere other than Time Out. A powerful global proposition."[5] Nevertheless, despite these accolades from the PPA and the earlier cash injection from Oakley Capital Limited, the newly formed Time Out Group[6] had consecutive losses in the years ending December 31, 2014, and December 31, 2015 (see Exhibit 2). Group revenues for 2014 and 2015 were £26.9 million and £28.5 million, respectively, while adjusted EBITDA losses for the same two years were £5.5 million and £12.4 million, respectively.

Bruno joined Time Out Group as executive chairman in September 2015. Bruno had previously served as global vice-president of sales at TripAdvisor and had held senior executive roles at Travelport, Regus Group Companies, and Diageo. He had been based in New York and was looking for a new leadership challenge back in Europe in the media, travel, and entertainment space when he had singled the company out, later commenting, "They didn't find me . . . I found them." He was particularly interested in the challenge of transforming the company from print to digital, and had expressed his ideas for growing the company to Oakley Capital Limited, convincing the firm to appoint him as executive chairman. The intention was for Bruno to be based between London and New York.[7]

---

4 "Swinging 60s—Capital of Cool," History, accessed November 18, 2016, www.history.co.uk/topics/history-of-london/swinging-60s-capital-cool; "Worldwide Brand of the Year . . . Again!," TimeOut, July 15, 2014, accessed November 18, 2016, www.timeout.com/about/time-out-group/latest-news/worldwide-brand-of-the-year-again.

5 Ibid.

6 Time Out Group came into being with the company's investment in Time Out Market. Initially, this was a 10 per cent stake, with Oakley Capital having a majority stake. Just prior to the IPO in June 2016, Time Out acquired the remaining equity.

7 Graeme Davies, "Boardroom Talk: Time Out's Growth Quest," Investors Chronicle, December 16, 2016, accessed January 5, 2017, www.investorschronicle.co.uk/2016/12/16/shares/news-and-analysis/boardroom-talk-time-out-s-growth-quest-A6G831XbmtFZpibEv1bGmJ/article.html.

Bruno spearheaded the group's IPO on the Alternative Investment Market, a sub-market of the London Stock Exchange. The IPO, which became effective on June 14, 2016, was completed in a record two and a half months under the leadership of Bruno, who became group CEO at that time. The company had £59 million net after paying off shareholder debt;[8] it used the IPO not only to pay off debt but also to raise funds for continued investment and transformation into digital and e-commerce initiatives. Statements in the IPO admission document indicated five areas of investment: expansion of Time Out Market to other locations, sales and marketing, technology and product, commercial teams, and general corporate purposes (see Exhibit 3). While the largest single item for post-IPO investment was related to Time Out Market (£20 million), digital and e-commerce investments together added up to over £30 million.

TIME OUT DIGITAL

Time Out had been engaged in a process of digital transformation since 2010, and had attained a monthly global audience reach of 111 million, growing to 137 million in June 2016. It had started to move away from a reliance on revenue from printed materials to new revenue sources based on the Internet and online technologies. Continued investment in developing the company's technology and sales and marketing of new digital products was seen as an important driver for growth and profitability (see Exhibit 3). For example, in 2015, the company had sold 262,000 tickets through a combination of click-throughs and direct sales via its own and other systems.[9] Bruno commented that "we need to invest in 'clicks and mortar' . . . our customer can be digital [clicks] or physical [mortar] by visiting a live event or the Time Out Market."

Development of new and enhanced digital platforms was central to Time Out's post-IPO strategy. It would provide new capabilities such as content offerings and social media functionality that would result in an increase in the number of transacting users. While these technology developments were aimed at increasing revenue from users, they also provided opportunities for the company to grow revenue from advertisers

---

8 "Time Out* - Buy a Ticket," accessed April 3, 2017, 1, http://oakleycapital.com/media/170328-Time_Out_BUY_TP_195p_Buy_a_ticket_22_pgs.pdf.

9 Click-throughs occurred when web users clicked on advertisements to open up advertisers' websites to make purchases electronically.

by enhancing advertising solutions on its platforms. Innovations in video and social media and creative applications of technology would broaden the appeal of Time Out as a platform for advertisers around the world. The company also wanted to improve its electronic interface with local business partners, offering them self-service solutions such as the ability to list their own events and issue electronic discount vouchers, which would make interacting with the Time Out platform more attractive.

While Bruno continued to drive the company's efforts in digital products, he also provided fresh impetus for a new venture that had been successfully launched in Lisbon, Portugal, in May 2014. This new venture was known as Time Out Market.

TIME OUT MARKET

Time Out Market brought together the best of a city, based on Time Out's editorial curation, under one roof. It was a market-style food-hall space within a fashionable area of a well-known global city, where consumers were offered food, drink, and cultural experiences. It was first launched and trialled in the Mercado da Ribeira, in Lisbon, Portugal, in May 2014. In addition to the physical experience, the market had its own website (in Portuguese and English), which informed consumers on the latest chefs, menus, and cultural experiences; consumers could also get information via the market's email address and direct telephone line. The Lisbon market offered an open space for consumers to enjoy dining experiences from 14 chefs in 30 restaurants.[10] It was open from 10:00 a.m. to 12:00 a.m. from Sunday to Wednesday, and from 10:00 a.m. to 2:00 a.m. from Thursday to Saturday. The market included a cooking academy as well—a space in which consumers could "learn, perfect, and share" their love of food.[11]

The initial results were highly encouraging for Time Out. The market received 1.9 million visitors in 2015, which was noteworthy because the population of the greater Lisbon area was 2.8 million people. The company also reported receiving 1.3 million visitors in the first half of

---

10 "Muitos Mas Bons," TimeOut Market Lisboa, accessed November 18, 2016, www.timeoutmarket.com/en/highlights/muitos-mas-bons/.

11 "Academia Time Out," accessed November 18, 2016, www.timeoutmarket.com/en/academy/.

2016, and 3.1 million for the full year. The Lisbon market showed a positive EBITDA within 18 months of opening.

Bruno and the board of Time Out felt that the Time Out Market was a scalable opportunity. Bruno believed the company's early experiences from the Lisbon market would allow it to build and develop successful markets in other locations around the world. He saw this as a way of differentiating the company from the competition, noting, "Time Out sells experiences . . . our markets are experiences . . . who else out there is doing this?"

Based on these experiences with the Lisbon market, the company considered expanding the Time Out Market. First, it considered further penetrating Portugal with a market in Porto, in Northern Portugal. It also considered London in the United Kingdom and Miami in the United States. Other possible locations considered for opening within the following two years were Berlin in Germany and New York City in the United States. Bruno noted, "We receive requests from around the world—places such as Sydney, Tel Aviv, and Tokyo, and many more—to come and set this up as they would love to have a Time Out Market there. If we could accelerate this using management contracts, then great . . . the scalability is there."

Given these possibilities, Bruno decided to focus on opening new Time Out Markets in Porto, London, and Miami in 2017 and early 2018, and having a dedicated CEO responsible for setting up in these locations. This resulted in plans to open a new Time Out Market in the iconic São Bento train station in Porto in 2017, subject to planning permission. This market would provide 500 seats over 2,043 square metres, and would include 15 restaurants, four bars, four shops, one café, and an art gallery. The London site, which was also subject to planning permission, would be a converted Victorian stable in Shoreditch, close to the famous Old Spitalfields Market. It would be 1,788 square metres and would accommodate 450 seats surrounded by 17 food stalls, four bars, a permanent shop, an art gallery, and a cooking academy.[12] Shoreditch was seen as a trendy area of London. In December 2016, a conditional lease agreement was signed for a Time Out Market in South Beach, Miami. A number of exh4_people in Time Out Market's central team,

---

12 "FY16 Interim Results Presentation," Time Out Group plc, October 2016; Jillian Ambrose, "Time Out Market to Open in Shoreditch in 2017," *The Telegraph*, October 12, 2016, accessed November 17, 2016, www.telegraph.co.uk/business/2016/10/12/time-out-market-to-open-in-shoreditch-in-2017/.

including designers, architects, and operations specialists, worked closely with local designers and architects in each location.

GOVERNANCE OF TIME OUT GROUP

At the time of the IPO in June 2016, the group's board consisted of Bruno, Peter Dubens (non-executive chairman and partner in Oakley Capital), Richard Boult (chief financial officer), and non-executive directors Lord Rose of Monewden, Alexander Collins, Christine Petersen, and Tony Elliott. Only Elliott, the founder, had been involved in the company since its early days. Dubens and Collins had joined the group in 2010; Bruno and Lord Rose of Monewden joined in 2015; and Bruno recruited Petersen, his boss at TripAdvisor, in 2016.

In terms of operating structure, Time Out Group was divided into two subgroups: Time Out Digital (TOD) and Time Out Market (TOM). While Bruno was CEO of the combined group, each subgroup had its own CEO, who reported to Bruno. TOD was further divided into Europe, North America, International, Content/Editorial, Marketing, E-commerce, Engineering, and Product. The CEO of TOM had four direct reports from Time Out Markets in Lisbon, Porto, London, and Miami, as well as central support groups (see Exhibit 4).

In 2016, the group owned and operated business in 65 cities and 14 countries. In 25 other countries (43 cities), the group used international licensing arrangements with partners (see Exhibits 5 and 6). Under the licensing model, Time Out Group retained ownership of rights, title, and interest in the brand and content. The majority of revenue in owned and operated business came from the United Kingdom and the United States, which represented 59.6 per cent and 32.1 per cent of group revenue in 2015. The group generated £26.7 million in revenue through the owned and operated models in 2015, compared to £1.7 million in fees and royalties revenues in 2015 from international licensing arrangements. The international licensing arrangements were made with local media companies and provided between 7 and 15 per cent of revenue generated through the licence. These were all fixed-term agreements.

ORGANIZATIONAL CULTURE

Bruno strongly believed that the company's employees needed to be content and happy themselves in order for this to translate into satisfied consumer experiences. He said, "We sell happiness, so we need happy people." Recalling the atmosphere around the time he joined the company, he noted a "need to nurture our culture . . . it was a big problem . . . . [There was] no clear sense of purpose and a lack of entrepreneurial spirit." In his view, the company was a "48-year old start-up," and he wanted to inject the kind of entrepreneurial culture that he had experienced working in start-ups in the United States. He felt there had been a silo mentality in the organization, with departments not communicating effectively and some employees not understanding the company's strategy. Bruno was concerned about mistrust and suspicion between departments, and a lack of creativity and innovation.

In order to address profitability concerns as well as concerns about the company's culture, Bruno laid off around 20 per cent of staff globally in November and December 2015. Throughout 2016, Bruno established a number of new organizational routines designed as opportunities for employees to socialize, be recognized, and develop a common sense of purpose around the company's new vision. He set up Time Out café/bar areas within the offices in London and New York. Every week, external contacts and representatives from the wider entertainment and media sectors would be invited to showcase their brands and companies, and socialize with Time Out staff in the café/bar area. Music, pizza, alcohol, and soft drinks were served for free. These external representatives included distributors, entrepreneurs, and founders of other companies (for example, the founder of a new vodka company based in London) who would then get exposure for their products among the staff at Time Out.

Bruno also established a variety of meeting types for the key offices in major cities. "Stand-up" meetings took place every two weeks and allowed all employees to stand up and give a short presentation on their current projects. New joiners were introduced to the rest of the team in the location at these meetings. "Shout-outs," whereby employees gave accolades regarding the quality and impact of their colleagues' work, were encouraged, and staff could also anonymously submit questions to be read out and answered by the senior executives. "Town hall" meetings were also run by Bruno, who visited every major city office once every three months throughout 2016 to share the company's new mission and vision. These formal meetings took place in the United Kingdom, the United States, Spain, Portugal, and France. Finally, "show and tell" meetings involved product demonstrations by the technology (engineering and product) team. In these meetings, staff could show what they were actually working on and elicit feedback from all others in attendance.

Appendix: Cases

COMPETITION AND DIGITAL DISRUPTION

Time Out Group faced competition from different sources and industries. The company was present not only in e-commerce and digital advertising but also in the area of offering experiences to customers through live events produced and sold by Time Out and Time Out Market. Bruno emphasized that his vision for the company did not align Time Out Group with a single traditional industry: "We don't consider ourselves publishers . . . Time Out is the only global brand you can read, eat, drink, and enjoy."

On the content side (events and culture), Time Out Group faced competition from traditional and new publishers of content. The publishing industry for entertainment, culture, and events was broadly defined as including publishers that provided information or content related to events, travel, food, art, theatre, lifestyle, and so on. However, this industry had been affected by digital disruption with competitors that increasingly offered content online. Digital disruption meant that publishers now had to contend with a much bigger field of competition. Several other companies offered similar content and information online and for free, competing for the audience's attention and advertisers' budgets.

Direct competition came from companies such as TripAdvisor and Yelp, which had become well-known and established online platforms for users to gain information and provide reviews about businesses offering services in the travel, entertainment, and hospitality sectors. By 2016, TripAdvisor, with 3,000 employees, had reached 390 million average monthly unique visitors and operated in 49 countries. Yelp, with 4,050 employees, had a mission to "connect people with great local businesses." By 2016, it had a monthly average of 25 million unique visitors via its app, and 72 million visitors to its mobile web platform.[13] Competition came from other magazine publishers who utilized the "freemium" business model (that is, they complemented free print publications with an online presence and mobile applications) and who shared a similar or overlapping audience with Time Out. These included general news and lifestyle magazines like *Metro*, *Evening Standard*, *ShortList*, and *Stylist* in the United Kingdom, and *Billboard*,

---

13 "About TripAdvisor," TripAdvisor, accessed January 10, 2017, https://www.tripad visor.co.uk/PressCenter-c6-About_Us.html; "About Us," Yelp, accessed January 10, 2017, https://www.yelp.co.uk/about.

Appendix: Cases

Entertainment Weekly, and *The New Yorker* in the United States. Competition also came from websites such as Vice, Buzzfeed, and New York Magazine.

Indirect competition came from a range of sources, including technology and social media companies like Google and Facebook, which had entered the entertainment, culture, and events markets and were solidifying their presence there. Such companies had introduced applications (apps) such as Google Trips, Google Maps' "explore" features, and Facebook's events features and new "Events" app. Further, travel and online booking companies like Expedia, Ticketmaster, and StubHub competed for revenue from e-commerce commissions and offered ticketing options that were similar to those of Time Out. Despite this competition, there was a trend towards co-opetition[14] in the industry: Time Out Group sold tickets through Facebook, and consumers came to the Time Out web pages through Google searches.

Print magazine publishers had been forced to transform themselves into primarily digital publishers and to adopt a freemium model—offering high-quality content for free and using digital advertising and e-commerce for revenue. Publishing no longer focused on a product but on a user-centric platform that provided content from contributors and advertisers (e.g., retailers), and publishers' audiences were no longer seen as readers but instead as consumers. These new breeds of publishers competed for consumers to interact with their sites and worked to monetize their website traffic through e-commerce activity and digital advertisements that influenced their consumers' purchasing behaviour.

Digital disruption had also given rise to the phenomenon of "big data," as publishers tried to use data to understand consumer behaviour and optimize and personalize content according to consumers' profiles and needs. Big data could further be used to develop key performance indicators to demonstrate the value of websites to digital advertisers.

Changes in consumer behaviour also affected the publishing industry. As a result of digital disruption, the publishing industry's audience increasingly overlapped with the audience of companies that offered

---

14 Mechanisms that encouraged firms to simultaneously cooperate and compete; see Adam M. Brandenburger and Barry J. Nalebuff, *Co-Opetition*, (New York: Crown Publishing Group, 2011).

information and content related to entertainment, events, and culture. Consumers became frustrated by advertising attempts such as pop-up advertisements, and native advertising and sophisticated content marketing, which could be used to discreetly advertise and market services or products without impeding a user's experience, were seen as the way forward.[15] Consumers favoured mobile apps that provided real-time events, culture, travel, and entertainment information using location-based services, and allowed them to make reservations or book tickets for events very quickly.

Many consumers had started to prioritize experiences over material goods, and they increasingly wanted to experience new cuisines, events, and cultures, and to share these experiences with others. This desire took the form of consumers exploring their own cities, as well as tourists exploring new places by touring as locals. Airbnb recognized this trend in its marketing, which promised to provide tourists with local, cultural experiences. Consumers flocked to trendy locations that were in the news, including countries such as Brazil, which hosted the FIFA World Cup in 2014 and was the first South American country to host the Olympic Games in 2016. At the same time, consumers from emerging economies such as China were starting to explore the Western world.

As the market became increasingly congested with information and content related to entertainment, culture, and events, consumers relied on trusted user-generated reviews. Companies such as TripAdvisor emerged as leading providers of such reviews. Analysts had observed that consumers increasingly demanded a seamless and tailored user experience,[16] and they were loyal to trusted and well-known brands that provided tailored and personalized content. Companies tried to build relationships with individual consumers rather than trying to reach out to the masses.

While there was no direct competition for the specific format used by Time Out Market, this new and relatively unique format faced competition from a wide range of restaurant types, particularly those that offered local or trendy new styles of cuisines. Restaurants that were local favourites or offered unique dining experiences—those places

---

15 Simon Das, "Magazine Publishing Innovation: Two Case Studies on Managing Creativity," Publications 4, no. 2 (2016): 15. doi:10.3390/publications4020015.

16 "Top 5 Customer Experience Trends for 2016," iperceptions, January 13, 2016, accessed April 3, 2017, https://www.iperceptions.com/blog/customer-experience-trends-2016.

Appendix: Cases

with good reviews that offered quick and efficient dining experiences in close proximity to shops and creative zones such as art galleries—were seen as potential competition to the Time Out Market.

JULIO BRUNO'S VISION

At the time of his appointment in 2015, Bruno explained his vision:

> I believe that the Time Out brand and our unique content approach will reach an even larger audience. Over the next few years, we have exciting plans to roll out our digital products globally as well as our unique Time Out Market. As I see it, Time Out is the global source for local entertainment, and I am very pleased to be joining at this exciting moment in time to lead this organization to greater heights.[17]

It was clear that Bruno no longer saw Time Out simply as a publisher. He later commented that he saw "the magazines as a marketing channel." In his view, Time Out was the global media and entertainment business, creating value through clicks and mortar. He also observed that "the consumer is not unidimensional," and that creating value from the entertainment needs of global consumers would require simultaneous competition and co-operation with other companies. In his view, the basis of competition had changed. In addition, Bruno was highly aware of the importance of carefully balancing global capabilities with local needs. For instance, when reflecting on Time Out Market, he observed that "the best of Porto is not the best of Lisbon . . . and the same for London. It's a city-by-city model. Brand colours may be the same, but tables and chairing are different and unique to that place. That's why it takes time."

BREXIT

On June 23, 2016, one week after Time Out Group's IPO, the United Kingdom held a referendum on its European Union (EU) membership—a democratic decision made by the British electorate on whether to

---

17 "Time Out Group Appoints Julio Bruno as Executive Chairman and Noel Penzer as CEO," TimeOut, October 1, 2015, accessed November 18, 2016, www.timeout.com/about/time-out-group/latest-news/time-out-group-appoints-julio-bruno-as-executive-chairman-and-noel-penzer-as-ceo.

165

Appendix: Cases

withdraw from the EU, commonly known as the "Brexit" decision. The country voted to leave the EU by 17,410,742 votes to 16,141,241 votes. The result took many by surprise, including currency markets. Within days of the vote, the United Kingdom's currency, the pound, had fallen to a 31-year low against the U.S. dollar, and the Financial Times Stock Exchange 100 Index had lost £100 billion in value amidst market volatility.[18] While stock indices recovered in subsequent weeks, the pound remained suppressed, and the outlook for pound-to-dollar and pound-to-euro exchange rates remained uncertain. Imports into the United Kingdom became more expensive, and foreign direct investments in U.S. dollars or euros could be up to 30 per cent more expensive than they were before Brexit, all other factors remaining equal. Uncertainty over the impact of Brexit on British businesses remained.

Prior to the IPO, Time Out Group had not developed a currency hedging strategy and had not believed the Brexit vote would materially impact its strategy. However, the company had bought modest amounts (low millions) of U.S. and European currencies before June 23 in order to cover ongoing operating expenses in those currencies.

STATUS AND DECISION POINT

Bruno was facing challenges in multiple areas. There had been overall losses in 2014 and 2015, and flat or even declining revenue in traditional lines of business. Some good news had come from the growing revenue in digital and e-commerce and from Time Out Market, the fastest growth area in the non-digital and non-traditional area of the company. Indeed, by the middle of 2016, Bruno's work appeared to be having a positive effect on the company's bottom line. Figures for the first half of 2016 were £16.6 million in revenue with a loss (adjusted EBITDA) of £4.8 million.[19] This was encouraging news for the company: for the first half of 2016, pro forma revenue was up 16 per cent, and losses improved by £0.8 million.

---

18 Angela Monaghan, "Sterling Hits New 31-Year Low against the Dollar," *The Guardian*, July 6, 2016, accessed August 17, 2016, https://www.theguardian.com/business/2016/jul/06/brexit-pound-plunges-to-30-year-lows-as-eu-fears-bite-into-global-markets-again; Tara Cunningham, "FTSE 100 Loses £100bn in Four Days as Brexit Paralyses Markets and Pound Crumbles," *The Telegraph*, June 15, 2016, accessed November 18, 2016, www.telegraph.co.uk/business/2016/06/14/ftse-100-slides-towards-6000-and-pound-falls-as-brexit-fears-dri/.

19 "FY16 Interim Results Presentation," Time Out Group plc, October 2016.

Yet Bruno was mindful of potential hazards. While he had £59 million to invest, he was aware of the risks of rushing into overseas investment. "I want to spend it very carefully," he commented. "Even if you gave me £200 million right now and said, 'Go and open 20 new Time Out Markets,' I wouldn't because of the amount of management resources and curation needed to open one market, let alone 20. We will eventually open many, but not in one go. It takes time and expertise, not just money." Nevertheless, competition remained fierce, and the effect of Brexit on the attractiveness of foreign investment opportunities was unclear.

Returning to Profitability

This was the biggest challenge. Bruno was under pressure to get Time Out back to a position of sustainable profitability quickly. How should he lead the recently listed company back to profitability? How should he balance foreign direct investment in physical Time Out Markets around the world with investments in digital transformation and the company's global online presence? Did the areas for investment indicated in the pre-Brexit IPO admission document (see Exhibit 2) make sense in light of the post-Brexit impact on the pound?

Reinforcing Culture and Staff Satisfaction

Bruno had started to build a new organizational culture within Time Out through new meeting formats, socialization activities, and café/bar areas within the offices in London and New York. What else could he consider doing in order to promote the type of internal culture needed to fulfil the corporate vision?

Maintaining the Vision

Bruno was acutely aware of the fast pace of change and levels of disruption in the industry. He himself saw Time Out Group's new strategy as a disruptive force—but was his vision sustainable? How should it change going forward, and how could he revise the vision in line with changing events?

Appendix: Cases

EXHIBIT 1: LIST OF TIME OUT'S NON-ENGLISH WEBSITE LOCATIONS AND LANGUAGES

Location	Language
Paris	French
Barcelona, Madrid, Girona, Mexico City	Spanish, Catalan (Barcelona only)
Lisbon, Sao Paolo, Rio	Portuguese
Moscow	Russian
Istanbul	Turkish
Tel Aviv	Hebrew
Beijing, Shanghai	Chinese
Bangkok	Thai
Tokyo	Japanese
Seoul	Korean

Source: Created by the case authors based on company documents.

EXHIBIT 2: TIME OUT—SEGMENT REVENUE 2014–2015 (IN £ MILLIONS)

Segment	2014	2015
Digital advertising and e-commerce	£9.8	£11.7
Print advertising and circulation	£15.0	£15.0
Other, principally international licensing	£2.1	£1.8

Note: Figures were for years ending December 31.

Source: Created by the case authors based on Time Out Group, *Time Out Admission Document*, 2016, 74, accessed November 17, 2016, http://media.timeout.com/www_timeout_com_uploads/wp-content/uploads/2016/06/Admission-Document.pdf.

Appendix: Cases

EXHIBIT 3: TIME OUT—INDICATED AREAS FOR INVESTMENT (IN £ MILLIONS)

Area of Investment	Amount
Capital expenditure to roll out Time Out Market: • geographical expansion of the concept to new cities • sourcing and design of new leased premises • physical infrastructure improvements • recruitment of local management teams • local marketing • technology, including point of sale and free wi-fi	£20
Investment in sales and marketing for e-commerce offerings: • increasing in-house headcount • engaging in paid social media • increasing use of direct advertising and Google Ad Awards • enhancing "gamification" (rewards via membership and mobile app) • developing customer relationship management tool	£15
Investment in technology and product: • expansion into new product verticals • development of new user interface • improvement of premium profiles service • development of data warehouse • improvement of user integration and integration of Flypay • development of management information system (MIS)	£10
Commercial teams: • expansion of teams, focusing on premium profiles, brand solutions, creative solutions, content moderation, and e-commerce partner acquisitions	£5
General corporate purposes	£8

Source: Created by the case authors based on Time Out Group, *Time Out Admission Document*, 2016, 32, accessed November 17, 2016, http://media.timeout.com/www_timeout_com_uploads/wp-content/uploads/2016/06/Admission-Document.pdf.

Appendix: Cases

EXHIBIT 4: TIME OUT—COMPANY STRUCTURE

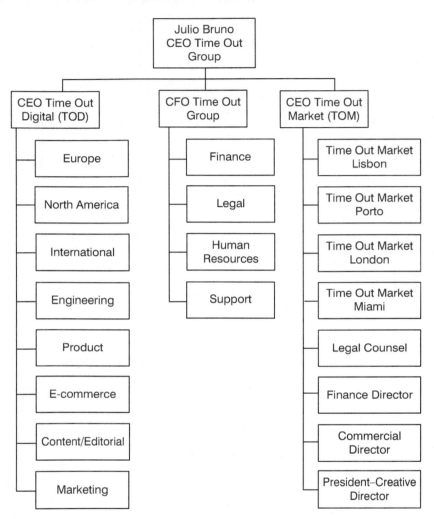

Source: Created by the case authors.

Appendix: Cases

EXHIBIT 5: TIME OUT—OWNED AND OPERATED BUSINESSES

Region	Countries
Americas	United States, Canada, Argentina
Europe	United Kingdom, France, Germany, Portugal, Netherlands, Czech Republic, Sweden, Ireland, Italy
Africa	South Africa
Middle East	None
Australasia	None
Asia	India

Source: Adapted from Time Out Group, Time Out Admission Document, 2016, 14, accessed November 17, 2016, http://media.timeout.com/www_timeout_com_ uploads/wp-content/uploads/2016/06/Admission-Document.pdf, and company input.

EXHIBIT 6: TIME OUT—INTERNATIONAL LICENSING ARRANGEMENTS

Region	Countries
Americas	Mexico, Brazil
Europe	Croatia, Spain, Switzerland, Turkey, Russia, Cyprus, Malta
Africa	Ghana
Middle East	United Arab Emirates, Lebanon, Oman, Bahrain, Qatar, Israel
Australasia	Australia (includes the right to operate in New Zealand)
Asia	Japan, China, Malaysia, Singapore, Sri Lanka, Korea, Hong Kong, Thailand

Source: Adapted from Time Out Group, Time Out Admission Document, 2016, 15, accessed November 17, 2016, http://media.timeout.com/www_timeout_com_uploads/ wp-content/uploads/2016/06/Admission-Document.pdf, and company input.

⚗ IVEY | Publishing

9B11M014

INTERNATIONAL ENTREPRENEURSHIP AT INFUSION

Christopher Williams and Melissa Davis wrote this case solely to provide material for class discussion. The authors do not intend to illustrate either effective or ineffective handling of a managerial situation. The authors may have disguised certain names and other identifying information to protect confidentiality.

This publication may not be transmitted, photocopied, digitized, or otherwise reproduced in any form or by any means without the permission of the copyright holder. Reproduction of this material is not covered under authorization by any reproduction rights organization. To order copies or request permission to reproduce materials, contact Ivey Publishing, Ivey Business School, Western University, London, Ontario, Canada, N6G 0N1; (t) 519.661.3208; (e) cases@ivey.ca; www.iveycases.com.

Copyright © 2011, Richard Ivey School of Business Foundation   Version: 2017-09-29

In the late summer of 2010, Alim Somani, president of Infusion Development Corporation (Infusion), returned from vacation to his 11th floor office in downtown Toronto. He had some tough decisions to make. Since joining Infusion as its sixth employee a decade earlier, Somani had seen Infusion grow to become a $50 million per annum international software services business with 350 employees. Somani had joined as a co-op student. Now president, Somani pondered how he could use organic growth and initiatives with partners to move the company toward becoming a $100 million per annum international business. In many ways, the entrepreneurial vision of Infusion's original founders lived on, but the company had found it necessary to install an administrative structure with a professional management layer to underpin delivery in both domestic and international markets. It had not been an easy ride. The company had encountered problems in India and had experienced periods of staff attrition and challenging deliveries to clients. Clients were now beginning to pull the company in new directions. The pace of technology change appeared to be relentless. Although the entrepreneurial spirit was still encouraged in the form of an incubator called Infusion Angels, Somani was faced with some critical decisions: How could the company remain nimble and innovative enough to continue to compete on the back of constantly emerging technology? How could the company ensure its staff would continue to have opportunities to engage in entrepreneurial behavior and pursue rapid personal growth?

INCEPTION

Greg Brill and DeBorah Johnson were the original co-founders of Infusion Development Corporation. Brill had always had a passion for computers and computer science. After graduating from University in the mid-1990s, he joined a company called MediaServ, based in New York and Toronto. MediaServ was staffed by University of Waterloo graduates and co-op students. After about a year, Brill felt he wanted to set up on his own. He met Johnson (who later became his wife), and she introduced him to Johnson and Hayward, a family business and one of the largest international mailing companies in the United States. Johnson and Hayward needed help with its information technology (IT) systems. So Brill and Johnson started Infusion with Johnson and Hayward as the company's first client.

Because of Brill's background in English literature and drama, he proved to be a very good trainer. The idea was that Infusion would go into an IT-challenged organization and infuse the staff with sufficient knowledge that they became empowered to solve their own problems. It was the late-1990s, in the heat of the dot-com boom in New York City. The IT departments of Wall Street banks were struggling to cope with the turnover of technical staff. The banks paid well, but many young technical staff left to try to become dot-com millionaires. Brill and Johnson's idea was for Infusion to fill the gap. Lehman Brothers was Infusion's first major Wall Street client.

LEHMAN BROTHERS

Infusion's first contract at Lehman Brothers (Lehman) was to run a technical employee training program in New York: their so-called "New Hire" program. Every new technical hire recruited by Lehman attended approximately eight weeks of training, put together and delivered by Infusion: four weeks of classroom training on different

Appendix: Cases

technologies followed by a four-week project course. The latter would entail Infusion getting to know a Lehman Brothers manager and identifying an actual system that the manager was looking to build. Over the course of four weeks, a new hire would take over that system or a component of that system as a real project. The new hires would move into their permanent roles after the eight-week period, which was supplemented by Lehman Brothers' custom training. In the early years, Infusion delivered three or four graduating (hiring) classes each year to Lehman Brothers.

On the back of this experience, Infusion started to deliver custom training to other investment banks in Lower Manhattan, which often included training on the latest software technologies. Infusion started to find that technical managers approached the trainers after class with a request for them to take a closer look at their production systems. Managers were often highly complimentary on the quality of Infusion's training. The training then evolved into consulting engagements. Brill was open to the consulting work and started to diagnose and then design a way to solve the client's specific problem. As a result, consulting revenue increased, particularly in architecting solutions for global securities trading.

Increased demand for technical consultants at Lehman Brothers meant Brill and Johnson had to start hiring. One of the key lessons Brill took from his experience at MediaServ was the concept of co-op hiring from the University of Waterloo in Canada. He found that he could not source the required level of technical talent at a competitive price in the United States. Meanwhile, sales became very concentrated: approximately 80 per cent of Infusion's revenue came from Lehman Brothers. Brill and Johnson immediately turned to the University of Waterloo and recruited Alim Somani and Sheldon Fernandez as co-op students.

OPENING THE TORONTO OPERATION

In 2000, Somani and Fernandez were the sixth and seventh employees at Infusion and delivered successful co-op placements. On their return to the University of Waterloo after their co-op term, and with one year of school left to go, Brill and Johnson offered Somani and Fernandez permanent jobs. They initially declined, pointing out they had a year of school to complete and wanted to remain in Canada. They also wanted to start their own software services business, and they had some leads for work at the College of Optometry. On hearing about their plans to start up on their own, Brill and Johnson showed immediate interest and offered the opportunity to have Infusion as their client. As a result, Somani and Fernandez started S-Squared Solutions, which they ran out of their basement, and Infusion was their main client. Brill continued to hire other co-op students from the University of Waterloo.

During late 2000, just as the dot-com bubble was bursting, Brill flew to Waterloo, Ontario, and made a proposal to Somani and Fernandez to incorporate S-Squared Solutions into Infusion and for Somani and Fernandez to run Infusion Canada. The idea was for Somani and Fernandez to drum up business in the Canadian market, targeting financial institutions, such as the Bank of Montreal, the Royal Bank of Canada and the Canadian Imperial Bank of Commerce (CIBC). With the addition of two other former Infusion co-op students, Infusion Canada was born. Somani and Fernandez were optimistic they would succeed in finding business in Canada delivering the same kind of services Infusion had been delivering on Wall Street.

While working at drumming up that business in Canada, Somani and Fernandez had a fall-back option. When Infusion had a shortfall of resources to fulfill the U.S. work, it would provide enough overflow work to keep the Toronto operation utilized. This arrangement required extensive travel for the Canadians, but, because of the exchange rate at that time, the model was profitable (see Exhibit 1 for the 10-year trend in the Canadian and U.S. dollar exchange rates). Even when including the cost of flights and expenses, using Canadian resources was cheaper than finding and using talent in New York.

Initially, prospects looked good. Following a chance meeting at a job fair in Waterloo with two new hires to Infusion (Bill Boldasti and Steve Ellis), Ralph Lauren showed keen interest in using Infusion Canada for a major contract on polo.com. The project was scheduled to start just as Somani and Fernandez finished school. At the last minute, however, the project was cancelled. Indeed, the model for Canada rolled out very differently from what had been envisioned. As Somani recalled, "We were young and naïve and we were knocking on the Canadian banks' doors and we were a new company . . . we learnt a few things and it was difficult."

In fact, Infusion Canada did not close a deal with a Canadian bank for two more years. In the meantime, the Canadian office, rather than being

Appendix: Cases

a sales arm, became a low- to mid-cost development center for the New York office. The exchange rate acted in the company's favor at a time when more and more IT work was being outsourced by U.S. firms, especially to India. Canadian talent, specifically talent from the University of Waterloo, became the engine of the company. By the end of 2001, approximately 80 per cent of the total company comprised Canadian hires. These young Canadians were sent to Manhattan to work in the banks in what became known in the company as a "Tour of New York." They were provided with apartments and full expenses. On returning to Canada, they could work out of the Toronto office and continue to service the U.S. clients.

THE PUBLISHING INITIATIVE

Meanwhile, in January 2000, Brill had secured a contract with New Riders, a book publisher, to write a book titled *Applying COM+*. Brill had realized during the dot-com era that one of the elements that built credibility was authorship of technology books, in particular books on the latest emerging software technologies. He had previously published in numerous technology and trade magazines, but had yet to publish a book. He also learned that Random House had wanted to start publishing technology books and was toying with the concept of e-books. Infusion created a joint venture with Random House called CodeNotes. The deal involved Infusion developing 11 titles in a book series (see Exhibit 2).

At the same time, Microsoft was in the process of releasing a technology platform called .NET. Infusion decided not to put all its eggs in one basket: writing some of the CodeNotes books on .NET and some on the competing JAVA platform. The book series became an important development for Infusion, giving the company enormous credibility with clients. As a result of this initiative, Infusion started to get to know the emerging Microsoft platforms. Until then Microsoft had not played a big role in enterprise solutions but its .NET platform represented Microsoft's big push into this area.

Soon the Microsoft field team picked up on Infusion's growth and expertise. Microsoft recognized that Infusion had gained expertise in a few very important areas. Infusion understood banking clients very well. Infusion also knew Microsoft's emerging technology, arguably as well as Microsoft did. Microsoft also acknowledged that Infusion understood the competitor (e.g., JAVA) technology. The published book series was a clear sign of Infusion's specialist knowledge base. Microsoft was facing criticism that its new effort to penetrate enterprise computing was a marketing hype and that it lacked understanding of industries such as corporate banking. Microsoft's proposal was that Infusion help Microsoft's efforts to teach its new enterprise technology platform, .NET, to the financial sector.

PARTNERING WITH MICROSOFT

As part of a partnering deal with Microsoft, Infusion staff were assigned to educate potential enterprise clients about Microsoft's technology. This arrangement started in New York and Northeastern United States, but eventually expanded throughout the United States and eventually to locations around the world. The purpose was for Infusion to explain to companies what .NET was, how it compared with JAVA, where to use it, where not to use it and how to make it relevant to the industry. This deal gave Infusion huge exposure, especially to other banks. Based on Infusion's success in training bank clients, Microsoft asked Infusion to train in other sectors, such as the public sector. Infusion thus gained exposure to state and local governments. After 9/11, the economy slowed down and many banks curbed their IT spending; however, the public sector was a counter-cyclical market. Infusion was thus able to diversify out of financial services into the public sector, which strengthened its relationship with Microsoft.

Infusion made it a mission to learn any new significant Microsoft product that was announced. Importantly, Infusion was able to help sales teams sell the new technology and articulate its application and benefits to clients. Infusion employees would spend time at Microsoft's Redmond campus prior to going into the field, which enabled Infusion to position itself as adding value.

SOMANI TAKES OVER AT THE HELM

In 2002, Brill and Johnson decided they needed someone to manage the day-to-day running of the company. The company had 40 employees, and the number and size of projects was growing. Sales had reached $3 million a year. Brill felt his passion lay in new initiatives and wanted to stay at Infusion but concentrate on these entrepreneurial ventures. After careful consideration of alternatives, Brill and Johnson approached

Somani, 22 years of age at the time. Somani had been running Infusion Canada for approximately a year, while also executing projects in the United States. Brill and Johnson asked Somani to become Infusion's chief operating officer (COO). Somani agreed to take on the role on the condition that Brill and Johnson spend time mentoring him, which they both readily agreed to. Gradually, through a process of mentorship, full responsibility for execution and sales moved to Somani. He was confident that the two central thrusts of the company's strategy (the Canadian development model and partnering with Microsoft) were strong pillars for success.

IN AND OUT OF INDIA

Lehman Brothers continued to represent a large slice of Infusion revenues when Somani took the COO role. However, it was shortly to drop a bombshell that Infusion was not prepared for. Lehman Brothers announced its intention to offshore a third of its IT work to India as soon as possible. The trend for offshoring and offshore outsourcing had been increasing among the investment banks since Y2K conversion projects at the end of the century. Lehman Brothers sent a clear message to its permanent in-house IT staff: their jobs would be protected as much as possible by eliminating external consultants. Somani, new in his position, soon realized that this decision did not bode well for Infusion. Somani and Brill quickly arranged meetings with Infusion's champions within Lehman Brothers to ask whether the company could continue to work with Infusion if Infusion also had a presence in India. The response was qualified. Lehman Brothers was set to work with Wipro and Tata Consulting Services (TCS) in India for the most strategic IT work. But was Lehman Brothers still prepared to give a small amount of project work to Infusion, as long as it was co-located in Bangalore?

Infusion's selling point was that it already had an embedded relationship with Lehman Brothers, and it was delivering. The Wipro and TCS relationships would take some time to set up and embed. Infusion took advantage of the situation and, within six months of setting up a development site in India, Infusion had secured a fairly large deal with Lehman Brothers. Infusion recruited locally to resource this work. However, the company soon realized the whole Infusion operation in India faced failure. Even in these early days, Indian software engineers had high rates of turnover. Infusion found it difficult to manage quality and to manage across time zones, and it encountered problems in working with a very different culture. Infusion had not previously faced these problems. Most project work had been based on high-quality deliverables in the same time zone and in very similar cultures. In addition to these issues, many of the client systems were not well documented. Formal training on client systems and development projects for the Indian recruits was therefore hampered.

Infusion eventually decided to close shop in India and move the development capability back to Canada. According to Infusion's calculations, by moving back to Canada, the company would break even on the project. Infusion realized that, for its size, it had no recruiting competitive advantage to attract and retain great talent in India. As Infusion made the decision to shut down the India operation, Lehman Brothers was already a year into its work with Wipro and TCS, which ended up acting in Infusion's favor. Lehman began to experience downsides to working with Indian providers for complex software development where requirements were ambiguous and emerging. Database migrations worked, infrastructure projects worked, but the more complex development projects suffered. On reviewing the situation of offshore outsourcing, Lehman Brothers came to the conclusion that the only place it had experienced success with outsourcing complex projects was with Infusion, delivering out of Canada.

Lehman's technology executives visited Infusion in Toronto to learn more about why Infusion had pulled out of India and how it was able to deliver successfully from Toronto. The result was Infusion landing a new deal with Lehman Brothers to work in collaboration with Wipro and TCS. Lehman invested hundreds of thousands of dollars running dedicated lines to Toronto and setting up the Infusion office with Lehman hardware. Infusion Canada was designated as a Lehman branch office. The Canadian dollar was still relatively weak, but Infusion was not able to charge Indian rates. The justification for this new set-up was that Infusion's cost of delivery for critical projects worked out to be less than Lehman's cost of delivery from India. Twenty-five Infusion consultants were allocated to the Lehman account, working out of the Toronto office.

EXPANSION INTO LONDON

On the financial services side of the business, Infusion's relationships with Lehman Brothers and other banks continued to be strong. Because these banks were global organizations, Infusion had mused for some

Appendix: Cases

time about securing business from these clients on a more global basis, particularly in London, England. Some of the banks had also discussed this opportunity with Infusion.

Because of the company's many focuses — on India, Microsoft and other initiatives, such as mapping — Infusion found that it did not have the resources or bandwidth to set up an operation in London. In addition, the IT sector in the United Kingdom was mature and competitive. Microsoft already had an established network of partners in the United Kingdom. Given Infusion's experience with India, Somani was cautious.

Finally, in 2007, Infusion's operations manager decided the matter. Shelina Hirji, who had originally joined Infusion as a part-time receptionist, gave notice that she wanted to move to London to be with her fiancé. Somani immediately made the connection and asked whether she would be willing to help set up an office in London. Two more home-grown Infusion employees, Bryan Shiffman and Syd Millett, also said that they wouldn't mind moving to London. Both Shiffman and Millett had been heavily entrenched in the financial services business at Infusion in New York. In 2007, along with a fourth employee from Toronto, Joseph Lai, the London office opened up just over the bridge from Canary Wharf.

After its first year, Infusion London had 10 people, and by the end of year two, 45 employees. A little more than three years later, in late 2010, Infusion London had grown to 78 employees. Shiffman and Millett were the co-managing directors in the first year. Millett moved back to Toronto at the end of that year, and Shiffman stayed on as managing director. Hirji was appointed director of operations. Over the three years, Shiffman reduced Infusion London's dependency on investment banking from 100 per cent of sales in the first year, to 90 per cent in the second year. The expectation was that services to investment banking would represent approximately 65 per cent of sales at the end of the third year. The remaining sales came from retail banking. On the basis of this success, Somani promoted Lai to global sales director for Financial Services, taking on responsibility for New York in addition to London. Lai expressed interest in opening an Asian office.

The global financial crisis of 2008 caused major concerns within Infusion. The pain was felt particularly heavily in the London operation. Lehman Brothers — which represented the largest single account over the years — ended up in bankruptcy, and other big accounts dramatically slowed their spending on Infusion. However, Infusion had managed to diversify its sales across a number of London banks that were located along the Wharf. Outside of the Wharf, Infusion also managed to sell projects into what it called its tier-two banks, in contrast to its top clients in London, referred to as its "stable of seven." Spreading the sales and delivery proved to be vital: as some accounts closed or slowed down, others actually ramped up.

Infusion London also managed to grow its relationship in the United Kingdom with Microsoft. Kevin Lasitz, who had been Infusion's North American lead for everything related to both Microsoft and the public sector, was recruited from New York. Lasitz had been with the company since 2003 and had been central to growing the relationship with Microsoft in North America. Infusion London gained access to Lloyds, BNP-Paribas and Deutsche Bank all through Microsoft work. The London operation also became involved in Microsoft's Industry Solutions University (ISU), where Infusion held keynote speeches at major marketing events sponsored by Microsoft in the United Kingdom.

By late 2010, Infusion London had between 25 and 35 employees permanently located in the Infusion office. The rest went into the office at various frequencies: ranging from once a week to once a month. Being embedded in the client organization was necessary in professional services organizations. One of the issues recognized by the local management team was how to keep the utilized employees engaged with Infusion, by feeling a part of Infusion and its developing global activities. Infusion London was the company's most important foreign operation: much of the work in London was helping Infusion elsewhere. The strengthening relationship with Microsoft, especially within the globalized public sector space was seen as promising. Lasitz often was called on by Microsoft to examine opportunities in locations such as Haiti, Pakistan, Australia, China, the Middle East and within Europe. Infusion London was thus able to gain knowledge of those locations and evaluate new opportunities signaled by Microsoft. Knowledge gained from these links was continuously shared with Somani.

EXPANSION INTO DUBAI

Microsoft's Gulf Region faced a deficiency in its local partner community. The key struggle was in finding a partner that could provide both superior technical skills and business know-how. In early 2008,

Appendix: Cases

Brill and Somani met with Vimal Sethi, who ran Microsoft's development platform in Dubai. Somani was keen to strengthen the relationship with Microsoft where possible. As he recalled, "The mortgage market was in trouble and things didn't seem to be going so well on the financial services side."

The purpose of the Dubai meeting was to discuss Microsoft operations in the Middle East. After hearing about the lack of strong Microsoft partners in Dubai, Brill and Somani immediately saw an opportunity for Infusion.

Sethi stressed the importance of having employees on the ground. Heeding this advice, in the second quarter of 2008, Infusion began developing its business in the region. Somani considered the need to have an experienced Infusion consultant to spearhead its activities. As a result, Cortez Lapalme, who had also joined Infusion in 2001 from the University of Waterloo, was relocated to Dubai. Leveraging Microsoft's business contacts, Infusion was introduced to Jumeirah Group, a Dubai hotel management company that needed assistance with its digital strategy and online revenue growth. Infusion was successful in winning the bid for this project. Infusion hoped this project would open doors for more business in the region.

Somani felt he needed to appoint someone to lead operations locally. Past experience showed that the leader needed to have a good understanding of how to do business in the region. Sethi was appointed to set up and lead operations in Dubai. In January 2009, Sethi joined Infusion, bringing with him nine years of valuable Microsoft experience and a firm understanding of the Middle East. Within one year, Sethi had established an office in Dubai that provided clients with premium services in a fully integrated solution package. He built brand awareness locally and increased headcount from six to 30 employees comprising more than 20 different nationalities. New contracts were signed with some of the biggest brands in the region: Jumeirah, Etihad Airways, Aramco and Mubadala.

Infusion's initial success in Dubai was underpinned by two factors: the company's talented and skilled employees and its growing partnership with Microsoft within the region. Sethi was adamant about the need to hire top talent and not accepting mediocrity. The superior level of Infusion's employees was visible in its employment of numerous Microsoft MVPs (Most Valuable Professionals) and top-rated Microsoft Subject

Matter Experts. Infusion's relationship with Microsoft continued to be critical to its business: approximately 99 per cent of its work in the region was done on the Microsoft platform. The success of the partnership was seen through partnership initiatives such as Infusion's involvement in Microsoft's Technology Adoption Programs (TAP) and partnership awards won by Infusion, such as the Microsoft Gold Partner award and the Microsoft Worldwide Public Sector award. Although young, the Dubai office had become recognized as early adopters, highly technical, very creative and innovative.

Most of Infusion's competitors in the region had only local sales offices with development and innovation located elsewhere. Infusion's Dubai office offered all of these services in one location, with the ability to draw on resources from the company's network. Clients wanted to work with Infusion because of its premium services and ability to design creative and innovative solutions. However, these same clients also began to express a desire for less costly resources in the implementation phase.

In a very short period, the Dubai office had grown very fast. Although its growth was in some ways organic in the beginning, the company began 2010 with plans for a more structured approach. Plans for the Dubai office included adding a new local management structure, diversifying its business into new areas and looking at ways to effectively manage global versus local communication flows and processes. As the office continued to grow, it faced the challenge of balancing the pull to add more structure with the need to stay agile. As Sethi asked in late 2010, "How do we keep innovation as part of our business model in a very structured way?"[1]

The answer may have already been started in Infusion's North American operations, where the company had been developing an idea incubator called Infusion Angels, while also installing a more structured management layer for service delivery.

INFUSION ANGELS

Infusion had always encouraged the entrepreneurial spirit in its employees. In 2004, Infusion signed a single-client strategic deal with Microsoft to provide support for Microsoft's mapping business. One of the support

---

1 *Interview with Vimal Sethi, Dubai, September 2010.*

Appendix: Cases

engineers in the mapping group was Tyler Davey. After a number of months supporting Microsoft, Davey approached Somani with an idea to develop the mapping into a much broader support, development and hosting business. Somani agreed and Infusion's mapping practice was born, with Davey at the helm. Davey had enough success with the mapping business that he was promoted to general manager of Global Channel Sales, which was part of Infusion's new strategy to diversify and become less dependent on financial services. Vertical diversification included non-core business sales, such as travel and hospitality, training and writing, infrastructure mapping and managed services.

In 2007, Infusion set up a sister company, Infusion Angels, in Waterloo, Ontario, which had two main goals. The first was to allow Infusion to re-invest its profit in companies and ideas that the management felt passionate about. The second goal was to signal to employees that to be entrepreneurial was a desirable quality to have in the company. As Somani recalled:

> The company was always very entrepreneurial. And we hired a lot of people who wanted to start their own businesses. People like us who wanted to be entrepreneurs. And so people would come at various times wanting to run their own businesses.[2]

Sheldon Fernandez became chief technology officer (CTO) of Infusion Angels. Fernandez had always been involved on the technical side of the business, having run the Technology and Architecture Group in Toronto in the early years. The basic mandate of this group was to ensure that the firm was abreast of the newest technologies. Fernandez ran technology boot camps for new hires and included lessons on soft skills, such as writing professional emails and the proper conduct at client locations.

At the outset, Infusion Angels ran as a "Dragon's Den" format. Every Friday, Fernandez would come into the office to hear professionals and students pitch their ideas and ask for funding. It was Fernandez's responsibility to vet the ideas from both a technical and commercial standpoint. Just as in TV's *Dragon's Den*, the pitches exhibited a wide variety of ideas and a great deal of enthusiasm, especially among the undergraduates who often made up for a lack of business acumen with

---

2 *Interview with Alim Somani, Toronto, August 2010.*

Appendix: Cases

their sheer energy. In 2006, news of how Infusion was helping budding entrepreneurs was covered in the *Globe and Mail*, Canada's leading broadsheet newspaper (see Exhibit 3).

It had never been Infusion's ambition to abandon services and become a product company, but Somani and Fernandez viewed the Angels initiative as a way of becoming involved in emerging technologies and ideas that could be profitable in the long run. Infusion Angels allowed the company to gain an interest in two new business areas: video gaming and entertainment.

Infusion Angels invested in a video gaming company called Frozen North. By late 2010, Frozen North was due to launch its first published title on the Nintendo Wii platform.

In 2009, Infusion invested in a company called Audition Booth, which provided a platform for reality TV and commercial auditions. This investment was seen as a major departure for the company because Audition Booth was in the media and entertainment space. Fernandez became the lead for the Audition Booth project, which was a large-scale effort with risks attached. The project intended to deliver a standard back-end system for Hollywood auditioning. Fernandez found himself spending much of his time in Hollywood, working with high-profile producers. Infusion wanted to make a technical imprint in an industry that was very different from its existing markets, one that the company was not used to working with. As Fernandez commented:

> It's quite exciting because you may find yourself in some very creative conversations with individuals who don't know what technology can do for them, but once they find out they're extremely motivated and excited to get you involved.[3]

Despite this progress, the Angels initiative created new challenges and tensions in the company. For example, one issue related to raising the attention of other executives when an interesting idea arose in Waterloo. Services projects in New York and London were bringing in the money. Thus, many of the other senior managers were less interested in what they saw as speculative product initiatives, expressing concerns that product initiatives would cannibalize services revenue if existing

---

3 *Interview with Sheldon Fernandez, Toronto, September 2010.*

Infusion staff were used in uncertain projects in new areas such as gaming and entertainment. Another discussion among the management team was how to decide where to put the organization's best resources. As Infusion announced internally it was doing the development for Audition Booth, many of the company's technical employees showed an interest in being assigned to the project. Some employees were disappointed not to be brought on board. Most of the high-performing resources were already being utilized on client projects and were needed where they were. Some who worked on the product initiatives eventually showed more interest in working in London or Dubai.

INSTALLING THE MANAGEMENT LAYER: HRM AND GLOBAL DELIVERY

Guided by Brill's early philosophy for Infusion, the company's policy was for the core management team to hire people directly. They looked for individuals with the right attitude and aptitude, and then helped them build the experience needed to deliver quality services. Clients would refer to Infusion consultants as the "Infusion guys." Unlike some of their competitors' résumés, Infusion consultants did not have 20 years of Wall Street experience; they were more likely to have two years. But they were seen as talents that could be molded into the right form.

By 2005, Infusion had used this approach to recruit approximately 60 people. The new hires had an average age of 25 years, which was rising. Worryingly for Somani, turnover of staff was also increasing. Somani then recruited Andrea Richardson as the company's first senior human resources (HR) manager. Richardson had come from a larger corporate environment and, on her first day, was a little shocked to find no formal HR systems in place. The company had a template for a job offer letter and some employee guidelines that formed part of the offer letter. She also found some employee files and a basic payroll system. But not a lot of thought had been put into HR. For many at Infusion, HR and recruiting had been considered to be the same thing.

In her first year at Infusion, Richardson put into place formal annual reviews and basic HR programs, such as structured social events. But the need was still very much on recruiting: Infusion was growing rapidly. Fortunately, staff turnover slowed to below the industry average. Richardson implemented a professional development program as a way to guide employee growth and success within the company. At the core of this program was a career path model: an initial attempt to give employees an overview of all the career paths available in the company. Up until this time, technical staff tended to leave after two or so years of service. As Richardson recalled:

> In their minds there was just nowhere else to go. You were a software consultant that moved into a senior consultant role that moved into a technical account manager role. And then from there, there were director roles. There was no career path . . .. At some point we realized that that model was just not a scalable model.[4]

The career path model was implemented in January of 2008 (see Exhibit 4). Richardson identified individual competencies: the skills needed to be successful in the company. After various management meetings, 12 individual competencies were drawn up, which proved to be unworkable and were reduced to five competencies. The focus of this program was not on support and administrative staff but on those who filled billable roles (solution delivery, applied technology, project management, leadership and business development). Infusion took each of the billable roles and identified the level of competency expected; that is, what it meant to be at each level of each competency.

Richardson also set up career coaches. Individuals would be assigned career coaches who were at least two levels ahead of them in the organization. Coaches, who tended to be those employees who had been with the company for a while, were asked to meet with their mentees and to help them fill out their professional development plan (called ProD), a goal-setting plan to be completed twice a year. Billable staff were asked to meet with their career coaches once a month. In reality, the meetings took place approximately once each quarter. Coaches were asked to send follow-up emails to resource managers to maintain a repository of billable staff skills and experience.

The new HR systems provided structure to new employees and created HR information that could be used when staffing new projects. One problem was that the system was adopted by only approximately 70 per cent of the billable staff. Furthermore, the system failed to link goals to

---

4 *Interview with Andrea Richardson, Toronto, September 2010.*

Appendix: Cases

compensation. The annual reviews, self-assessment and ProD goals would be packaged up and kept, but they were not tied to any bonus or pay increase. The system was adopted, however, by Infusion in Dubai.

The company's growth had continued (see Exhibit 5). To help deal with the ongoing HR changes, Infusion turned to a local Toronto-based management consulting firm for advice in 2010. The outcome was to create performance metrics for the entire company. The management consultant helped to facilitate a number of changes. First, the management team decided they needed to be measured on five new metrics: financial goals, employee engagement goals, Microsoft-related goals, strategic goals and innovation. These metrics were trickled down through the company, which was seen as a success. In terms of employee engagement, for example, the whole executive team signed off on goals for 2011 employee engagement as one of the factors they would be evaluated on at the end of the year. As a result, vice presidents were required not only to keep staff motivated but also to do a certain amount of employee engagement. A new employee survey was due to start in November 2010 to gauge the extent to which supervisors had engaged with their employees.

In 2009, Infusion embarked on a project to implement an integrated, online tool for HR functions, called OSS. Up to that point, Infusion did not have one integrated system for HR processes. Resource planning had been done using desktop tools, whereas payroll was done using ADP, accounting was done using Great Plains (part of a Microsoft Dynamics system), time tracking for billable staff was done using Quick Arrow and a separate CRM system was not used by all sales and marketing staff. The idea was for OSS to be an all-in-one solution that would support these various functions. Infusion decided to build the system in-house and set up an internal team to work on it.

By mid-2010, the system was only partially up and running. Project managers and resource managers were using it; however, further development was needed before it could replace all the systems used in HR functions. The in-house development team had consisted of technical consultants who also were counted as billable roles. As client requests increased, Infusion became less able and willing to sacrifice consulting revenue for internal development work.

Another pressure on Richardson was her involvement in global recruiting. When Infusion entered Dubai for example, the company had no

Appendix: Cases

experience of recruiting in the Middle East. Because there was no one responsible for HR at the start, Richardson ended up hiring people for the Dubai operation from her office in Toronto. As she recalled, "It's really been a race to recruit people there and get people there."[5]

In 2006, Infusion hired Carl Thomson as a senior project manager. At that time, a typical client project was worth approximately $20,000. But the company had recently started to bid for projects in the $100,000 to $300,000 range, and was winning contracts. However, Infusion experienced problems with these larger and more complex projects. Some of them were over budget, some were delivered late. Client satisfaction was dropping.

Thompson's mandate was to bring structure and process to the projects. For his first six months Thompson ran three to four key projects, ensuring they were structured, had clear communications and that their budgets were managed. The results were impressive, client satisfaction was restored and Thompson was given six employees to manage in the company's new project management office (PMO) in Toronto. He ensured his team understood the project execution process in order to increase the capacity for executing larger projects. In 2007, Infusion started executing projects in the $500,000 range and eventually won its first million-dollar project.

By 2010, Thomson was vice president of Global Delivery, running a 60-person professional services team globally. Those services included a global PMO, a support group, a user experience and design team, a technical architecture group, and the training and writing team. Infusion now offered a choice of industry-standard Project Management Institute[6] (PMI) processes. For the software development life-cycle, Infusion offered two methods: Agile Scrum and the traditional waterfall method. Infusion's policy was to discuss the choice of method with clients before commencing the project. If the Agile approach was chosen, the client needed to be prepared to commit a significant amount of resources to ensure the project ran successfully.

Somani had made a significant investment in Thompson's organization in 2009 and 2010. Thompson's challenge was to grow the people under

---

5 *Interview with Andrea Richardson, Toronto, September 2010.*
6 *Project Management Institute website, available at http://www.pmi.org/, accessed February 7, 2011.*

Appendix: Cases

him to ensure that the delivery arm was scalable, to enable Infusion to continue to grow. One problem had been staff attrition in the technical architecture group. Thompson had to recruit a new manager into that group and develop competencies in that area. Infusion offices in London and Dubai were also asking to have members of the technical architecture group stationed in those offices. Technical architects were seen as key for delivering large, complex projects. One of the biggest contracts in 2010 was for a U.S. travel company, requiring 40,000 person hours of effort. The overall solution for this project was drawn up by one of the architects. The result was a success: the client was happy, and Infusion had a strong possibility of gaining repeat business. Thompson recognized the need to grow the technical architecture capability globally, especially in Dubai where an increasing number of complex projects were being developed.

ENTERING POLAND

As a result of the increase in both project size and complexity, Infusion faced different competitors. Clients were also being pitched to by the likes of Accenture, TCS and InfoSys. Many of these larger players were able to offer lower-cost solutions, on the basis of their vast offshore resource pools. Infusion felt renewed pressure to source and develop talented "Infusion guys" at competitive rates. Clients were increasingly telling Infusion they were looking for the high-quality consultants that Infusion offered, in particular those who could deliver at a higher rate of productivity than the competition. The decision was made in 2010 to set up a new low-cost center in Krakow, Poland. The strategic thinking behind this decision was to seek to emulate the success that the company had experienced in Canada nearly a decade earlier: to build a presence in a location that had an abundant source of talent but where currency rates enabled competitive bids. The idea was that this strategy would create capacity and bring in projects requiring a range of priced components to be competitive.

The office was due to start in the first quarter of 2011, and planning was already underway. The Polish resources would be involved in global projects and initially would focus on three key existing global accounts. Thompson wanted to keep the initial operation small, at three to four employees per account. The plan was to first move these employees to Infusion in Toronto for a three-month induction period, where they would execute client projects. During this time, the infrastructure and administration for the office would be set up in Poland. The employees would then be moved back to Poland to a fully functional office from which they would execute projects remotely.

Thompson expected to be spending significant time in Poland and planned to bring senior staff members with him to help ensure the new site was up and running swiftly. The first recruits that Infusion was looking to bring into the new Poland operation were to be partners in the company. Somani and Thompson wanted to avoid the type of attrition problem encountered in India. As Thompson said:

> I think the big thing for us is to make sure it's manageable and small and it's not trying to grow this thing into hundreds of people in the very first day . . . . So we don't get into the India problem that we had the first time.[7]

CHALLENGES AND CHOICES GOING FORWARD

In the late summer of 2010, as Infusion's president, Somani, looked out over the Toronto skyline from his office, he knew he had some tough decisions to make. The company had managed to navigate through some stormy waters: overcoming the impact of the global financial crisis, reducing its exposure to Lehman Brothers, turning its misfortunes in India into a success story, becoming a successful Microsoft partner in Dubai and the competitive U.K. market, and making progress with risky investments in the media and entertainment space. Entrepreneurship was in the company's DNA. But professional management practice had been needed for the company to deliver increasingly large and complex projects. How could the company remain nimble and innovative enough to continue to compete on the back of constantly emerging technology? How could the company ensure its staff would continue to have opportunities to engage in entrepreneurship and pursue rapid personal growth?

---

7 *Interview with Carl Thompson, Toronto, September 2010.*

Appendix: Cases

Exhibit 1

10-YEAR CANADIAN AND U.S. DOLLAR EXCHANGE RATE

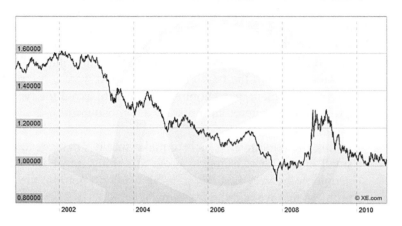

Source: XE.COM.INC, www.xe.com,

Exhibit 2

TITLES IN THE RANDOM HOUSE CODENOTES SERIES

CodeNotes for XML
CodeNotes for .NET
CodeNotes for Java
CodeNotes for VB.NET
CodeNotes for Web-Based UI
CodeNotes for J2EE
CodeNotes for Oracle 9i
CodeNotes for ASP.NET
CodeNotes for C#
CodeNotes for Web Services in Java and .NET
CodeNotes for J#

Source: Random House

Exhibit 3

INFUSION ANGELS COVERAGE IN THE GLOBE AND MAIL

A new generation discovers the benefits of 'giving back'

Young employees who have the opportunity to volunteer while working find it valuable on many levels, **VIRGINIA GALT** writes

Alim Somani and Sheldon Fernandez have barely begun their careers, but they already feel compelled to give back to their alma mater.

Both 28 years old and with just five years in the business world, the young electrical engineers believe they have something to offer the future generation of entrepreneurs — drawing on the lessons they have learned since starting up their Canadian operations of New York-based software firm Infusion Development Corp. fresh out of university.

"We can give them some of the grey hairs from our university days," says Mr. Somani who, with Mr. Fernandez, has created an organization called Infusion Angels to provide advice and seed money to support business ventures developed by current students at the University of Waterloo in Waterloo, Ont.

In many respects, they are representative of their generation: The opportunity to volunteer during working hours, or to make a charitable contribution on behalf of an employee, is one of the major benefits able to be offered by young Canadians, say human resource consultants.

Indeed, a survey this week by Hewitt Associates found that more employers plan to provide time off for charitable work in a bid to attract and engage these employees.

Like many of their cohorts, Mr. Somani and Mr. Fernandez grew up volunteering. Statistics Canada recently reported that the percentage of Canadians with the volunteer generally decreases with age: 55 per cent of 15-to 24-year-olds volunteer — compared with 32 per cent of those 65 and older — but it is by reversing this altruism into the workplace.

"It's wonderful for me," says Mr. Fernandez, who helps the students determine whether their ideas can be taken to market.

"It is fun to hear what they are thinking. It is fun to play with new ideas and consider new angles on things," says Mr. Fernandez, who also volunteers with the Big Brothers organization.

Mr. Somani says he and Mr. Fernandez both benefited from the mentorship of professors and from their current chief executive officer, Gregory Brill, who first hired them as co-op students for his New York operations.

"Now, we are spending a lot of time lecturing on entrepreneurship, advising students and meeting them for lunch and chatting about their ideas partly because that's the kind of support we got. You want to give back," he says.

According to a recent report by Statistics Canada, 92 per cent of Canadians who volunteer say they do so to make a contribution to the community. Almost half view volunteering as a way to explore their strengths, and 47 per cent see it as a way to network and meet new people. Just 22 per cent of Canadians covered in the surveys say they volunteer to advance their career opportunities.

Nonetheless, volunteering is something recruiters look for, say human resource specialists. "Certainly, it broadens their skill set and adds to the portfolio that they bring to the organization," says Cathy Webster, vice-president of human resources at Hydro One. Mr. Fernandez and Mr. Somani both have high-level responsibilities with Infusion Development, which provides software and consulting services to the investment banking industry as well as to state and local governments in New York. The firm is currently working on a system that will help the New York City school board implement its No Child Left Behind program.

Aim Somani, left, and Sheldon Fernandez, shown at their Toronto office, help University of Waterloo students determine whether their ideas can be taken to market. The electrical engineers, both 28, have created an organization called Infusion Angels to help their alma mater's next generation of entrepreneurs.

Employer support for volunteering by employees is becoming more common.

I gave at the office . . .

57% of employed volunteers received some form of non-monetary support from their employer for their good works.
33% were allowed to reduce or change their work schedules in order to volunteer.
32% were allowed to use work facilities or equipment.
23% received recognition or a letter of thanks from their employer for their good works.
21% received paid time off to volunteer.

And this is why . . .

92% of volunteers want to make a contribution to the community.
77% want to use their skills and experience.
60% are personally affected by the cause they are supporting.
49% want to explore their own strengths.
47% want to network.
22% want to fulfil their religious reasons.
22% hope to improve their job opportunities.
7% say they were forced to "volunteer" by their employers, schools or some other authority.
Source: Statistics Canada

prospective employees want to know, coming in, whether the company will support their volunteer efforts.

"People are time-starved, as you know, so we give people time," says Ms. Webster, who recently spent a day reading to kids, talking to seniors, Ms. Webster says.

"They were at daycare centres, community centres, seniors' homes, Boys' and Girls' Clubs, . . . doing clean-up projects, gardening, reading to kids, talking to seniors, Ms. Webster says.

Mr. Somani and Mr. Fernandez both have high-level responsibilities

However, they have also made their work with the University of Waterloo students a priority and are committed to providing start-up funds of between $50,000 and $100,000 for viable business projects. "The money is part of it," Mr. Somani says. "But so much more is the mentoring and volunteering."

Source: Virginia Galt, "A New Generation Discovers the Benefits of 'Giving Back.'" *Globe and Mail*, June 17, 2006, reprinted with permission.

Appendix: Cases

Exhibit 4

INFUSION'S CAREER PATH MODEL

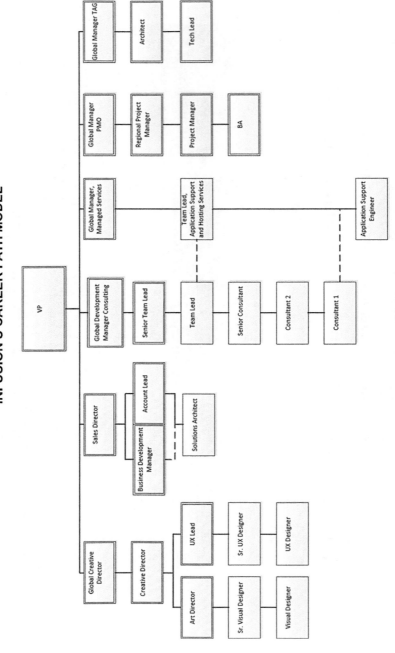

Exhibit 5

ORGANIZATION GROWTH 2006–2010

	Number of Employees at Year End	Sales (in US$)
2006	81	$15,084,292
2007	176	$26,347,583
2008	188	$33,561,333
2009	233	$36,885,975
2010	333	$55,160,900

Source: Internal company document

IVEY | Publishing

9B12M076

INFUSION'S GREENFIELD SUBSIDIARY IN POLAND

Christopher Williams, Wendelien van Eerde, and Danielle Thé wrote this case to provide material for class discussion. The authors do not intend to illustrate either effective or ineffective handling of a managerial situation. The authors may have disguised certain names and other identifying information to protect confidentiality.

This publication may not be transmitted, photocopied, digitized, or otherwise reproduced in any form or by any means without the permission of the copyright holder. Reproduction of this material is not covered under authorization by any reproduction rights organization. To order copies or request permission to reproduce materials, contact Ivey Publishing, Ivey Business School, Western University, London, Ontario, Canada, N6G 0N1; (t) 519.661.3208; (e) cases@ivey.ca; www.iveycases.com.

Copyright © 2012, Richard Ivey School of Business Foundation   Version: 2017-05-25

In April 2012, Alim Somani, president of Infusion Development Corporation (Infusion), was reviewing the progress of a new subsidiary (Infusion Poland) that the company had set up 15 months earlier in Krakow, Poland. The purpose of the subsidiary was to work in conjunction with other Infusion offices around the world to provide innovative software development services to global clients. The company saw the investment as a big success. The subsidiary had grown in size from eight to 40 staff in 2011, and there were plans to double that number of employees by the end of 2012. The issues facing Somani were threefold. Firstly, how could he work with the country manager, Ryan Hunter, to continue to grow the subsidiary moving forward? Attracting the right talent was vital to Infusion's culture and business model. Initial growth in Poland was based partly on local referrals in the community of .NET[1] professionals in Krakow. It was also based on being a new start-up with an entrepreneurial culture. Somani and Hunter were

---

1 *NET (pronounced "dot net") is a software development framework from Microsoft that supports different programming languages in a common software environment.*

Appendix: Cases

concerned that there were limits to these factors. Secondly, what role should Infusion Poland have in the wider company in the future? Should it become a global centre of excellence and a pivotal hub for the company's innovative capability? If so, how could this be achieved? Thirdly, what kind of succession planning should be put in place for the country manager in Poland? If, as was expected, Hunter would move on to another post in Infusion, should the company seek a local country manager instead of transferring one from headquarters?

COMPANY BACKGROUND

Infusion Development Corporation was founded by Greg Brill and DeBorah Johnson in the late 1990s. The company started out by providing information technology (IT) services to Johnson & Hayward, a large family-owned mail order company in the United States. Infusion expanded through Brill's drive and enthusiasm for emerging IT. Brill delivered training to investment bank clients on Wall Street using a small number of staff, including co-op students from the University of Waterloo in Canada. Brill also published a series of technical books on various programming languages, including the emerging .NET platform offered by Microsoft.

A breakthrough came when Lehman Brothers became one of Infusion's first major clients for customized training for its new technical hires. Infusion was able to nurture a relationship with Lehman Brothers and sell development projects in addition to the new hire training. In 2000, Somani and Sheldon Fernandez were recruited by Brill to set up a development office in Toronto. At that time the exchange rate favoured Canadian employees. Infusion began expanding by selling projects to other investment banks and moving into other sectors. Infusion managed to build a relationship with Microsoft through its training capabilities. The company eventually became a specialist in Microsoft's enterprise platforms. Through its relationship with Microsoft, Infusion diversified out of financial services and into the public sector.

Somani became chief operating officer (COO) in 2002, and presided over a rapid expansion of the company in the following eight years. By 2010, the company was making $50 million[2] in revenue and had 350 employees in various locations around the world. The main locations

_____

2 *All dollar amounts in Canadian dollars unless otherwise noted.*

197

were Toronto, London and Dubai. The company had entered India in 2003, but backed out within a year due to problems with staff turnover and quality. The company also found it necessary to implement a professional management layer: a set of management structures and processes for handling increasingly large and complex client projects.

By 2010, Infusion started to look for a new offshore location due to various motives. The Canadian dollar had become much stronger. Clients were increasingly stressing the need to reduce overall blended rates, but they were also seeking high-quality and talented consultants, such as those offered by Infusion. In addition to these factors, the company was under pressure to maintain or improve both its high level of productivity and the transparency through which clients could assess the progress of projects.

BACKGROUND TO POLAND

Geographically centred between European Union member states and non-member states, Poland represented a type of gateway between the former Eastern Bloc and the West. Throughout the mid-to-late 20th century, Poland operated under a communist regime.[3] When communist powers fell in the late 1980s, a democratic Poland began to emerge.[4] In 1989, the adoption of a "shock therapy" program[5] enabled Poland to successfully transition from a state-owned economy to a capitalist market economy.[6] Due to its progress by 2012, Poland represented a great economic success story for transitioning economies.[7]

AN EMERGING ECONOMIC POWER IN EUROPE

On May 1, 2004, Poland became an official member of the European Union (EU). Poland had been steadily increasing its influence in European

---

3 Anna Zorska, "Foreign Direct Investment and Transformation: Evolution and Impacts in the Polish Economy," *Eastern European Economics*, 43 (4), 2005, p. 56.
4 Ibid.
5 Also known as the Balcerowicz Plan in the Polish context, a shock therapy program referred to immediate trade liberalization within a country. This included large-scale privatization and commercialization of previously public-owned assets.
6 Anna Zorska, "Foreign Direct Investment and Transformation: Evolution and Impacts in the Polish Economy," *Eastern European Economics*, 43 (4), 2005, p. 56.
7 "Poland," *Central Intelligence Agency: The World Factbook*, last modified May 3, 2012, www.cia.gov/library/publications/the-world-factbook/geos/pl.html, accessed May 28, 2012.

Appendix: Cases

political affairs as it was both one of the fastest-growing economies in the EU and the sixth most-populous member state. The country had also gained economic influence in the European community. Between 2008 and 2010, Poland averaged 3.5 per cent growth during the European recessionary crisis.[8] This made Poland the only European nation to avoid the recession.[9] A combination of Poland's low private debt, large foreign direct investment (FDI) inflows and flexible currency (Poland had not adopted the euro) had helped the country achieve this economic stability.[10]

INCREASINGLY POPULAR LOCATION FOR FDI

Over the previous two decades, Poland had become a popular destination for FDI. Between 2000 to 2004, over US$84 billion of FDI had flowed into Poland, making the country a top investment destination in the EU.[11] Principal forms of FDI in Poland were mergers and acquisitions (47 per cent) and greenfield investment (37 per cent).[12] Only 14 per cent of foreign investments came as a result of privatization.[13] While increases in FDI were common for transitioning economies, Poland's FDI focus on mergers and acquisitions and greenfield investments demonstrated that the country could achieve a sustainable growth in FDI beyond its trade liberalization from the early 1990s. Poland's FDI had also been reinvigorated by the country's entry into the EU. Membership in the EU had both aligned Polish business practices with those of the other European nations and granted the country access to EU structural funding.[14,15] These factors provided foreign investors with confidence in the nation's economic environment.[16]

---

8 *Ibid.*

9 *Catriona Davies, "How Poland became only EU nation to avoid recession," CNN World News, June 29, 2010, http://articles.cnn.com/2010-06-29/world/poland.economy. recession_1_poland-transition-economies-eastern-europe?_s=PM:WORLD*

10 *Ibid.*

11 *"Advisory Report: Why Poland? Strengths and Weaknesses of Running a Business in Poland, from the Perspective of Foreign Investors," KPMG, Warsaw, 2006, p. 7.*

12 *Ibid., p. 8.*

13 *Ibid.*

14 *Between 2004 to 2010, Poland was boosted by UN Structural Funding.*

15 *Catriona Davies, "How Poland became only EU nation to avoid recession," CNN World News, June 29, 2010, http://articles.cnn.com/2010-06-29/world/poland.economy. recession_1_poland-transition-economies-eastern-europe?_s=PM:WORLD*

16 *"Over the hill? Foreign investment in Eastern Europe may be at a peak," The Economist, June 25, 2007, www.economist.com/node/9392733*

Foreign investors also had a high satisfaction rate with the decision to commit financial resources to Poland. A study conducted in 2005 noted that over 80 per cent of foreign investors surveyed would choose Poland again.[17] Notably, investors viewed Poland as an investment destination with "low labour costs and highly skilled people."[18] With a social, economic and geographic proximity to Western Europe, Poland offered an advantageous cultural fit for Western investors.[19]

SHIFTING INDUSTRIAL LANDSCAPE

In 2010, Rafal Szajewski, project manager of the Polish Foreign Investment Agency, noted that Poland's economy had been making an important transition from manufacturing to service industries such as IT.[20] The development of the IT industry in particular had made cities such as Krakow attractive outsourcing destinations for large multinational firms. Since 2000, IBM, Motorola and Google had all established research hubs in Krakow.[21] These firms were initially drawn to this historic city in southern Poland as it boasted more than 150,000 students in a community of reputable universities (see Exhibit 1).[22] The potential relationship with these universities, the calibre of students and the fact that Poland's average salary was lower than that in Europe had made Polish cities like Krakow attractive ecosystems for research-intensive outsourcing.[23]

POTENTIAL CHALLENGES OF DOING BUSINESS IN POLAND

Culturally, Poland showed signs of social residue from its former state-owned economy. Businesses had noted an inefficient commercial court

---

17 *"Advisory Report: Why Poland? Strengths and Weaknesses of Running a Business in Poland, from the Perspective of Foreign Investors," KPMG, Warsaw, 2006, p. 10.*
18 *Ibid., p. 3.*
19 *"Over the Hill? Foreign Investment in Eastern Europe May be at a Peak," The Economist, June 25, 2007, http://www.economist.com/node/9392733*
20 *Catriona Davies, "How Poland Became Only EU Nation to Avoid Recession," CNN World News, June 29, 2010, http://articles.cnn.com/2010-06-29/world/poland.economy.recession_1_poland-transition-economies-eastern-europe?_s=PM:WORLD*
21 *Colin Woodard, "Why Google Put a Research Lab in Poland," USA Today, March 13, 2007, www.usatoday.com/tech/techinvestor/industry/2007-03-13-google-poland_N.htm.*
22 *Jack Ewing, "Why Krakow Still Works for IBM," Bloomberg Businessweek, September 25, 2007, www.businessweek.com/globalbiz/content/sep2007/gb20070925_228125.htm.*
23 *Ibid.*

system, rigid labour code, burdensome tax system and bureaucratic red tape as operational hostilities in the Polish private sector.[24] Particularly, bureaucracy within Poland had been described as "ubiquitous."[25]

While Poland had experienced economic stability and investment attractiveness, it also faced economic concerns. In 2007, Poland joined the Schengen Area[26] that enabled free labour mobility between the majority of EU member states. Effects of "brain drain" had been observed, as educated individuals left Poland for greater employment opportunities and salaries.[27] The annual average salary in Poland had been steadily increasing by 7 per cent per year with domestic firms attempting to compete with salaries offered by other nations in the Schengen Area.[28,29] Costs of operating in Poland were also on the rise as the country continued to become more economically prosperous.[30] Further economic changes were underway as the Polish government planned to enter the eurozone in 2016.[31] Preparation for eurozone transition was well underway, and pressure on currencies and labour costs were expected.[32] As global competition for FDI was aggressive, cost sensitivities could potentially lure future international investors away from Poland and into cheaper destinations.[33]

---

24 *"Poland," Central Intelligence Agency: The World Factbook, last modified May 3, 2012, www.cia.gov/library/publications/the-world-factbook/geos/pl.html.*

25 *"Advisory Report: Why Poland? Strengths and Weaknesses of Running a Business in Poland, from the Perspective of Foreign Investors," KPMG, Warsaw, 2006, p. 3.*

26 *The Schengen Area acted very much like a single state for travel. It comprised over 25 European countries. This agreement enabled freer mobility of labour between EU nations.*

27 *"Four Years of Poland's Membership in the EU," Office of the Committee for European Integration: Department of Analyses and Strategies, Warsaw, 2008, p. 43.*

28 *Catriona Davies, "How Poland Became Only EU Nation to Avoid Recession". CNN World News, June 29, 2010, http://articles.cnn.com/2010-06-29/world/poland. economy.recession_1_poland-transition-economies-eastern-europe?_s=P-M:WORLD.*

29 *"Four Years of Poland's Membership in the EU," Office of the Committee for European Integration: Department of Analyses and Strategies, Warsaw, 2008, p. 31.*

30 *Arjun S. Bedi, and Andrzej Cieslik, "Wages and Wage Growth in Poland: The Role of Foreign Direct Investment," Economics of Transition, 10 (1), 2002, p. 3.*

31 *"Official: Poland to be Ready for Euro in 4 Years," Bloomberg Businessweek, December 2, 2011, www.businessweek.com/ap/financialnews/D9RCGVPG2.htm.*

32 *"Four Years of Poland's Membership in the EU," Office of the Committee for European Integration: Department of Analyses and Strategies, Warsaw, 2008, p. 7.*

33 *"Over the Hill? Foreign Investment in Eastern Europe May be at a Peak," The Economist, June 25, 2007, www.economist.com/node/9392733.*

Appendix: Cases

INFUSION'S CHOICE TO ENTER POLAND

Infusion made the decision to enter Poland in 2010. Senior managers in the company spent 10 months investigating different locations around the world. They considered many options (see Exhibit 2). Three countries were shortlisted: Brazil (advantageous because it was in the same time zone as North America), Czech Republic (Prague) and Poland (Warsaw or Krakow). Poland had been chosen because of the cost advantages, an abundance of suitably qualified software engineers and time zone benefits. The quality of living, the creativity of the people in the field and the relative lack of competition for these people were also key factors that were decisive in choosing Krakow. The country manager, Ryan Hunter, was heavily involved in the decision process. He previously worked in the project management function in the company's Toronto office for about two years before getting involved in the expansion strategy. He then spearheaded the set-up of the office in Krakow.

Target recruits in Krakow were members of the local .NET community. Infusion learnt about this community through contacts and researched the recruits' blogs. The company became familiar with key members of the .NET community in Krakow. The presence of three universities and the creative climate in the community were good indicators that hiring appropriately talented people would be possible. As Infusion had an established strategy of building its business around the talent of its employees, it was very important for Somani and Hunter to find the right people.

INITIAL ENGAGEMENT IN POLAND

The presence of the .NET community and referrals by a key community leader proved to be crucial in the process of identifying talent as Somani and Hunter began the initial engagement in Poland. In 2010, Somani, Hunter and John Mitchell (Infusion's COO) visited Poland to learn about the technical communities and the .NET community in particular. They were joined by Monika Owsianna (from Infusion's human resource team in Toronto), who spoke Polish. Somani was especially interested in assessing the size of the .NET community, as well as its innovative capability, vibrancy and quality. These managers first went to Warsaw and met with Microsoft. They then visited Wroclaw and finally Krakow (partly on Hunter's suggestion). Through contacts they were introduced

202

to the leader of the .NET community in Krakow, Szymon Lewandowski. The Infusion representatives asked if they could attend some of the meetings that the .NET community held regularly in Krakow. They attended various meetings and also gave presentations as part of a speaking tour with demonstrations. Some of the presentations that Infusion gave were in Polish and others in English. These presentations were well-received. The Infusion managers also met with key people at the local universities. Their approach was to listen, rather than poach people from other employers. They were very keen not to be seen as poachers. Many of the technical people that they met were already working in local companies.

Lewandowski was a freelance contractor running his own business offering .NET consulting services. He was willing to meet with the Infusion team to discuss their needs. He did not receive any financial compensation from Infusion for his time and ended up referring a number of potential candidates for Infusion to interview.

One month later, Infusion visited Krakow to conduct initial interviews. This time Owsianna was joined by Dan Barkowski (from one of Infusion's technical teams in Toronto). Barkowski could also speak some Polish, although interviews were conducted in English. They attended a local job fair and had further appointments within the .NET groups. They obtained a "surface" from Microsoft (a large tablet device) and used this to demonstrate Infusion's innovative software. New recruits such as Szymon Pobiega were impressed by the style of the interviewing, which involved technical questions that really challenged the interviewee (rather than a fixed list of standard questions).

Infusion was attractive to .NET developers in Krakow who found Polish employers rather old–fashioned, bureaucratic and unable to understand or use agile software development methods.[34] Furthermore, the initial recruits were attracted to being part of a start-up from the beginning. The presentations given by Infusion contained examples of innovative software applications that the company had developed in the past. Awareness of these presentations spread throughout the community through word-of-mouth, and this also attracted candidates to the company.

---

34 *Agile software development methods involve engineers and users working collaboratively on repeated iterations of development.*

Appendix: Cases

2011: THE FIRST YEAR IN OPERATION

The initial target was to recruit 10 .NET engineers. Much less than this would have meant that the office could only work on one project at a time. Furthermore, the company would be exposed if one or two of the engineers left. Infusion was concerned that an initial intake much larger than 10 could mean that the initial team would be difficult to manage. This posed a risk for the company as it had no experience running an operation in Poland. Start-up costs also increased with the number of initial recruits.

Infusion initially hired eight engineers at the end of 2010, due to start working in January 2011. All of these engineers were referred by Lewandowski. A ninth employee was delayed due to transition issues in his existing employment contracts, but also started in the first quarter of 2011. Seven out of the initial eight employees knew each other from working in a local Polish company in the past and from being members of the .NET community in Krakow. They had respect for each other and experience working with each other. Eight employees were seen as a good number to manage and a sufficient number to work on two to three projects simultaneously.

In January and February 2011, these eight engineers were sent to Toronto to receive training and undertake initial onboarding. This became known as the Infusion boot camp. The objective was for new recruits to experience team building within the Infusion environment, improve their English and learn about the company culture. At the same time, they were to work on real client projects by shadowing employees in Toronto. There were potential risks for the initial intake. Infusion was seen as a pioneer rather than an established company in Poland. Infusion Poland had no office space at that point. However, the recruits embarked on this journey trusting that it would work out. The training was received very well and was repeated for new employees in the next batch that was hired four months later.

The Polish recruits were initially skeptical about the mission and vision statements given to them by the company: they were not used to these types of cultural symbols in Polish organizations. However, they were very impressed by the quality of the technical staff that they met in Toronto. Likewise, Infusion trainers and other technical staff were impressed by the quality of the new recruits. This established credibility and trust at an early stage and proved to be an important factor in ongoing international collaboration. There was a sense that if Infusion had told technical teams in Toronto to collaborate with the new Polish recruits on increasingly advanced work without the establishment of credibility, then there would have been some resistance. There was also a sense that the first batch of recruits did not feel the need to "sell" their skills. They impressed people in Toronto through simply exhibiting their intelligence.

There were two streams to the initial onboarding (see Exhibit 3). The first stream took four engineers and focused on SharePoint[35] and web development. The second stream took the remaining four engineers and focused on SmartClient[36] and WPF[37] development. Both streams involved an orientation week at the beginning of January and a job shadowing and full project integration phase (one month) at the end. Client projects for the eight engineers to work on were picked to suit the capabilities of the engineers.

Hunter accompanied the team when they returned to Krakow at the end of February. Once back in Poland they continued to work on the projects that they started while in Toronto. Within weeks, some members of the team were assigned to new projects.

During March and April, the team used temporary office space in the building next door to where the main office was due to be set up. During this period, the main building was being renovated. When they eventually moved into the main building, they all carried their own personal items to help in the relocation (see Exhibit 4). Infusion recruited a local office manager who was Polish-born but had lived in the United States for many years. She helped with the setting up of initial office space and with practicalities of dealing with local authorities.

The start in Krakow was cautious. Projects executed in Krakow were firmly tied to existing activities in other company locations (Toronto, London and Dubai). Managers soon realized that projects executed with the Polish staff were exceeding client expectations. It appeared that the company had hired very good people who clearly demonstrated their talent.

---

35 A platform from Microsoft for developing web applications.
36 A framework from Isomorphic Software for developing web applications on the client-side (rather than the server-side).
37 Windows Presentation Foundation.

Appendix: Cases

In May, Infusion recruited eight additional employees. This intake experienced a short boot camp in Toronto (two weeks) for training and onboarding. Each newcomer was then integrated into the team in Krakow by being paired up with one of the initial eight engineers.

By June, newer and less "safe," projects were started. These projects were in the user experience area, such as touch screen interactive presentations and mobile applications. Quality assurance eventually became another new area of competence for the Polish subsidiary.

In the second half of 2011, new waves of recruits joined Infusion Poland approximately every other month. All attended the boot camp in Toronto. By the end of the year there were 40 full time employees at Infusion Poland. In January 2012, the first boot camp for Polish recruits took place exclusively in Krakow. By April 2012, there were plans to hold boot camp training in Krakow for new employees joining the company in London and Toronto.

The growth of Infusion Poland was possible because the subsidiary delivered excellent quality work at a good price for clients. Infusion won projects that previously might have been lost due to a less-competitive price. Having the operations in Poland saved about 50 per cent on quotes to clients due to lower costs in salaries, office space and services. There was no sales team in Poland delivering to the Polish market. All projects delivered by Infusion Poland were developed and sold together with the other Infusion locations.

The organization of Infusion Poland involved a country manager (Hunter) and various team leads who reported to him. Project teams were constructed based on the prior experience of engineers and the nature and timing of the projects. The office was a very informal, open-plan setting (see Exhibit 5). The country manager had a separate office and some smaller rooms were available for meetings, videoconferencing and guests. In the middle of the office was a kitchen and some chairs and sofas. There was enough room for short-term expansion in the communal office space. One corner of the office was used for a specific project, where the engineers working on that project were co-located.

The employees working for Infusion Poland were part of a new generation in Poland that learned English quickly, mainly through applying their technical skills in that language. They generally made a much larger salary in comparison to the previous generation. Technically skilled Poles had previously gone abroad to work, but companies such as Infusion Poland were now coming to Poland. Initially, the informal North American culture of the company clashed with that which the Polish engineers were used to. Polish employees could be distrustful of bosses, but they would do exactly what was asked of them, even if they realized that there could be better ways of conducting a task. They were often accepting of bureaucracy, perhaps more so than North Americans. Their attention to detail to working conditions and contracts could be described as typically European. They were used to having many more days of vacation than their counterparts in North America. Infusion Poland's new recruits agreed to internalize Infusion's values and adopt the company's culture. During the course of 2011, most new recruits showed signs of adapting and being willing to speak up if they felt that things could be done better. Once invited to be more autonomous and express their opinions, they often would.

One of the most difficult issues encountered by Infusion Poland was the bureaucracy and paperwork involved. All paperwork needed to be both in English and Polish. Only signatures in ink were accepted, and on many occasions only persons higher in rank than the country manager could sign. This meant that mail needed to go back and forth to Canada, thus slowing down some of the processes. Some small things turned out to be a hassle, such as not being able to use a company credit card for minor expenses such as buying office lunches. The company discovered that there was a lot of paperwork involved in starting the business, as well as in employee contracts. Infusion Poland initially used a local agency to help prepare contracts. This agency also helped with practical aspects of preparing for the initial interviews, such as organizing space.

Despite these issues, over 40 successful projects were delivered by Infusion Poland in its first year for clients in North America, Europe and the Middle East. The company implemented a number of process changes as it grew in Poland, including improved productivity and transparency (e.g. bug tracking). The eight engineers recruited at the outset played important roles in the recruitment of the next 30 employees. Over 80 per cent of the next 30 came through referrals. Infusion implemented financial incentives for successful referrals (a cash payment if a new recruit was employed one year later).

THE SITUATION IN EARLY 2012

By the first quarter of 2012, Infusion Poland had about 40 employees working on global accounts. The subsidiary had matured to the point at which it worked on three project models: (1) split teams (the most common form of project) — the client team in another location (e.g. London, Dubai or Toronto) and the development team in Krakow; (2) direct client projects — projects that interfaced directly with client contacts in order to understand needs and develop solutions for the client; (3) development for other Infusion teams.

Engineers and managers from different locations met regularly; for example, they met to liaise and build relations with the split team model or to interface directly with client representatives. However, most internal communication was handled virtually by phone, email and video-conferencing. The Polish time zone was a benefit: when the work day ended in Dubai, Krakow could continue. At around 2 p.m. or 3 p.m., calls from Toronto started and work from there could be handled as well. London and Krakow only had one hour difference and could easily be in contact with each other during the day.

In addition to the Krakow location, Infusion Poland also opened a small office in Wroclaw during 2011. Infusion Wroclaw was set up to service one specific key client in the financial sector that had set up a back-office processing centre in that city. This client was an important global account for the company and Infusion was engaged with the client in London and New York. Infusion Wroclaw grew to around 25 employees by the end of 2011.

For the near future, Infusion Poland planned to make Krakow more independent through having a local manager so that the current manager could focus more externally on the relations with the other locations. In particular, it planned to grow operations in Krakow to about 100 employees. Next, the plan was to expand Wroclaw (also to 100 people) and to do activities for clients other than the one in financial services. Any restriction of this growth was mostly caused by how many people with the right technical skills could be recruited. In some sense, the market was competitive because many IT companies were expanding in Poland. On the other hand, Krakow and Wroclaw could be seen as two different areas from which to recruit. Also, the type of developers that Infusion Poland needed were somewhat niche-oriented, thus competition was within a specialized area.

Appendix: Cases

DECISIONS FACING SOMANI AND HUNTER

Somani had followed the progress of Infusion Poland very closely. His view was that there was considerable room for the company to grow in that location. Poland had a cost advantage over other Infusion locations. The level of talent was extremely high and the fit with Infusion's culture had appeared to work. Infusion London had recently started to sell to clients in Europe, and the European business was set to grow.

Despite the initial success of the investment in Poland, continued growth could not be guaranteed. Somani wondered how he and Hunter could continue to grow the subsidiary moving forward. The use of referrals to tap into the .NET community was limited. Wage inflation was picking up, and international competitors could follow Infusion's approach. Somani also pondered how the role of Infusion Poland might need to change in the future.

Appendix: Cases

Exhibit 1

UNIVERSITIES IN KRAKOW PRODUCING TECHNICAL GRADUATES

University	Year founded	Number of students in 2011
Jagiellonian	1364	51,601 (includes non-technical)
AGH University of Science and Technology	1919	37,996
Politecknike Krakowska (Cracow University of Technology – CUT)	1945	17,101

Sources: Case authors.

Exhibit 2

INFUSION'S EVALUATION OF OFFSHORE LOCATIONS

City	Country	Total	Cost	Language	Labour Pool	Education	Timezone	Travel	Visa	"Insiders"	Infrastructure	Gvt Support	Political & Econom.	Cultural	Legal	Data & IP	Tier
Warsaw	Poland	34	●	3	3	3	3	2	2	3	3	1	2	3	3	2	1
Krakow	Poland	34	●	3	3	3	3	2	2	3	3	1	2	3	3	2	2
Sao Paulo	Brazil	34	●	1	3	3	3	3	2	1	3	3	2	3	3	2	1
Wroclaw	Poland	33	●	3	3	2	3	3	2	3	3	1	2	3	3	2	3
Curitiba	Brazil	33	●	2	2	2	3	3	2	1	3	3	2	3	3	2	2
Guadalajara	Mexico	33	●	2	3	3	3	2	2	3	0	2	3	2	3	2	2
Rio de Janeiro	Brazil	32	●	1	2	3	2	3	2	1	3	3	2	3	3	2	1
Mexico	Mexico	32	●	1	3	3	3	2	2	3	0	2	3	2	3	2	1
Recife	Brazil	29	●	3	1	1	2	3	1	1	3	2	2	3	3	2	3
Prague	Czech Rep	28	●	2	2	2	2	2	2	3	0	2	2	3	2	2	2
Budapest	Hungary	27	●	3	1	2	2	2	2	3	0	2	2	2	2	2	3
Santiago	Chile	27	●	2	1	1	2	3	1	2	0	3	3	3	3	2	2
Bucharest	Romania	26	●	3	1	2	2	2	2	3	0	1	2	2	2	2	3
San Jose	Costa Rica	25	●	2	2	1	2	2	2	3	0	2	2	1	3	1	2

Source: Company documents.

Appendix: Cases

Exhibit 3

STREAMS OF INITIAL ONBOARDING

Source: Company documents.

Exhibit 4

COMPANY OFFICE BUILDING IN KRAKOW

Source: Case authors.

Appendix: Cases

Exhibit 5

INTERNAL OFFICE FEATURES

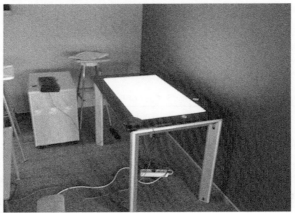

Source: Company documents and case authors.

213

IVEY | Publishing

9B15M074

TESLA: INTERNATIONALIZATION FROM SINGAPORE TO CHINA[1]

Umair Shafique, Agata Barczyk, Lukasz Gluszynski, Adnan Kayssi and Wanyi Zhao wrote this case under the supervision of Christopher Williams solely to provide material for class discussion. The authors do not intend to illustrate either effective or ineffective handling of a managerial situation. The authors may have disguised certain names and other identifying information to protect confidentiality.

This publication may not be transmitted, photocopied, digitized or otherwise reproduced in any form or by any means without the permission of the copyright holder. Reproduction of this material is not covered under authorization by any reproduction rights organization. To order copies or request permission to reproduce materials, contact Ivey Publishing, Ivey Business School, Western University, London, Ontario, Canada, N6G 0N1; (t) 519.661.3208; (e) cases@ivey.ca; www.iveycases.com.

Copyright © 2015, Richard Ivey School of Business Foundation   Version: 2017-09-28

In late December 2012, U.S.-headquartered Tesla Motors (Tesla) was faced with a challenge in terms of how to continue with its internationalization strategy. It had been more than a year since Tesla exited Singapore — six months after having entered that market. In considering China as a possible location for investment, several questions needed to be addressed. What could the company learn from its experiences in the United States and Singapore? Was it the right time to enter the Chinese market? How could Tesla prevent a repeat of the Singapore experience in China?

ELON MUSK — A SERIAL ENTREPRENEUR

Born in South Africa, Elon Musk immigrated to Canada at the age of 15. He later relocated to the United States for further education.[2] In 1995, he co-founded Zip2, an Internet map and directory company, which he sold to Compaq Computer for more than US$300 million in 1999.[3]

He went on to co-found PayPal — an e-payments service — which was sold to eBay for $1.5 billion in 2002.[4] Not content with revolutionizing the online payments market, Musk then founded SpaceX — a company that developed spacecraft and reusable rockets, and with which he hoped to revolutionize space travel.[5] He joined the board of Tesla in 2004 and helped shape its vision.[6] He also had plans to develop a new high-speed transit system, called Hyperloop, which would transport commuters between Los Angeles and San Francisco in only 30 minutes at 1,287 kilometres per hour.[7]

Despite these apparent successes in entrepreneurship, Musk's most recent ventures had suffered setbacks, such as delays in the production of the all-electric Roadster sports car in 2007, and the failure of the first three rocket launches by SpaceX between 2006 and 2008.[8] It had been noted how Musk's calculated risk-taking and persistence ensured that his companies were able to overcome hurdles. In fact, such was Musk's determination that he had even risked personal bankruptcy to ensure Tesla survived.[9]

TESLA — COMPANY BACKGROUND

Tesla was an automaker headquartered in Palo Alto, California. The company designed, manufactured and sold fully-electric vehicles (EVs) as well as EV powertrain components.[10] Tesla was formed in 2003 and went public in 2010. Musk joined the company in 2004. He set the company's mission, which was "to accelerate the advent of sustainable transport by bringing compelling mass market electric cars to market as soon as possible."[11]

While the concept of fully-electric vehicles was not new, automakers had struggled to balance design with performance. Furthermore, the batteries used for these vehicles were not optimal, and a single battery charge only offered a short driving distance.[12] However, by partnering with Panasonic, a major Japanese electronics corporation, Tesla was able to develop a lithium-ion rechargeable battery for EVs, which solved the driving-distance-per-battery-charge issue.[13] In doing so, Tesla succeeded in developing technology that other major automakers, such as General Motors, had been pessimistic about.[14] Tesla also formed partnerships with other automakers and component manufacturers, such as Daimler and Toyota. This enabled Tesla to overcome design and performance issues and to develop fully electric and optimally designed vehicles.[15]

By December 2012, Tesla had established a presence in the United States and Europe. Furthermore, it had also opened up stores and galleries in Japan and Australia.

Corporate Strategy

Consistent with its vision to eventually create a mass market for cost-effective, fully-electric vehicles, Tesla set out with a strategy to "go down the market." This involved starting by developing and marketing high-end products for affluent customers, and as the company, its products and its customers became more mature, the company would use the profits and experience generated to refine the technology.[16] This strategy was similar to that employed by companies in fast-moving technology industries such as Apple, but was quite unique in the automotive industry, where major companies like General Motors and Ford tended to start at the lower end of the market.[17]

Vehicles and Complementary Products

In 2008, Tesla introduced its first vehicle, the Tesla Roadster, to the North American market. Priced at about $109,000[18] and aimed at the richest individuals, it was a two-seat convertible and the first high-performance electric sports car. It had the ability to accelerate from zero to 97 kilometres per hour in 3.7 seconds, with a maximum speed of about 193 kilometres per hour, and a range of 394 kilometres on a single charge of the battery.[19]

Tesla stopped production at the end of 2011 because its contract with Lotus Cars had expired, and Lotus had provided the case component for the Roadster.[20] Tesla sold its remaining Roadsters throughout 2012 in Europe and Asia. By December 31, 2012, it had sold a total of 2,450 Roadsters in a four year period.[21]

Tesla's second vehicle, the Model S sedan, was released in North America in June 2012. The Model S offered customers a lower cost of ownership compared to other sedans that were available at the time.[22] The Model S was a fully-electric, four-door vehicle, with a range of 426 kilometres for each charge of its battery. It also boasted an acceleration capability of zero to 97 kilometres per hour in 4.4 seconds.[23] It was offered with several battery pack options (40, 60 and 85 kilowatt-hours).

Depending on the option chosen, Tesla priced the Model S between $52,400 and $72,400.[24] By December 2012, Tesla had sold 2,650 Model S cars, mainly in the United States. It had also announced plans to sell the vehicle in the European and Asian markets from 2013 onwards.

The Model S was different from the Roadster in that it had an adaptable platform architecture and its own electric powertrain. This common base would be used for newer Tesla models, and would help shorten both the cost of, and time needed for, developing future models. This would help to fulfil Tesla's vision to accelerate the creation of a mass market for cost-effective EVs.

Tesla unveiled a prototype of a third vehicle, the Model X, in February 2012, with an intention to produce it after 2014. Tesla had intended to set a price for the Model X that would be appropriate to a comparable version of the Model S.[25] The Model X was designed to be a hybrid and to feature both the roominess of a minivan, and the style of a sports utility vehicle, while still offering high-performance features such as a dual-motor all-wheel-drive system. In the long term, Tesla had outlined plans to release a car priced between $30,000 and $40,000.

TESLA IN THE UNITED STATES

Tesla opened its first retail stores in Los Angeles and Menlo Park, California, in the summer of 2008.[26] By December 2012, it operated a network of more than 30 stores, sales and service centres, and galleries around the world. Locations included Seattle, New York City, Osaka, Sydney and Toronto.

Showrooms

Tesla's ability to adapt and innovate in uncertain times came under examination in 2008. Such uncertainty was characterized by a decline in automotive industry sales due to the credit crisis and a general lack of acceptance of the "electric car" concept by U.S. consumers. The appeal of electric cars suffered from a steep drop in fuel prices in the United States at the end of 2008.[27] Tesla needed to be creative in order to develop a successful strategy to sell its vehicles to consumers.

Appendix: Cases

While a traditional dealership-based franchise model had been implemented by all other car manufacturers in the United States, Musk believed that such a model would not meet Tesla's needs. He felt that this model had two major disadvantages for the sale of EVs. First, dealers would encounter a fundamental conflict between the sale of gasoline-dependant cars and EVs. They would not be able to explain the benefits of an EV without undermining the advantages of their traditional business.[28]

Second, Musk believed that when consumers visited a local dealership, the majority of potential buyers had already come to a tentative decision about which vehicle they would purchase. This could potentially reduce the dealer's opportunity to educate those consumers on the benefits of Tesla's EV. Tesla decided to pursue an alternative strategy to sell its vehicles by making them available through their own dealerships.[29]

Tesla's strategy allowed the company to offer a compelling customer experience while operating efficiently. The company was also able to capture sales and service revenues that other automobile manufacturers would not be able to attain through the use of the traditional model.

Tesla also believed that it would be have better control over the sales process if it sold its own vehicles. Factors such as the costs of inventory, management of warranty services and the pricing of the products could be better maintained. All of this would serve to strengthen the Tesla brand, and obtain rapid customer feedback.[30]

However there was one problem: U.S. law-makers in some states had prevented the direct sale of vehicles to customers by their manufacturers. This created a barrier for Tesla to overcome in its pursuit of company-owned dealerships.[31] In 48 of the 50 states, Tesla was required to sell and service its automobiles through a middleman franchise — a dealer.[32] Once dealers had invested in inventory and facilities, automotive companies could pressure dealers to accept shipments of cars. If the dealer did not comply they could face the possibility of the manufacturer finding another local dealer to use instead. In such a situation, the dealer would lose the money that had been invested in the dealership. To prevent such situations from occurring, the states had begun to enact laws to provide dealers with exclusive rights in local markets. Tesla overcame this obstacle with a revolutionary solution.

On July 8, 2010, Tesla announced the appointment of George Blankenship as the vice-president of design and store development for Tesla.[33]

Blankenship, the former vice-president of real estate for Apple, was best known for his work on Apple's brand-building retail strategy — one of the most successful retail growth strategies in history.[34] Blankenship, through the use of his knowledge acquired at Apple, was able to devise an innovative strategy to adapt to the laws that prohibited the sale of vehicles by a manufacturer. His strategy would also maximize the number of consumers that would be exposed to and educated about the product.

Blankenship recommended that Tesla position its new stores, which they called "showrooms," in retail venues that had high foot-traffic and visibility. Places such as malls and shopping districts, where people were regularly in a relatively open and buying mood, were considered the ideal places for the "showrooms." He believed this would satisfy the company's need to educate consumers because Tesla would be able to interact with potential consumers before they had decided on which new vehicle they wanted to purchase.[35] Also, implementing these showrooms in high foot-traffic areas ensured maximum exposure for the company's brand.

More importantly, Blankenship's showrooms enabled Tesla to sell its own vehicles in the United States without violating the dealership laws. Each showroom was used to display the vehicles and to educate consumers on the benefits of EVs and Tesla's other products. If the consumer did decide to purchase a Tesla vehicle, a company employee would direct the consumer to the company's website, where they would complete their order. By having the customer purchase the vehicle online, Tesla would not infringe on state laws and would be allowed to sell its own vehicles.

Charging Stations

Consumers had questioned the vehicles' potential to serve as a primary form of transportation. This was due to limitations on long-distance travel associated with EVs and their power sources. Without an improvement in the vehicle's range, the product would be considered impractical. This would prevent Tesla from producing vehicles on a mass scale. Similarly, questions were being asked about the practicality of a vehicle that required a long time to charge its battery. Tesla products had two feasible charging options: The wall charger and the universal mobile connector. The wall charger would be installed in the consumer's home, and could refuel a Model S at a 90-kilometre range per hour (approximately four hours). The universal mobile connector was designed to allow consumers to travel longer distances. It could charge the vehicle at a 52-kilometre range per hour (six hours for a full charge).[36] With the high-end Model S able to travel only a 426-kilometre range between charges, the time required to refuel would cause the vehicle to be considered impractical for everyday use.

In response to this challenge, Tesla developed a solution that satisfied both the charging-needs of its vehicle and the requirement for the vehicle to be able to travel longer distances. These challenges were ameliorated with the introduction of Tesla's "supercharger stations." A charging station allowed a consumer to recharge a vehicle at a much higher speed then previously possible. Tesla vehicles could now replenish half of their battery power in as little as 20 minutes.[37] The significant improvement in charging time eliminated a portion of consumer concerns related to using a Tesla vehicle as a primary mode of transportation.

The supercharger stations also addressed long-distance travel concerns. As of December 2012, Tesla had implemented supercharger stations in two separate corridors in the United States that allowed for efficient long-distance travel. The first corridor used six charging stations to connect San Francisco, Lake Tahoe, Los Angeles and Las Vegas. The second corridor connected the District of Columbia, New York City and Boston.[38] Tesla announced further expansions in 2013 for its supercharger stations which included a network that featured a "supercharger highway" that would connect Los Angeles to New York.

Battery Swap

Tesla's implementation of Supercharger stations placated many critics that questioned the Model S's potential to serve as a primary vehicle. However, a few detractors remained. Some believed that without an option for instant charges, Tesla products would be too time consuming for many customers. If the cars could not refuel instantly like their gasoline-using counterparts, the issue would continue to be seen as a weakness. To address this issue, Tesla designed a system that would allow consumers to "swap" batteries in their vehicles, allowing for immediate refuelling. The swap option was implemented in 2013.

Appendix: Cases

TESLA IN SINGAPORE

In the 2000s, Singapore was one of the wealthiest economies in the world. The real gross domestic product per capita was fourth and fifth in the world, in 2009 and 2010, respectively, exceeding US$60,000 (purchasing power parity).[39] Singapore's population amounted to around five million people, while the number of cars used in Singapore exceeded half a million (see Exhibit 1).[40] Alongside a high tax policy for conventional fuel-using cars, the Singaporean government pursued a policy of maintaining a green and clean city that included limiting air pollution. Singapore was technologically advanced and offered local expertise in electronics, power and precision engineering. These factors, together with its small size, compact urban environment and robust power grid, as well as an information and communications technology infrastructure, made Singapore an ideal location for testing EVs.

Singapore generated around 80 per cent of its power from natural gas. It was estimated that a 30 per cent penetration of EVs in private car ownership would provide the benefit of a 7 per cent reduction in carbon emissions in the country.[41] Moreover, the size[42] of Singapore meant short average driving distances (55 kilometres per day). This put passenger vehicle distance requirements within the range of a fully charged EV (90 to 160 kilometres).[43] Another benefit of moving over to EVs was the potential reduction in the Singaporean preoccupation with cars as status symbols. This was hoped to be an added benefit if EVs could be seen only as functional vehicles with the single purpose of getting from point A to point B. The move over to EVs would potentially shift consumer focus from the fastest, most powerful cars to the most environmentally friendly ones.[44]

In May 2009, the Singaporean government announced its decision to establish a two-year test-bed program for EVs.[45] The program was dubbed the Transport Technology Innovation and Development Scheme (TIDES). The program prompted the government to look for commercial partnerships with foreign companies. There were two different types of investments within the program. First, companies were needed that were able to provide EVs. Second, companies were needed that could help develop a charging-station infrastructure in the city.

Singapore had already offered a 40 per cent discount for EVs on the Additional Registration Fee (ARF), but TIDES was a great opportunity for electric car manufacturers to build their presence in Singapore.[46]

221

Appendix: Cases

When TIDES was announced, the Renault–Nissan Alliance was already appointed as a partner, but applications from other players were still being accepted.

Tesla's Response and Subsequent Outcome

Tesla opened its first store and service centre in Singapore in 2010. In order to take advantage of the opportunities offered by the Singaporean government, Tesla applied for participation in the program. Tesla felt that it met the government's criteria.[47] Although it had already taken advantage of a 40 per cent rebate for the ARF, the company endeavoured to obtain additional tax breaks through TIDES; this would allow it to decrease the initial price of the cars offered in Singapore by 50 per cent.

Meanwhile, a new player had joined the program: Mitsubishi i-MiEV. The i-MiEV had an open market value (i.e. dealership price) of about SG$85,000, which would increase to about SG$190,000 after payment of full ARF, Certificate of Entitlement[48] and road taxes.[49] Under TIDES, each i-MiEV was priced at only SG$90,000, with exemption from the above duties and taxes for a maximum period of 10 years.[50]

Tesla's price for the Roadster was much higher — SG$500,000 (more than SG$400,000 without any tax exemptions). By becoming part of TIDES, the price for the Roadster would come down to SG$250,000.

Despite all of the favourable conditions, Tesla did not receive the afore-mentioned tax breaks. Only four companies managed to obtain the grant from the Singaporean government (Daimler, Mitsubishi, Nissan and Renault).[51] It was reported that Tesla did not meet the technical requirements for EVs.[52] Consequently, Tesla did not sell a single car in Singapore.[53] The company had garnered about a dozen orders, most on the condition that the tax break be granted.[54] A few people were willing to buy the car without the tax break, because they perceived Tesla as the car manufacturer of the future, but the numbers were too small to justify Tesla's presence in Singapore. Tesla Motors' Asia-Pacific director Kevin Yu told *The Straits Times*: "Unfortunately, Singapore has not turned out to be the market we hoped it would be." He followed: "Given the Roadster's limited production run and the enthusiastic support from both customers and governments for the vehicle in other markets, Tesla has decided to focus our limited resources elsewhere."[55]

Appendix: Cases

Failing to Meet World Demand

By the end of 2012, Tesla's automotive sales revenue had increased to $385.7 million from $148.6 million due to a dramatic increase in demand.[56] 2,650 units of the Model S were delivered in 2012, but the total number of reservations was 15,000. Those vehicles that were delivered were all in North America — none were delivered in Europe or Asia. In addition, the supply of the Tesla Model S significantly lagged the demand. Tesla could not provide vehicles in any of the countries where it operated in 2012. Tesla explained that the delays were due to "difficulties in training new employees to use new equipment, and in part to delays from suppliers."[57]

CONSIDERING CHINA

The electric and hybrid automotive industry in China consisted of well-known car manufacturers such as Mercedes-Benz, Hyundai and Toyota, as well as other Asian brands, like Chery and BYD. Customers with high incomes, who wanted to have high social recognition, preferred well-known manufacturers, while customers with lower incomes, who were also concerned about environmental issues, tended to choose the Asian brands. The market was already competitive and Tesla had no reputation amongst such players.

China had been suffering from severe air pollution, and the Chinese government had taken a variety of approaches to reduce emissions. One of those approaches was to encourage EV purchases. At the end of 2012, the Chinese government planned to provide tax credits for those who purchased EVs and also implied that potential subsidies would be issued to some EV manufacturers in the future.

If Tesla could apply for said subsidies it would be able to offer more competitive prices for its vehicles. However, nothing concrete had been confirmed. In addition, Tesla did not have much information on the demand conditions in the Chinese market. It was thought that Tesla would need to invest in measures to educate local customers on its business vision, design and manufacturing. Another important issue was the electric charging infrastructure. In China, most people lived in apartments with limited parking space, which they often shared with others. Chinese customers were going to experience difficulty charging EVs which would result in less incentive to purchase one. A similar issue

Appendix: Cases

existed for supercharger stations: there were not enough of them, despite high population density in some regions.

DECISION POINT

Given the outcome in Singapore, as well as the mixed performance in the United States and Europe, was the time right for Tesla to enter China? If Musk took Tesla into China, what could he learn from the experiences Tesla had had elsewhere in order to make China a success? How could he deal with some of the unknowns that confronted the company in China? What should the company's entry strategy consist of?

EXHIBIT 1: NUMBER OF CARS IN SINGAPORE

	2006	2007	2008	2009	2010
Total vehicles	799,373	851,336	894,682	925,518	945,829
Cars*	465,482	505,987	540,455	566,608	584,399

*Includes station-wagons.

Source: Singapore Land Transport Authority, "Annual Vehicle Statistics — 2014: Motor Vehicle Population by Vehicle Type," January 19, 2015, www.lta.gov.sg/content/dam/ltaweb/corp/PublicationsResearch/files/FactsandFigures/MVP01-1_MVP_by_type.pdf, accessed August 10, 2015.

Appendix: Cases

ENDNOTES

1 *This case has been written on the basis of published sources only. Consequently, the interpretation and perspectives presented in this case are not necessarily those of Tesla Motors or any of its employees.*

2 *A. Vance, "Elon Musk, the 21st Century Industrialist," Bloomberg Business, September 13, 2012, www.businessweek.com/articles/2012-09-13/elon-musk-the-21st-century-industrialist#p2, accessed March 27, 2015.*

3 *All figures are in USD unless stated otherwise; USD$1 = SGD$1.22 on December 31, 2012.*

4 *A. Vance, op. cit.*

5 *Space Exploration Technologies Corp., "About SpaceX," SpaceX, www.spacex.com/about, accessed April 4, 2014.*

6 *M. Burns, "A Brief History of Tesla," Tech Crunch, October 8, 2014, http://techcrunch.com/gallery/a-brief-history-of-tesla/slide/2/, accessed July 6, 2015.*

7 *J. M. Chang, "Hyperloop Designed for a Quick, Convenient Commute like No Other," ABC News, August 12, 2013, http://abcnews.go.com/Technology/hyperloop-designed-quick-convenient-commute/story?id=19936169, accessed March 27, 2015.*

8 *J. Hsu, "SpaceX's Falcon 1 Falters for a Third Time," Space.com, August 3, 2008, www.space.com/5693-spacex-falcon-1-falters-time.html, accessed July 6, 2015.*

9 *O. Thomas, "Tesla's Elon Musk: 'I Ran out of Cash'," May 28, 2010, Business Insider, www.businessinsider.com/teslas-elon-musk-i-ran-out-of-cash-2010-5-2, accessed March 27, 2015.*

10 *Edgar Online, "Tesla Motors Inc.: Form 10-K (Annual Report)," 2012, http://files.shareholder.com/downloads/ABEA-4CW8X0/496765154x0xS1193125-13-96241/1318605/filing.pdf, accessed March 27, 2015.*

11 *E. Musk, "Blog: The Mission of Tesla," Tesla Motors Blog, November 18, 2013, www.teslamotors.com/blog/mission-tesla, accessed March 27, 2015.*

12 *M. Eberhard, "Blog: Attitude," Tesla Motors Blog, July 19, 2006, www.teslamotors.com/blog/attitude, accessed March 27, 2015.*

13 *Panasonic Corporation, "Panasonic Enters into Supply Agreement with Tesla Motors to Supply Automotive-Grade Battery Cells," Panasonic Newsroom Global, October 11, 2011, http://news.panasonic.com/press/news/official.data/data.dir/en111011-3/en111011-3.html, accessed March 27, 2015.*

14 *T. Friend, "Plugged In: Can Elon Musk Lead the Way to an Electric-Car Future?" The New Yorker, August 24, 2009, www.newyorker.com/magazine/2009/08/24/plugged-in, accessed March 27, 2015.*

15 *Trefis Team, "Tesla's Strategic Relationships with Daimler and Toyota Getting Stronger," Trefis, November 17, 2011, www.trefis.com/stock/tsla/articles/86006/teslas-symbiotic-relationship-with-daimler-and-toyota-getting-stronger/2011-11-17, accessed March 27, 2015.*

16 *E. Musk, "Blog: The Secret Tesla Motors Master Plan (just between you and me)," Tesla Motors Blog, August 2, 2006, www.teslamotors.com/blog/secret-tesla-motors-master-plan-just-between-you-and-me, accessed March 27, 2015.*

17 *R. Carlson, "Why Tesla Has It Right and GM, Ford and Nissan Have It Wrong," Seeking Alpha, October 5, 2012, http://seekingalpha.com/article/907751-why-tesla-has-it-right-and-gm-ford-and-nissan-have-it-wrong, accessed March 27, 2015.*

18 *R. Valdes-Dapena, "5 Electric Cars You Can Buy Now," June 18, 2008, CNN Money, http://money.cnn.com/galleries/2008/autos/0806/gallery.electric_cars_now/, accessed August 7, 2015.*

19 Edgar Online, "Tesla Motors Inc: Form 10-K (Annual Report)," 2011, http://files. shareholder.com/downloads/ABEA-4CW8X0/496765154x0xS1193125-11-54847/1318605/filing.pdf, accessed August 7, 2015.

20 M. Eberhard, "Blog: Lotus Position," *Tesla Motors Blog*, July 25, 2006, www. teslamotors.com/blog/lotus-position, accessed March 27, 2015.

21 Edgar Online, op. cit.

22 Ibid.

23 L. Ulrich, "Top Tech Cars 2013: Tesla Model S: The Year's Most Significant Car Just Happens to be Electric," March 29, 2013, *IEEE Spectrum*, http://spectrum.ieee.org/ transportation/advanced-cars/tesla-model-s, accessed August 7, 2015.

24 D. Reisinger, "Tesla Kills 40 kWh Battery for Model S Over 'Lack of Demand'," April 1, 2013, *CNET*, www.cnet.com/news/tesla-kills-40-kwh-battery-for-model-s-over-lack-of-demand/, accessed August 7, 2015.

25 A. Davies, "How Elon Musk is Revolutionizing Two Major Industries at the Same Time," *Business Insider*, March 13, 2013, www.businessinsider.com/how-elon-musk-overcomes-challenges-2013-3, accessed March 27, 2015.

26 T. O'Leary, "Blog: Tesla Store Los Angeles," *Tesla Motors Blog*, May 14, 2008, www.teslamotors.com/blog/tesla-store-los-angeles, accessed July 15, 2015; Tesla Motors, "Tesla Motors Opens Second Store in Menlo Park," *Tesla Motors Blog*, April 20, 2010, www.teslamotors.com/blog/tesla-motors-opens-second-store-menlo-park-ca, accessed July 15, 2015

27 M. Krebs, "2008 U.S. Auto Sales Are Worst Since 1992," *Edmunds Auto Observer*, January 5, 2009, www.edmunds.com/autoobserver-archive/2009/01/2008-us-auto-sales-are-worst-since-1992.html, accessed March 27, 2015; M. Smith, "U.S. Gas Prices See Sharpest Dip Since 2008," *CNN*, November 5, 2012, www.cnn. com/2012/11/04/travel/gas-prices/index.html, accessed March 27, 2015.

28 E. Musk, "Blog: The Tesla Approach to Distributing and Servicing Cars," *Tesla Motors Blog*, October 22, 2012, www.teslamotors.com/blog/tesla-approach-distributing-and-servicing-cars, accessed March 27, 2015.

29 Ibid.

30 Edgar Online, 2012, op. cit.

31 M. Lao, D. Feinstein and F. Lafontaine, "Direct-to-Consumer Auto Sales: It's Not Just About Tesla," *Federal Trade Commission*, May 11, 2015, https://www.ftc. gov/news-events/blogs/competition-matters/2015/05/direct-consumer-auto-sales-its-not-just-about-tesla, accessed June 22, 2015.

32 M. C. O'Connor, "Tesla's Sales Model? It's Simple: Don't Sell Cars," *ZDNet*, December 20, 2012, www.zdnet.com/article/teslas-sales-model-its-simple-dont-sell-cars/, accessed July 15, 2015.

33 Tesla Motors, "About Tesla: Tesla's Missions is to Accelerate the World's Transition to Sustainable Transport," *Tesla Motors*, www.teslamotors.com/about/press/ releases/tesla-hires-apple-gap-veteran-revolutionize-car-buying-experience, accessed March 27, 2015.

34 K. Jade, "Former Apple Retail Mastermind Jumps Ship from Microsoft to Tesla," July 8, 2010, *AppleInsider*, http://appleinsider.com/articles/10/07/08/former_apple_retail_ mastermind_jumps_ship_from_microsoft_to_tesla, accessed August 7, 2015.

35 P. Valdes-Dapena, "Shop at the Mall for Your $100,000 Tesla," *CNN Money*, June 8, 2012, http://money.cnn.com/2012/06/08/autos/tesla-mall-stores/index. htm, accessed July 15, 2015.

36 Tesla Motors, "Charging: Plug it In, Top it Off," *Tesla Motors*, www.teslamotors. com/roadster/charging, accessed March 27, 2015.

37 Tesla Motors, "Supercharger," *Tesla Motors*, www.teslamotors.com/supercharger, accessed March 27, 2015.

Appendix: Cases

38 Tesla Motors, "Tesla Motors Launches Revolutionary Supercharger Enabling Convenient Long Distance Driving," *Tesla Motors Blog*, September 24, 2012, www.teslamotors.com/blog/tesla-motors-launches-revolutionary-supercharger-enabling-convenient-long-dista, accessed July 15, 2015.

39 Knoema, "GDP Statistics from the World Bank," *Knoema*, http://knoema.com/mhrzolg/gdp-statistics-from-the-world-bank#Singapore, accessed July 24, 2015.

40 Singapore Land Transport Authority, "Annual Vehicle Statistics — 2014," www.lta.gov.sg/content/dam/ltaweb/corp/PublicationsResearch/files/FactsandFigures/MVP01-1_MVP_by_type.pdf, accessed March 27, 2015.

41 EV Hub, "Singapore: as an Ideal Test Bedding Environment for Electric Vehicles," 2011, www.evhub.co/SingaporeEVTestBed.htm, accessed March 27, 2015.

42 Singapore is estimated to be 718.3 square kilometres, making it the 190th largest country in the world.

43 EV Hub, op cit.; Eco-Business, "Singapore Concludes Electric Vehicle Test Bed, May Conduct Further Trials," *Eco-Business*, January 14, 2014, www.eco-business.com/news/singapore-concludes-electric-vehicle-test-bed-may-conduct-further-trials, accessed March 27, 2015.

44 K. Mahbubani, "Can Singapore 'Electrify' the World?" *The Straits Times*, October 12, 2013, www.straitstimes.com/breaking-news/singapore/story/can-singapore-electrify-the-world-20131012, accessed March 27, 2015.

45 Z. Shahan, "Singapore Jumpstarting Electric Vehicles," *CleanTechnica*, August 17, 2009, http://cleantechnica.com/2009/08/17/singapore-jumpstarting-electric-vehicles, accessed March 27, 2015.

46 Globe Business Publishing Ltd., "Green Tax and Fiscal Incentives for General Business, Shipping and Land Transport in Singapore," *Lexology*, June 30, 2011, www.lexology.com/library/detail.aspx?g=7835d77c-e98f-4a17-b32a-80e86e099d52, accessed March 27, 2015.

47 Z. Shahan, op. cit.

48 Land Transport Authority of Singapore, "Certificate of Entitlement (COE)," *Singapore Government*, www.lta.gov.sg/content/ltaweb/en/roads-and-motoring/owning-a-vehicle/vehicle-quota-system/certificate-of-entitlement-coe.html, accessed July 24, 2015.

49 `Eco-Business, "Electric Cars to Receive Special Rebates in Singapore," *Eco-Business*, January 13, 2010, www.eco-business.com/news/electric-cars-receive-special-rebates-singapore, accessed March 27, 2015.

50 SGD$1 = USD$0.81 on September 30, 2012.

51 Eco-Business, "Singapore Concludes Electric Vehicle Test Bed, May Conduct Further Trials," Op. cit.

52 Admin, "Tesla Abandon Singapore, No Thanks to the Government," *Zero Emission Motoring*, February 13, 2011, www.zemotoring.com/news/2011/02/tesla-abandon-singapore-no-thanks-to-the-government, accessed July 15, 2015.

53 K. Mahbubani, op. cit.

54 sgCarMart, "Tesla Withdraws from Singapore," February 14, 2011, *sgCarMart*, www.sgcarmart.com/news/article.php?AID=4151, accessed July 15, 2015.

55 C. Tan, "Electric Car Firm Pulls Plug on Singapore," *Eco-Business*, 2011, http://wildsingaporenews.blogspot.ca/2011/02/electric-car-firm-pulls-plug-on.html#.UzwUVFcXXCs, accessed March 27, 2015.

56 Edgar Online, op. cit.

57 K. Bullis, "Tesla Blames New Delays on Production Difficulties," *MIT Technology Review*, September 25, 2012, www.technologyreview.com/news/429343/tesla-blames-new-delays-on-production-difficulties, accessed June 22, 2015.

⊗IVEY | Publishing

9B11M101

3M TAIWAN: PRODUCT INNOVATION IN THE SUBSIDIARY[1]

Chya-Yi Liaw (Emily) wrote this case under the supervision of Christopher Williams solely to provide material for class discussion. The authors do not intend to illustrate either effective or ineffective handling of a managerial situation. The authors may have disguised certain names and other identifying information to protect confidentiality.

This publication may not be transmitted, photocopied, digitized or otherwise reproduced in any form or by any means without the permission of the copyright holder. Reproduction of this material is not covered under authorization by any reproduction rights organization. To order copies or request permission to reproduce materials, contact Ivey Publishing, Ivey Business School, Western University, London, Ontario, Canada, N6G 0N1; (t) 519.661.3208; (e) cases@ivey.ca; www.iveycases.com.

Copyright © 2011, Richard Ivey School of Business Foundation   Version: 2017-09-28

In 2004, Tao-Chih Chung, departmental head of the health care business division of 3M Taiwan, initiated a project intended to exploit local market needs for 3M's hydrocolloid dressing, a technology that had existed within the company for many years without any practical applications. 3M hydrocolloid dressings were sterile wound dressings consisting of a hydrocolloid adhesive covered by an outer, clear adhesive film impermeable to liquids, bacteria and viruses.[2] The product was regarded as a medical material in Taiwan, sold only to hospitals and drug stores affiliated with clinics.

A product development review was conducted to examine the product's potential in the local market. The local project team suggested marketing

---

1 *This case has been written on the basis of published sources only. Consequently, the interpretation and perspectives presented in this case are not necessarily those of 3M or any of its employees.*

2 *"Product Information, 3M Tegaderm Hydrocolloid Dressing," 3M, www.3m.com/ product/information/Tegaderm-Hydrocolloid-Dressing.html, accessed July 5, 2011.*

Appendix: Cases

the material as an acne treatment. The product would be known as Acne Dressing. There was no standardized solution for acne treatment in Taiwan. If launched, Acne Dressing would be a new and innovative product in the local market as well as 3M's first application of hydrocolloid dressing technology. Since there were no similar products in the market, the project team had limited information: potential sales and volume estimations were largely speculative. With little previous experience in product development and no similar products to base development on, Chung had to decide whether or not to proceed with the product launch.

3M OVERVIEW

3M, formerly known as The Minnesota Mining and Manufacturing Company, was founded in Two Harbors, Minnesota in 1902. Five businessmen planned to mine a mineral deposit for grinding-wheel abrasive but the deposits proved to be of poor quality. The company quickly moved to nearby Duluth and focused on sandpaper manufacturing. Although the company was dedicated to manufacturing industrial products from the beginning, it gradually diversified into consumer markets. 3M became one of the world's most innovative and recognized companies with widely-known brands such as Scotch, Scotch-Brite, Nexcare, Post-it and Comment.

Headquartered in St. Paul, Minnesota, 3M had gradually extended its global presence in the United States, Europe, the Middle East, Africa and Asia Pacific. In 2004, 3M generated US$20 billion in sales and US$2.9 billion in net income.[3] International sales represented 60 per cent of total sales (see Exhibit 1). The company had 189 sales offices worldwide, with 15 in the United States and 174 internationally. By December 31, 2004, the company employed 67,071 people, with 32,648 employed in the United States and 34,423 (approximately 51 per cent) located internationally.[4]

THE 3M WAY TO INNOVATION

Innovation and product development constituted an important part of 3M's activities. 3M invested approximately US$1.1 billion (5-6 per cent

---

3 *3M 2004 Annual Report, Standard & Poor's NetAdvantage, www.netadvantage. standardandpoors.com.proxy1.lib.uwo.ca:2048/NASApp/NetAdvantage/index. do, accessed July 5, 2011.*

4 *Ibid.*

of sales) per annum in research development[5] and had 1,000 scientists and engineers dedicated to developing new ideas.[6] Most of the researchers in the United States were based in corporate research laboratories in St. Paul, Minnesota. Research and development activities included scientific research, application of scientific technology to the development of new products, technical support to customers and internal development of patents.

3M managed its operations in seven business segments: health care; industrial; display and graphics; consumer and office; electronics and communications; safety, security and protection services; and transportation (see Exhibit 2). The health care segment had the highest sales among all segments, accounting for more than 20 per cent of total sales (see Exhibit 3). Each business segment leveraged its own unique sales channels, customers, technologies, manufacturing facilities and selling processes. To encourage efficient distribution of business resources, the seven business segments shared common or related 3M technologies to facilitate innovation and product development.

Business segments were further segmented into divisions. Each product line represented an individual division that possessed its own sales, marketing and technical support staff. For example, the health care segment was comprised of a variety of divisions that included medical and surgical supplies, skin health and infection prevention products, pharmaceuticals, drug delivery systems, dental and orthodontic products, health information systems, microbiology products and closures for disposable diapers.[7] Each division was managed as an individual entity; this small, decentralized structure minimized bureaucracy and empowered business units to concentrate on new ideas and their own customer bases.[8]

3M's approach to innovation evolved from a distinctive corporate culture created by William L. McKnight. McKnight joined the company as

---

5 John Dwyer, "Dare you play R&D roulette," *Work Management*, September 26, 2008, p.16-18, www.worksmanagement.co.uk/features/dare-you-play-rd-roulette/15585/, accessed June 25, 2011.

6 "R&D Before All at Hewlett Packard, 3M and GE," *Strategic Direction*, 20 (10), October 2004, p. 15-17.

7 *3M 2004 Annual Report*, Standard & Poor's NetAdvantage, www.netadvantage. standardandpoors.com.proxy1.lib.uwo.ca:2048/NASApp/NetAdvantage/index. do, accessed July 5, 2011.

8 Ernest Gundling, *The 3M Way to Innovation: Balancing People and Profit*, Tokyo; New York: Kodansha International, 2000, p. 70.

Appendix: Cases

an assistant bookkeeper in 1907. He quickly rose in the company and became president and chairman of the board of directors.[9] McKnight's management philosophy was described in 1948:

> As our business grows, it becomes increasingly necessary to delegate responsibility and to encourage men and women to exercise their initiative. This requires considerable tolerance. Those men and women, to whom we delegate authority and responsibility, if they are good people, are going to want to do their jobs in their own way.
>
> Mistakes will be made. But if a person is essentially right, the mistakes he or she makes are not as serious in the long run as the mistakes management will make if it undertakes to tell those in authority exactly how they must do their jobs.
>
> Management that is destructively critical when mistakes are made kills initiative; and it is essential that we have many people with initiative if we are to continue to grow.[10]

These ideals promoted a company culture that emphasized innovation, risk taking and teamwork. As such, pursuing ideas that did not have immediate impact and learning from mistakes became an important part of 3M's culture of innovation; failure was seen as a learning experience.

McKnight's management philosophy affected many aspects of management at 3M. The company adopted a "15 per cent rule": employees in any area of the company could use 15 per cent of their working hours to pursue their own ideas or projects and had no obligation to report on progress of these ideas.[11] The 15 per cent rule empowered employees while encouraging managers not to over-manage operations (provided essential duties were performed adequately), promoting a corporate culture of freedom and innovation.

Each year, 3M allocated US$50,000 to the company's Genesis Grant program — a program designed to fund innovative projects that may not

---

9 *A Century of Innovation: The 3M Story, 3M, 2002, p. 9.*

10 *"McKnight Principles," 3M, http://solutions.3m.com/wps/portal/3M/en_WW/History/3M/Company/McKnight-principles/, accessed June 25, 2011.*

11 *Tim Stevens, "3M reinvents its innovation process," Research Technology Management, 47 (2), 2004, p. 3-5.*

receive funding through 3M's normal channels.[12] Project teams competed for grants by presenting their ideas to their peers. In this way, each staff member played an important role in building an innovative climate. Additionally, 3M unofficially practiced lifetime employment.[13] This job stability enhanced risk taking and allowed long-term career planning that could work for the company's benefit. The spirit of cooperation and teamwork within the organization derived from the fact that employees did not have to worry about looking for another job eventually.

Management at 3M had long realized that interaction with customers was an excellent way to garner new ideas and business solutions. In one of his early roles as a sales manager, McKnight had observed that salesmen were prime sources of innovative ideas due to their frequent interactions with the customers who used their products. Through constant interaction, the company identified users' problems and developed solutions accordingly; for example, in developing a material that limited the spread of skin infection, the company consulted its major users, including doctors and make-up artists, for ideas about how to use the product and apply it to the skin.[14]

3M's key growth driver was its investment in technologies. Technical innovation at 3M was based on more than 40 technological platforms (see Exhibit 4). The company also combined many of these technologies in order to invent new products that addressed different customer needs. This single set of assets was shared amongst all the business segments at 3M in order to allow free access to the company's technologies.

3M recognized innovation through both formal and informal mechanisms. The company had a tradition of celebrating important personnel in innovation (and motivating employees) by putting up photos and descriptions of early company success stories in 3M office hallways. In addition, 3M developed several programs and awards to recognize its most valuable employees. The most prestigious recognition was election into the Carlton Society, named after the company's first head of research and development (R&D).[15] Introduction into the Carlton

---

12 Felipe Lara-Angeli, "Encouraging innovation: Lessons from the 3M experience," China Staff, 13 (4), Apr 2007, p. 10-12.

13 彭芃萱，你不知道的3M: 透視永遠能把創意變黃金的企業傳奇 (Things you don't know about 3M), Business Weekly Publications, 2010, p.253-256.

14 Ruth Mortimer, "Customer Innovation: Inspirational Customers," Brand Strategy, London, July 12, 2005, p. 24.

15 Ernest Gundling, op cit, p. 95.

Society was the highest form of peer recognition at 3M. The award recognized individuals who made extraordinary contributions to 3M's science and technology. The Golden Step Award recognized teams whose new products achieved US$5 million in sales within three years of product launch.[16] Alpha Grants rewarded innovations in administrative, marketing and non-technical areas. Other 3M awards recognized achievements in areas such as technical excellence, engineering achievement and process technology.[17]

3M'S INNOVATION ACROSS BORDERS

In 1929, 3M made its first move towards international expansion by expanding to Europe.[18] By 2004, the company had a presence in more than 60 countries with geographic coverage in the United States, Europe, the Middle East, Africa and Asia Pacific. Within the United States, the company had 15 sales offices in 12 states and operated 58 manufacturing facilities in 22 states. Internationally, 3M had 174 sales offices and operated 74 manufacturing and converting facilities in 29 countries.[19] 3M products were sold through numerous distribution channels, including direct sales to users as well as sales through wholesalers, retailers, distributors and dealers around the world.

There were seven distinct but interrelated areas of innovative activities within 3M's global operations: sales and marketing techniques; product packaging; product adaptation; commercialization of new technologies; acquisition of technical information; co-design; and original inventions.[20] In many of 3M's subsidiaries, management's focus was on bringing the company's existing resources to meet local customer needs rather than inventing new technologies. Initially, the standard pattern was for new products to be developed by company headquarters and

---

16 Pedro Conceição, Dennis Hamill and Pedro Pinheiro, "Innovative Science and Technology Commercialization Strategies at 3M: A Case Study," Journal of Engineering and Technology Management, 19 (1), 2002, pp. 25-38.

17 Ernest Gundling, op cit, p.95.

18 "Historical timeline," 3M, http://solutions.3m.com/wps/portal/3M/en_WW/History/3M/Company/timeline/1920-profile/, accessed June 20, 2011.

19 3M 2004 Annual Report, Standard & Poor's NetAdvantage, www.netadvantage.standardandpoors.com.proxy1.lib.uwo.ca:2048/NASApp/NetAdvantage/index.do, accessed July 5, 2011.

20 Ernest Gundling, op cit, p.123-134.

Appendix: Cases

tested in the American market; once the product launch proved successful, the products would then be gradually introduced to subsidiary customers.[21] However, as the company continued to expand globally, subsidiaries were given more power and freedom to initiate local product developments that addressed customer needs.

3M cultivated global innovation through its organizational structure. The company followed a matrix management structure in which each international operation reported to the international operations authority for its respective country as well as its corresponding business segment. This organization structure intersected with and was balanced among all 3M's business subsidiaries; furthermore, all business units had their own reporting lines.

3M supported the exchange of personnel between countries and headquarters as a way to enhance the transfer of information and create better personal ties towards innovation. Each country's managing director was frequently an expatriate from another region or country. Sending staff to headquarters was another important part of 3M's expatriate strategy. If a potential innovator within a subsidiary needed information, his or her personal network became a powerful search engine. When a question emerged that had been answered by another 3M employee before, personal contacts could save the time and effort of information searching and speed the exchange of information.

Communication was another essential part of 3M's success. To facilitate communication between staff in technical expertise, marketing, sales, manufacturing and customers, the company encouraged networking activities that would ensure coordinated actions. Technical forums provided opportunities to share technology, best practices, policies and procedures; for example, the European Management Action Team (EMATs) Forum regularly brought together relevant personnel from the United States and European subsidiaries to share information and make decisions.[22] Lectures and problem-solving discussions were also held during the forums. These meetings enabled subsidiaries to present their thoughts and facilitated cooperation and accelerated pace in markets in which there were significant growth opportunities.

---

21 *Ibid.*
22 *Ernest Gundling, op cit, p. 137-138.*

Among all geographic areas, the Asia-Pacific region contributed to approximately 25 per cent of 3M's sales.[23] Asia Pacific was an extremely high-growth region for the company. In 2002, 3M's Asia-Pacific sales grew 12.7 per cent, compared to the company's 1.6 per cent overall growth; and in 2003, the region grew 26.3 per cent, compared to the company's 11.6 per cent.[24] In the early 2000s, 3M invested heavily in its Asian facilities. The company began relocating its R&D and manufacturing facilities for high-end optical components from Austin, Texas, to Singapore in 2002.[25] 3M extended its business model at the headquarters and established a co-location of manufacturing with development and product customization capabilities at the Singapore laboratory. An Optoelectronics Centre of Excellence was also established at the Singapore facility. In 2005, the company announced an investment of US$40 million to create its third-largest R&D centre (after Minnesota and Japan) in Shanghai.[26] The new centre in China served as an important platform for 3M's technological innovation activities on a global scale.

3M TAIWAN: AN OVERVIEW

Taiwan had a population of 23 million people[27] and an area of 35,801 square kilometres (km).[28] Strategically located in the middle of a chain of islands stretching from Japan in the north to the Philippines in the south, and only 160 km from the southeast coast of the Chinese mainland, Taiwan was a natural gateway to East Asia.

Established in 1969, 3M Taiwan was based in Taipei City with offices in Taichung and Kaohsiung, a logistics centre in Taoyuan and a plant

---

23 *3M 2004 Annual Report, Standard & Poor's NetAdvantage, www.netadvantage. standardandpoors.com.proxy1.lib.uwo.ca:2048/NASApp/NetAdvantage/index. do, accessed July 5, 2011.*

24 *3M Annual Reports, 2002-2003, Standard & Poor's NetAdvantage, www.net advantage.standardandpoors.com.proxy1.lib.uwo.ca:2048/NASApp/NetAdvantage/i ndex.do, accessed July 5, 2011.*

25 *"3M Opens Optoelectronics Lab," Light Reading, April 26, 2002, www.lightreading. com/document.asp?doc_id=14508, accessed June 25, 2011.*

26 *"3M sets up its third largest R&D center in Shanghai," People's Daily Online, August 25, 2005, http://english.peopledaily.com.cn/200508/25/eng20050825_ 204613.html, accessed June 24, 2011.*

27 *"Taiwan population," AsiaRooms.com, www.asiarooms.com/en/travel-guide/taiwan/ taiwan-overview/taiwan-population.html, accessed June 22, 2011.*

28 *Ibid*

Appendix: Cases

and R&D centre in Yangmei City, Taoyuan.[29] In 2005, 3M Taiwan Optronics Corporation was established as the only manufacturer of prism sheet films in Taiwan.

3M Taiwan sold more than 30,000 products locally, with product coverage of electrical devices, transportation, health care, information, security systems, automotive, construction and home improvement.[30] The company had approximately 1,000 employees. In 2002, 3M Taiwan had been ranked among the top 10 in sales performance of the 60 3M subsidiaries.[31] 3M Taiwan was also one of the company's most innovative subsidiaries. Products such as Magic Mop, 3M Polarizing Task Light (3M's first lighting product) and Filtrete Ultra Clear Air Purifier had been developed in 3M Taiwan and had been bestsellers around the world.[32]

3M Taiwan managed its operations under eight business segments: health care; industrial; display and graphics; consumer and office; electronics and communications; safety, security and protection services; transportation; and electronic key account. The additional electronic key account segment was created by the subsidiary to facilitate serving major electronic customers.[33] As was consistent with 3M's corporate approach, each business segment in 3M Taiwan leveraged its own sales, customers, technologies, manufacturing facilities and selling processes.

THE EVOLUTION OF 3M TAIWAN

3M initially positioned 3M Taiwan as a sales office in 1969. A small office with several people, 3M Taiwan sold products directly imported from headquarters. When sales became stable, headquarters began to involve the subsidiary in simple product processing. For example,

---

29 *"3M Taiwan," 3M Taiwan, http://solutions.3m.com.tw/wps/portal/3M/zh_TW/about-3M/information/more-info/history/local/, accessed June 28, 2011.*

30 張鴻, *"帶頭衝, 也要懂得適時放手 (Leaders should learn how to keep an eye closed)," Manager Today, June 2007, www.managertoday.com.tw/?p=889, accessed June 28, 2011.*

31 李筑因, *"美商3M台灣子公司24小時創意不休息 (Creativity never stops at 3M Taiwan)," Career, August 2008, http://future.sce.pccu.edu.tw/reading/digi_reader/pages/new_kp_dtl.aspx?publication_cls_id=A004&publication_dt_uid=dc7431fa-d04e-4c1d-804d-30e760fd0ab1, accessed June 24, 2011.*

32 彭芃萱, 你不知道的*3M: 透視永遠能把創意變黃金的企業傳奇 (Things you don't know about 3M), Business Weekly Publications, 2010, p.27.*

33 *Ibid.*

Scotch Brite pads for kitchenware cleaning were imported from the headquarters as jumble roll materials. The materials were cut by 3M Taiwan before being sent to local third-party agents and distributors for packaging and selling.[34]

In the late 1970s, the Taiwanese government launched 10 major construction projects, including rail electrification, construction of the North Link railroad, development of nuclear energy, construction of a steel mill at Kaohsiung and construction of the new port of Taichung.[35] The need for infrastructure materials provided the perfect opportunity for 3M Taiwan. The subsidiary persuaded local government to adopt some of the company's traffic control products, such as reflective materials (used in road signs, number plates on vehicles, emergency exit markings and display and graphics technologies).[36] 3M Taiwan also cooperated with the government to establish construction procurement regulations and procedures, as well as standards for roadway signage systems.

In the 1980s, the Taiwanese government promoted strategic industries with a high level of technology and low energy consumption. The Industrial Technology Research Institute (ITRI) and, later, the Hsinchu Science-based Industrial Park — which had been called the Taiwanese "Silicon Valley" — were established during this period, with a focus on R&D in information technology (IT) and biotechnology.[37] The national policy to promote R&D encouraged 3M Taiwan to transform from manufacturing to product development.

After 15 years of operating in Taiwan, a new national manager was appointed at 3M Taiwan. Kenneth Yu was expatriated from headquarters to Taiwan in 1984. Yu transformed 3M Taiwan into a subsidiary that went beyond simply meeting basic goals set by headquarters by conducting product development as well. Within four years, 3M Taiwan's

---

34 *Ibid.*

35 *"Taiwan-Economic development," Encyclopedia of the Nations, www.nationsencyclopedia. com/Asia-and-Oceania/Taiwan-ECONOMIC-DEVELOPMENT.html, accessed June 22, 2011.*

36 張鴻, *"*帶頭衝, 也要懂得適時放手 *(Leaders should learn how to keep an eye closed)," Manager Today, June 2007, www.managertoday.com.tw/?p=889, accessed June 28, 2011.*

37 *Sara Robinson, "Taiwan's chip plants left idle by earthquake," The New York Times, September 22, 1999, www.nytimes.com/1999/09/22/business/taiwan-s-chip-plants-left-idle-by-earthquake.html, accessed July 11, 2011.*

sales increased sevenfold.[38] Yu made several changes to the subsidiary. Knowing that sales were critical to expanding the business, Yu started offering a dynamic selling skills course that was required for sales, marketing and technical service staff. The course was developed based on the standard operations procedures for sales employees at headquarters. By translating the material according to local language and practices, Yu created eight steps to help sales employees approach and learn from customers.[39] This systemized approach established a company culture based on customer needs. By requiring staff from different divisions to take the course together, Yu strengthened teamwork and ties between divisions. The relationships among 3M Taiwan's researchers, marketers and salespeople were thus closely linked.

Projects such as "a marketer's dream" and the "advanced growth program" were launched to facilitate creative ideas from the team.[40] Product managers with ideas on product development or brand management were given permission to apply for company-level sponsorship, even without approval from their departments. The projects encouraged employees to pursue new concepts or applications of existing technology without being limited by financial concerns.

3M Taiwan gradually improved its ability to apply products with U.S. specifications to local needs (including making changes in format, thickness/solidity and formula and sourcing materials locally rather than buying and shipping them from headquarters); however, Yu believed that the subsidiary could do more. First, manufacturing facilities were extended to meet the increase in local sales. In 1987, the company set up its first large-scale manufacturing plant in Taoyuan. Additionally, the Kaohsiung Customer Centre was built to provide service and direct contact with customers in southern Taiwan.

The Yangmei plant was established in 1992 as a relocation of the Taoyuan plant. The strategic placement of new manufacturing facilities provided a tremendous boost to subsidiary innovation by making it easier to modify existing products and create customer-focused applications. A total of nine production lines, including tapes, electrical products, consumer products, surface mount suppliers and optical

---

38 彭芃萱, 你不知道的*3M:* 透視永遠能把創意變黃金的企業傳奇 *(Things you don't know about 3M), Business Weekly Publications, 2010, p.98.*
39 *Ibid.*
40 *Ibid.*

Appendix: Cases

contrast films, were established at the Yangmei plant to facilitate the process of local product development.[41] Products manufactured in Yangmei included a variety of tapes, electrical products, Scotch-Brite products, original equipment manufacturer (OEM) tapes, 3M carrier tapes, automotive graphics, 3M blackout films, contrast enhancement film die-cutting, pad conditioner and dark retro-reflecting stripes.[42] Following this first phase of development, Yangmei's research laboratory was opened in 1993 for technical and R&D development. By strategically locating the research laboratory and manufacturing facilities together, 3M Taiwan could update product manufacturing with the latest technical developments. With substantial sales growth, the second and third factories opened in 1995 and 1997 to support the manufacture of multiple product lines. 3M's Yangmei plant (29,792 square metres) served as the subsidiary's major manufacturing and R&D site and Taoyuan (12,500 square metres) functioned as the primary logistical centre (see Exhibit 5).[43]

Taiwan's increasing industrialization and rapid growth during the 20th century had sometimes been referred to as the "Taiwan Economic Miracle."[44] In particular, the economic ties between Taiwan and China grew significantly. Many Taiwanese manufacturers in the labour-intensive, electronics and IT industries set up manufacturing plants in China to take advantage of its cheap labour.

3M categorized 3M Taiwan as part of the Chinese region of Asia Pacific, together with China and Hong Kong. The more established operations in 3M Taiwan provided the company with resources to enter the newer, high-growth market in China. While Taiwanese companies moved operations to China, 3M followed its Taiwanese customers to China by establishing 3M manufacturing and sales operations there. As such, 3M started working directly with domestic Chinese enterprises, which further expanded its business activities in China. Building on the similarity of culture and language between Taiwan and China, it was much easier

---

41 *"3M Yangmei, Taiwan," 3M Taiwan, http://solutions.3m.com.tw/wps/portal/3M/ zh_TW/Yangmei/Plant/, accessed June 28, 2011.*

42 *"Products & services," 3M Yangmei, Taiwan, http://solutions.3m.com.tw/wps/ portal/3M/zh_TW/Yangmei/Plant/Facility/Products/, accessed June 28, 2011.*

43 *"3M Yangmei, Taiwan," 3M Taiwan, http://solutions.3m.com.tw/wps/portal/3M/ zh_TW/Yangmei/Plant/, accessed June 28, 2011.*

44 *"Taiwan's Economy," AsianInfo, www.asianinfo.org/asianinfo/taiwan/pro-economy. htm, accessed June 27, 2011.*

for 3M to import best practices from Taiwan to facilitate expansion into China. For example, "consumer and office" was the most innovative business segment in Taiwan; therefore, in 2004, Cheng-Kuan, Lin, department head of the consumer and office division of 3M Taiwan, was expatriated to China to lead the "consumer and office" business segment there.[45]

ACNE DRESSING DEVELOPMENT

While building a fire on a family and colleagues camping trip in 2004, Chung accidentally burnt his arm. Luckily, one of his colleagues was a nurse. After cleaning the wound with distilled water, she covered it with a piece of 3M hydrocolloid dressing.[46] After two days, Chung removed the hydrocolloid dressing pad to find that his arm had completely recovered — with no apparent scarring. Chung saw the potential for this product to be very successful if applied to the right market.

Hydrocolloid dressing was one of 3M's health care products. It was a sterile wound dressing consisting of a hydrocolloid adhesive covered with an outer adhesive film that was impermeable to liquids, bacteria and viruses. The product was indicated for partial- and full-thickness dermal ulcers, leg ulcers, superficial wounds, abrasions, first- and second-degree burns and donor sites (see Exhibit 6). In 2004, 3M hydrocolloid dressing products were regarded as medical materials sold only to hospitals and drugstores affiliated with clinics; the product was not available to local retailers. For the first time, after seeing how the dressing improved his burnt arm, Chung wondered if 3M could develop any new products from the company's existing hydrocolloid dressing technology.

With Chung's support, a project team was formed which consisted of employees from different divisions within the 3M health care business segment. At the outset, headquarters sent a U.S.-based engineer to 3M Taiwan to provide training on the product and demonstrate how the product was sold in the United States. In one of the meetings the engineer accidentally cut himself with a pair of scissors. A deep wound appeared on his hand, bleeding. The engineer opened a hydrocolloid dressing sample and placed the small, round dressing on the wound.

---

45 彭芃萱, 你不知道的3M: 透視永遠能把創意變黃金的企業傳奇 (Things you don't know about 3M), Business Weekly Publications, 2010, p.110.
46 Ibid, p.28-29.

Appendix: Cases

Soon after, he stopped bleeding.[47] The engineer's actions reminded a project team member of an earlier conversation with a medical instrument retailer. The retailer had told him that nurses were the primary consumers of 3M hydrocolloid dressings, as they often cut the product into small pieces and used it for superficial skin blemishes.[48] The team realized that there was marketable potential in applying the product to acne treatment.

Any product development idea in 3M Taiwan needed to go through a corporate-wide evaluation system, known as the new product implementation system (NPIS). All product development ideas had to successfully complete the full NPIS review process before being launched. NPIS evaluated the new product through seven stages: idea, concept, feasibility, development, scale up, launch and post-launch.[49] The review process helped to justify and evaluate the feasibility of the product development idea using figures such as potential sales, three- to five-year sales volume estimates, benefits that the product would bring to the existing product line, price setting, etc.[50] By evaluating in stages, 3M could use multiple operations (both internal and external) to diagnose potential risks that may occur in different areas. In addition, while the company's policy was to encourage innovative ideas, not all ideas could proceed. NPIS enabled the company to achieve better cost control through funding only those product development ideas with high potential in the market.

The Taiwanese project team soon engaged in the NPIS procedure for Acne Dressing. First, the marketing division evaluated the sales potential of the product. A marketing survey was deployed to see whether existing acne-treatment products were of local consumer interest. The result was positive. Because of the humid subtropical climate in Taiwan, acne had long been a problem for the age group between 15 and 35. There was no standardized solution for acne treatment in Taiwan though

---

47 彭芃萱, 你不知道的3M: 透視永遠能把創意變黃金的企業傳奇 (Things you don't know about 3M), Business Weekly Publications, 2010, p.31.

48 呂馨玲, "別人的難題, 3M的致富商機 (Other's challenge, 3M's opportunity)," Cheers, January 2010, http://career11.mac.nthu.edu.tw/job/campintro/company/007/990107b.html, accessed July 20, 2011.

49 彭芃萱, 你不知道的3M: 透視永遠能把創意變黃金的企業傳奇 (Things you don't know about 3M), Business Weekly Publications, 2010, p.184-186.

50 邱莉玲,"創新要有聚焦、量化標準來管 (Innovation must be focused and managed quantitatively)," China Productivity Centre, February 14, 2006, http://library.cpc.org.tw/express/0217/example02.htm, accessed July 4, 2011.

many different treatments existed. 3M Micropore Surgical Tape was widely used by teenaged consumers for acne treatment because the tape was breathable, hypoallergenic and affordable. In addition, the idea of do-it-yourself home health care was becoming particularly popular in Taiwan as consumers began to pay more attention to personal health care.[51] Many over-the-counter products became available in local drug stores, including Cosmed, SASA, and Watson. Since there was no standardized approach for acne treatment, 3M's marketing department saw the situation as an excellent opportunity to exploit the market and segregate a new market demand for the company's Acne Dressings.

In the next stage of development, the technical aspects of the Acne Dressing product were evaluated. The local technical service and financial divisions became involved in identifying ways to transform 3M hydrocolloid dressings into marketable Acne Dressing products, including establishing the estimated dimensions and size of the product and the associated costs of manufacturing.[52] The review then proceeded to the packaging and distribution segments. These departments evaluated the potential cost and design for packaging and distribution of the product, working towards designs that would attract consumers in the age group of 15 to 35.

The NPIS process involved not only local interdepartmental communication but also information exchange with 3M headquarters. The Taiwanese project team reported their findings to company headquarters for feedback in each review stage. In the local technical service evaluation stage, headquarters warned that product development for Acne Dressing might be challenging. Since 3M hydrocolloid dressings were professional, clinical materials, they might prove too costly to apply to over-the-counter acne-treatment products, which were often relatively low in price.[53]

Headquarters' role in product development idea evaluation was variable. In most product applications based on 3M existing technologies, headquarters' involvement was minimal. 3M relied on the

---

51 *Ibid.*
52 彭芃萱, 你不知道的3M: 透視永遠能把創意變黃金的企業傳奇 *(Things you don't know about 3M), Business Weekly Publications, 2010, p.184-186.*
53 彭芃萱, 你不知道的3M: 透視永遠能把創意變黃金的企業傳奇 *(Things you don't know about 3M), Business Weekly Publications, 2010, p.32.*
54 *Ibid, p.142-145.*

corporate-wide product development review appraisal and local project team judgments in determining product development potential. For technology-related product developments, however, the role of headquarters was essential. In the development of 3M's Dual Brightness Enhancement Film (DBEF) and Brightness Enhancement Film (BEF) products, for example, the technical service division of 3M Taiwan worked closely with headquarters' laboratory on detailed data analysis and product-testing experiments.[54] Headquarters' role became dominant in technology-related product advancement because more technical support was needed and it was likely that these products would eventually be applied globally.

After months of product evaluation, the Acne Dressing product development project successfully completed the review process. During the review procedure, the project team realized two major challenges that might threaten subsequent development and market launch of the product. Firstly, local customers were accustomed to using traditional acne-treatment methods such as anti-acne facial washes, acne-vanishing creams, acne-control facial masks and pore-toning creams. If developed and launched, Acne Dressing would be a brand new product in the local market — one that would likely necessitate educating consumers in order to expose them to the new product and change their buying behaviour accordingly. Secondly, since there were no similar products in the Taiwanese market, the project team had only limited information to use for further decision-making processes. However, the project team ultimately reached the consensus that Acne Dressing had extremely high market potential and was a feasible idea to develop and launch locally. Optimistic about their conclusions, the team decided to report their findings to Chung.

DECISIONS FACING CHUNG

Now, in early 2005, T.C. Chung, function head in the health care division in 3M Taiwan, was in the dilemma of whether to proceed with Acne Dressing product development with the company's existing technology- 3M Hydrocolloid Dressing. Until that point, there had been no product applications based on Hydrocolloid Dressing technology in 3M anywhere in the world. Although the local project team was confident on the market potential of Acne Dressing, major challenges remained.

With no previous experience in product development, Chung had to decide how to proceed with the idea with limited data in hand. Should the team carry on with the project? If so, what options did the local project team have? What kind of resources and support should the local health care business segment seek from headquarters for product development? Should the local product development collaborate with other subsidiaries?

EXHIBIT 1: PERFORMANCE BY GEOGRAPHIC AREA

Net Sales by Area (millions)	2004		2003		2002		2001	
	Sales	% of Total	Sales	% of Total	Sales	% of Total	Sales	% of Total
United States	$7,878	39.4	$7,581	41.6	$7,426	45.4	$7,523	46.8
Asia Pacific	5168	25.8	4335	23.8	3431	21.0	3043	18.9
Europe, Middle East and Africa	5070	25.3	4624	25.4	4035	24.7	3960	24.6
Latin America and Canada	1844	9.2	1651	9.0	1392	8.5	1494	9.3
Other Unallocated	51	0.3	41	0.2	48	0.4	34	0.4
Total Company	$20,011	100.0	$18,232	100.0	$16,332	100.0	$16,054	100.0

Source: Annual report 3M 2001-2004, Standard & Poor's NetAdvantage, www.netadvantage.standardandpoors.com.proxy1.lib.uwo.ca:2048/ NASApp/NetAdvantage/index.do, accessed July 5, 2011.

Appendix: Cases

EXHIBIT 2: 3M'S SEVEN BUSINESS SEGMENTS

Business Segment	Major Products
Health Care	Medical and surgical suppliers, skin health and infection prevention products, pharmaceuticals, drug delivery systems, dental and orthodontic products, health information systems, microbiology products, and closure for disposable diapers
Industrial	Tapes, coated and nonwoven abrasives, adhesives, specialty materials, supply chain execution software solutions, and filtration products
Display and Graphics	Optical films and lens solutions for electronic displays, touch screens and touch monitors, reflective sheeting for transportation safety, and commercial graphics systems
Consumer and Office	Sponges, scouring pads, high-performance cloths, consumer and office tapes, repositionable notes, carpet and fabric protectors, construction and home improvement products, home care products, visual systems and consumer health care products
Electro and Communication	Packaging and interconnection devices, insulating and splicing solutions for the electronics, telecommunication and electrical industries
Safety, Security and Protection Services	Personal protection products, safety and security products, energy control products, commercial cleaning and protection products, floor matting, and roofing granules for asphalt shingles
Transportation	Automotive components, coated and nonwoven abrasives, tapes, abrasion-resistant films, structural adhesives, specialty materials for the transportation industry, and paint finishing and detailing products

Source: Annual report 3M 2004, Standard & Poor's NetAdvantage, www.netadvantage. standardandpoors.com.proxy1.lib.uwo.ca:2048/NASApp/NetAdvantage/index.do, accessed July 5, 2011.

EXHIBIT 3: BUSINESS SEGMENT PERFORMANCE

	2004		2003		% change
(Dollars in millions)	Net Sales	% of Total	Net Sales	% of Total	Net Sales
Business Segments					
Health Care	$4,230	21.1	$3,995	21.9	5.9
Industrial	3,792	19.0	3,354	18.4	13.1
Display and Graphics	3,406	17.0	2,962	16.2	15.0
Consumer and Office	2,861	14.3	2,607	14.3	9.7
Safety, Security and Protection Services	2,125	10.6	1,928	10.6	10.2
Electro and Communications	1,876	9.4	1,818	10.0	3.2
Transportation	1,683	8.4	1,538	8.4	9.4
Corporate and Unallocated	38	0.2	30	0.2	
Total Company	$20,011	100.0	$18,232	100.0	9.8

Source: Annual report 3M 2003-2004, Standard & Poor's NetAdvantage, www.netadvantage.standardandpoors.com.proxy1.lib. uwo.ca:2048/NASApp/NetAdvantage/index.do, accessed July 5, 2011.

EXHIBIT 4: 3M TECHNOLOGY PLATFORMS

Ab Abrasives	**Bi** Biotech							**Pm** Polymer Melt Processing	**Sm** Specialty Materials
Ac Acoustics	**Ce** Ceramics	**Em** Electronic Materials					**Nt** Nano-technology	**Po** Porous Materials & Membranes	**Su** Surface Modification
Ad Adhesives	**Dd** Drug Delivery	**Fc** Flexible Converting & Packaging				**Mi** Microbial Detection & Control	**Nw** Nonwoven Materials	**Pp** Precision Processing	**Tt** Track and Trace
Am Advanced Materials	**Di** Display	**Fe** Flexible Electronics	**Fs** Filtration, Separation, Purification	**Is** Integrated Systems Design	**Me** Metal Matrix Composites	**Mo** Molding	**Op** Opto-electronics	**Pr** Process Design & Control	**Vp** Vapor Processing
An Analytical	**Do** Dental & Orthodontic Materials	**Fi** Films	**Im** Imaging	**Lm** Light Mgmt	**Mf** Mechanical Fasteners	**Mr** Micro-replication	**Pd** Particle & Dispersion Processing	**Rp** Radiation Processing	**We** Accelerated Weathering
As Application Software	**Ec** Energy Components	**Fl** Fluoro-materials	**In** Inspection & Measurement	**Md** Medical Data Mgmt			**Pe** Predictive Engineering & Modeling	**Se** Sensors	**Wo** Wound Mgmt

Source: 彭芃萱, 你不知道的3M: 透視永遠能把創意變黃金的企業傳奇 (Things you don't know about 3M), Business Weekly Publications, 2010, p.230.

Appendix: Cases

EXHIBIT 5: 3M TAIWAN FACILITY LOCATIONS

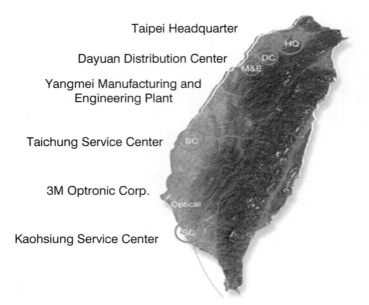

Taipei Headquarter

Dayuan Distribution Center

Yangmei Manufacturing and Engineering Plant

Taichung Service Center

3M Optronic Corp.

Kaohsiung Service Center

Source: "Company information,"3M Taiwan, http://solutions.3m.com.tw/wps/portal/3M/zh_TW/about-3M/information/more-info/contact-us/, accessed June 28, 2011.

Appendix: Cases

EXHIBIT 6: 3M HYDROCOLLOID DRESSINGS

Product Assortment	Product	Technical Specs
3M™ Tegaderm™ Hydrocolloid Dressing 90001		2-3/4 inch×3-1/2 inch (7cm×9cm) Hydrocolloid Dressing, Oval, Film border, Designed for long wear time. Overall size 4 inch×4-3/4 inch (10cm×12cm)
3M™ Tegaderm™ Hydrocolloid Dressing 90002		4 inch×4 inch (10cm×10cm) Hydrocolloid Dressing, Square
3M™ Tegaderm™ Hydrocolloid Dressing 90003		4 inch×4-3/4 inch (10cm×12cm) Hydrocolloid Dressing, Oval, Film border, Designed for long wear time. Overall size 5-1/8 inch×6 inch (13cm×15cm)
3M™ Tegaderm™ Hydrocolloid Dressing 90004		5-1/2 inch×6-3/4 inch (14cm×17cm) Hydrocolloid Dressing, Oval, Film border, Designed for long wear time. Overall size 6-3/4 inch×8 inch (17cm×20cm)
3M™ Tegaderm™ Hydrocolloid Dressing 90005		6 inch×6 inch (15cm×15cm) Hydrocolloid Dressing, Square
3M™ Tegaderm™ Hydrocolloid Dressing 90007		5-1/2 inch×4-7/8 inch (13.9cm×12.3cm) Hydrocolloid Dressing, Sacral Design, Film border, Designed for long wear time. Overall size 6-3/4 inch×6-3/8 inch (17.1cm×16.1cm)

Source: "3M Product Catalog," 3M, http://solutions.3m.com/wps/portal/3M/en_US/ 3MSWC/Skin-WoundCare/ProductDirectory/Catalog/?PC_7_RJH9U52300 OBC0IEI3TR643482_nid=65H4WS9TPBbeB385P3RT67gl, accessed July 9, 2011.

IVEY | Publishing

9B14M034

XEROX INNOVATION GROUP – FROM PRODUCTS TO SERVICES

R. Chandrasekhar wrote this case under the supervision of Professor Christopher Williams solely to provide material for class discussion. The authors do not intend to illustrate either effective or ineffective handling of a managerial situation. The authors may have disguised certain names and other identifying information to protect confidentiality.

This publication may not be transmitted, photocopied, digitized or otherwise reproduced in any form or by any means without the permission of the copyright holder. Reproduction of this material is not covered under authorization by any reproduction rights organization. To order copies or request permission to reproduce materials, contact Ivey Publishing, Ivey Business School, Western University, London, Ontario, Canada, N6G 0N1; (t) 519.661.3208; (e) cases@ivey.ca; www.iveycases.com.

Copyright © 2014, Richard Ivey School of Business Foundation   Version: 2017-05-25

In April 2007, Sophie Vandebroek, chief technology officer, Xerox Corp (Xerox), and head of Xerox Innovation Group (XIG), was facing strategic and organizational challenges related to supporting the company's competitiveness and growth going forward.

Through a network of dedicated research establishments, XIG was the spearhead of innovation at Xerox, a global documents company at the time. The first to be set up in the late 1960s was the Xerox Research Centre Webster, based in New York. It was focused on innovations in xerography and ink-jet systems. The Palo Alto Research Centre, based in California, was focused on inventing the office of the future, shifting its emphasis in later years to what it called the "business of breakthroughs." The Xerox Research Centre Europe, based at Grenoble in France, was focused on innovations in work practices and agile workflows. The Toronto-based Xerox Research Centre of Canada was focused on innovations in materials for various Xerox products.

For over a decade, Xerox had been a pioneer in providing a service dimension to its product sales. The service dimension was a blend of three areas in which the company had built up expertise: "knowledge, content, and document management."[1] The company had stationed its own employees at customer sites around the world to provide a comprehensive range of device management services which it called Managed Print Services (MPS). As an organization, it was moving from providing technology products to providing a combination of products and services. The combinations would be customized to the individual needs of large corporate customers which were themselves global in their operations. Xerox would no longer sell printers or copiers separately to each far flung location of a customer; it would market a comprehensive device management capability, enterprise-wide. It would take custody of product maintenance, ensure steady supplies of consumables, simplify workflows at all sites around the world, generate a single point invoice and present a common face for each customer.

The transition was gathering momentum because of trends in the external environment. First, large corporations, operating in document-intensive industries (like healthcare and banking for example), wanted agile systems that enabled employees to process information efficiently. They wanted to ensure that devices could not only deliver output in response to commands from afar (from employees on-the-go, for example) but also self-restore in the event of malfunctions (without requiring operator intervention).

Second, large companies wanted to reduce their documentation costs which were often higher, as a percentage of revenue, than their outlays on research and development (R&D) or advertising. In a 2001 study, for example, the Gartner Group found that "mismanagement" of copiers, printers and fax machines alone cost between one and 3 per cent of the annual revenue of an enterprise.[2] According to Xerox's own estimates, document-related activities consumed up to 15 per cent of the annual revenue of an enterprise.[3]

Third, companies were regularly tracking their carbon footprint in response to the growing awareness of sustainability around the world. Printers were known to account for 6 per cent of the total emission of carbon dioxide from the global information and communication technology (ICT) industry.[4]

Finally, members of the Net Generation,[5] already part of the ranks of the workforce, were expected to make the prediction of a paperless office come true. But the prediction, made for the first time in 1975,[6] had not happened. However, members of Generation Next,[7] who would soon be entering the workforce, would be looking for office systems running on auto-pilot without human intervention.

Said Vandebroek:

> My strategic dilemmas in managing this transition were two-fold. Our researchers were used to working with Xerox business units managers. Together they developed new technologies and new product platforms. Moving into services requires researchers and engineers to step out of the box and be tuned to the needs of end users. How do researchers become customer focused? Xerox has been a hardware company with core competence in imaging technologies. As part of creating product-service combinations, we now need to develop an infrastructure that links all devices in customer premises and delivers solutions on a platform that is consistent across locations. It is software-based. At one level, it is unique to customer needs but, at another, it is a building block which is replicable across customers. How do we secure this client focus and services platform approach?

Managing the transition meant managing a fundamental contradiction at Xerox. The profitability of the company's strategic business units depended on selling more devices and supplies. As part of its foray into global services, Xerox would be pursuing a three-fold objective for the customer at the latter's premises: print for less (in terms of costs); print less (in terms of pages);[8] and reduce the user-to-device ratio (through optimization). The contradiction lay in the fact that device optimization at customer sites would lead to a reduction in device sales for Xerox because there would be more users per device.

The transition was also opening up new opportunities for Xerox and securing deeper engagement with its global customers. The opportunities were evident in three areas.

First, researchers in XIG working on information systems controls with devices, like printers, were beginning to see broader applications. For example, the skill in data classification could be used with equal ease in consumer applications (e.g., sorting holiday pictures) and industry applications (e.g., applying tolling rates on highways for different types of vehicles). The skill in automatic image enhancement was transferable to any situation calling for improvement in the quality of a document before being printed.

Second, optimization would help Xerox gain access to competitors' devices, in addition to its own, at customer sites.[9] As the customer gradually transitioned to Xerox's own devices, as part of device optimization, the post-sales revenue would go up in spite of a drop in device sales. Xerox could thus lock in the customer by increasing switching costs.

Finally, Xerox could build on its presence in the small and medium enterprises (SME) segment in which it had built up a network of concessionaires and resellers. There was an opportunity to develop technologies with which the prevailing offering of managing a fleet of devices for large customers could be scaled down to address the needs of the SME segment in a cost-effective way.

DOCUMENTS MANAGEMENT (DM) SEGMENT

The global print industry was of the order of $804 billion[10] in 2006.[11] Labels and packaging was the largest segment at about $300 million. The trends influencing the growth of the print industry included shorter lead times, greater volume of colour printing, personalization, cost reduction and digitization. Asia was the largest geographical region at 33 per cent of revenues followed by North America (29 per cent) and Western Europe (23 per cent).

The DM segment was valued at $117 billion. It consisted of four sub-segments: office ($71 billion); services ($21 billion); eligible offset printing ($17 billion) and production systems ($8 billion).[12] DM was characterized by several major shifts. The medium of communication was moving from physical (print) to virtual (electronic); centrally generated content was giving way to user-generated content; a few dominant media channels were being replaced by a multitude of media channels; and reverse publishing (taking online content to print) was a growing trend.

Notwithstanding the predictions about the arrival of a paperless era, the information explosion was not only of high magnitude but was also continuing to accelerate from year to year. International Data Corporation (IDC), a firm specializing in market intelligence for the global

Appendix: Cases

information technology (IT) industry, had reported that in 2006, for example, 161 exabytes of digital information had been created, captured and replicated.[13] The report stated that, by 2010, the information added annually to the digital universe would increase more than six fold – to 988 exabytes.[14]

An imminent trend in the industry was the adoption of MPS as a product-service combination which Xerox was pioneering. Typically, MPS would be a multi-year contract with corporate enterprises. The service provider would make an assessment of the customer's infrastructure related to imaging and printing, take over the management of data, and administer not only the hardware but consumables, maintenance and services. It would consolidate billings of all devices and report to the customer on a regular basis with analytics around usage. The latter was a crucial input to the customer in reducing costs. The service provider would take a proactive stance wherein problems in workflow would be resolved before the customer even noticed them.

There were six key success factors for a global player in the DM sector, according to IDC.

Consistency: The processes for delivery of products and services had to be consistent across geographies. There also had to be consistency in the products and services, per se. Uniformity was required in pricing. The sales force had to be integrated globally. The company's customer relationship management systems had to be seamless.

Services capabilities: This meant having the business process and vertical expertise to understand a customer's requirements and then craft the best combination of technology and services to meet those requirements in real time.

Support systems: A successful player had comprehensive systems in place to support indirect channels like third party distributors and sub-contractors. This might include systems such as sales force training, business development and marketing support.

Portfolio of offerings: The products and services extended beyond fleet management and included management of production print facilities and in the commercial purchase of print.

Cutting edge technology: The technology being deployed by the company had to be state-of-the-art so as to offer timely solutions to a range

Appendix: Cases

of emerging customer requirements such as data security, mobility and remote access.

Networks: The company had to provide its customers with access to its own network of partnerships.

COMPANY BACKGROUND

Xerox had revenues of $15.89 billion and a net income of $1.2 billion for the year ending December 2006 (see Exhibit 1). The United States was its single largest market at $8.4 billion (see Exhibit 2).

The company was founded in 1906 in Rochester, New York as Haloid Photographic Company to manufacture photographic paper and related consumables. It acquired commercial rights in 1947 for a process called "xerography" (meaning "dry writing" in Greek) which had been invented by Chester Carlson, an independent researcher in the United States. The process could instantly reproduce text and illustrations on plain paper. IBM and GE, whom Carlson first approached, had turned him down on the grounds that, in the wake of the popularity of the carbon paper, his invention did not have business viability. Haloid fine-tuned the process leading to the launch in 1959 of the world's first plain paper photocopier.

Xerox 914, as it was called, became a blockbuster product, generating not only high revenues for the company but also high unit margins at the time of about 70 per cent. Xerox had 95 per cent share of the photocopier market during the 1960s and 1970s.[15]

Sustaining growth on the basis of a single product – which was by then so ingrained into its DNA that Xerox had become a synonym for copying – was becoming difficult, notwithstanding the company's deeply rooted sales-driven ethos. The compulsion to come up with breakthrough innovations, commercialize new technologies and launch new products was strong.

Beyond Copiers

The 1970s was a decade of achievements for Xerox. The company had set up Palo Alto Research Centre (PARC) with a mandate to create "the office of the future."[16] PARC came up with a string of discoveries: a laser printer in 1971 which became another block-buster; a programming language called Smalltalk in 1972 which revolutionized the fledgling software industry; a local area network in 1973 called Ethernet which became a global standard; a graphical user interface (GUI) in 1975 influencing the development of the personal computer industry; a very large scale integrated (VLSI) circuit in 1977 that led to a new generation of computer-aided design tools; and computational linguistic technology in 1979 incorporating spell-checks, dictionaries and other language processing tools. The company spun off over 40 companies to commercialize some of its technologies.[17]

However, the 1980s was a troubled decade for Xerox. Its xerographic patents had expired. As part of encouraging competition, the Federal Trade Commission (FTC) of the United States had ruled that Xerox should license its core patents. The impact was not in line with FTC's original intent because the new competitors were not from within the United States – in fact, they were from Japan. PARC could not hold on to many of its pioneering technologies. By 1983, Xerox's market share in copiers fell to 18 per cent. Japanese firms like Canon and Ricoh were gaining market share as a result of price wars in the copier industry. Xerox fought back through the decade by paring down costs, searching for process efficiencies and improving quality.[18]

In 1994, Xerox rebranded itself as "The Document Company." The growth of desktop publishing was leading to a growth in the number of documents being created. Xerox moved from analog to digital products; from high-margin, high-end products to consumables; and from large, global customers to the small office home office (SOHO) segment.

The early years of the new millennium were again troubled. Revenues and margins fell and debt was mounting. Xerox restructured its operations on several fronts to preempt the risk of Chapter 11 bankruptcy proceedings – it divested non-core assets on a large scale, outsourced manufacturing, exited unprofitable businesses (like desktop inkjet), focused on operational cash flow and reduced capital spending. However, it continued to invest in R&D – an indication that Xerox was in a constant state of renewal, in both good and bad times. This was also evident in the number of patents granted to the company which was increasing year after year (see Exhibit 3).

Strategy

Xerox was driven by the vision of "helping people find better ways to do great work."[19] Its strategy in realizing the vision had three major planks in 2006: dominating in colour; targeting new business opportunities (like commercial printing and graphic arts) and new customer segments (like small enterprises); and leading with services.[20]

Colour pages represented 9 per cent of total pages printed on Xerox equipment. Out of about 333 billion pages printed on Xerox equipment in 2006, over 30 billion were in colour.[21] The company was keen on increasing the share since colour pages generated higher revenue and margins than black-and-white pages because they consumed a higher proportion of consumables like toner.

Small and medium enterprises (SMEs) represented a growing opportunity, particularly in the emerging markets. A major segment of the company's customers, comprising commercial printers and graphic arts firms, was also moving from offset to digital printing. Xerox was enabling this transition with products that helped them print on demand, take short production runs, and personalize documents – all faster and neater than before.

Expanding into providing managed print services, particularly for global customers, was an opportunity representing the "tip of an iceberg,"[22] as the company saw it.

The trend had in fact begun in early 2000 when the company shifted its focus from selling hardware to selling output management solutions to large customers. The solutions consisted of simplifying work processes of customers, as well as managing their IT needs and helping them bridge the paper and digital divide. Gradually, it was catering to a similar need in document-intensive industries (like health care, legal, banking, insurance and mortgage) where records had to be scanned, searched and stored. It had, in turn, led to some strategic changes like becoming an outsourcing vendor for companies, developing customized software and moving into colour. It led to some structural changes as well like reorganizing the sales force around industry groups rather than around geographies.

Business model

For many decades, Xerox sold its copiers and printers as capital equipment. Their gross margin averaged 36 to 37 per cent.[23] Xerox also provided service and maintenance at customer premises and leased out the equipment. It also sold toner and paper as consumables in addition to financing the purchase of capital equipment. The margins on the latter were higher; for example, they averaged 43 per cent on after-market service, outsourcing and rentals. Higher margins were one of the internal triggers for going deeper into services.

An integral part of Xerox's business model was "post-sale" revenue, also known as annuity, which comprised over 70 per cent of annual revenues. Annuity ensured regular cash flow to the company from revenue streams such as equipment maintenance, supplies of consumables (like ink and toner), contract services (like document imaging, archiving and managing print shops) and financing for purchase.

However, as Xerox extended the scope of its services and took end to end responsibility for managing the copiers and printers on the premises of a large customer, it started charging the customer only for the number of pages processed by each device. Xerox retained ownership of equipment; it thus converted fixed costs into variable costs for the customer. The offer was not limited to Xerox's own equipment but for all copiers and printers in customer premises, irrespective of their manufacturer or location.

Some of the metrics Xerox was tracking in this regard included growth in services signings (which reflected the year-over-year increase in estimated future revenues from contracts signed during the period); growth in services pipeline (which measured the year-over-year increase in new business opportunities); growth in the number of machines-in-the-field (also known as MIF, which showed new equipment installations) and growth in page volume and in colour pages printed (which indicated value-added since colour pages generated more revenue per page than black-and-white).

The company's value proposition to its customers was that it offered a "combination of painkiller and steroid."[24] Reducing costs and boosting productivity comprised the painkiller. Leveraging documents and making it easier for customers to grow their business comprised the steroid.

Services Orientation

It was in the 1990s that Xerox had developed, in-house, an online knowledge-sharing system for its community of mobile technicians,

Appendix: Cases

numbering about 25,000 worldwide at the time. Known as Eureka, the system was meant to help them resolve repair issues with the company's printers, copiers and fax machines at customer premises. Every technician carried a notebook computer containing a subset of the Eureka database around his or her area of expertise. It enabled them to connect with peers in the company on the web and solve a product glitch in a day as opposed to the weeks it would have taken previously. The pilot deployment in France in 1995 showed that Eureka saved an average of 5 per cent of a technician's time in diagnosing a problem and an average of 5 per cent in parts expenditures. With over a million service calls per month worldwide,[25] the results seemed promising.

Eureka was designed as a repository of product fixes. It gained ground because of two factors. Technicians everywhere generally "loved to talk about how they figured out nasty problems."[26] They also used all of their senses in documenting the trouble shooting – smells, noises and so on. Eureka had a short audio file in which the technician recorded the sounds a device made at various repair stages.

XEROX INNOVATION GROUP

XIG was founded on a conviction that "Something is only an innovation if it makes a difference to our clients or to the world."[27]

Said Vandebroek:

Our innovation projects have three time horizons: short, mid and long term. They tie up with three different roles we play at XIG: partner, incubator and explorer. In partnership projects, we provide direct support for business units who are commercializing the new technologies we incubated previously; they cover 35 per cent of our research investments. Incubation projects, led by XIG researchers, create options for the next generation technologies and services; they cover another 35 per cent of our investments. Exploration projects are meant to develop new insights into the potential of new technologies and create significant new intellectual property; they cover 30 per cent of our investments at XIG [see Exhibit 4].

The R&D activities at Xerox were characterized by a hybrid model. Business groups had their own R&D activities embedded into their

Appendix: Cases

operations; they were supported by XIG for more complex and strategic projects that had originated in the research labs. This generated economies of scale for Xerox since the innovation developed for one business group could often be applied to others. The relationship between XIG and the business groups was governed by annual contracts. Every year, business groups and XIG agreed on the technologies that would be investigated by XIG for which it charged an annual fee.

Customer-led Innovation

Xerox saw the beginnings of customer-led innovation when the Xerox Research Centre Europe set up a Technology Innovation Showroom at Grenoble in France in 1996.

Patrick Mazeau, who was among the early recruits at Grenoble, said:

> The Technology Showroom is a place where Xerox researchers and Xerox marketers get together for an informal exchange with Xerox customers. It provides a platform for researchers to showcase their innovative ideas and relate those ideas to the larger context of generating customer value. The Technology Showroom has a two-fold objective of demonstrating the results of ongoing research at Xerox and gather insights for further research.

The concept was extended to other research centres at Xerox and results were soon becoming evident.

As an example, in 2004, a team of researchers at the company's Webster centre conceived of a printer with two engines rather than one. The normal practice at the company until then was to build a prototype, pilot it, test the product for quality and launch it. Xerox had such a strong hold on the market that it could sell a new release without customer input and respond to complaints, if any, with changes in subsequent versions. But the development team at Webster had set up a focus group to get some preliminary feedback from existing and potential customers. The session was webcast live to the company's product developers who were surprised at how wrong they were in their assessment of customer needs. They had thought, for example, that a second engine would be no more than an accompaniment that a customer would switch on only for special requirements like colour prints.

The feedback, which was spontaneous, was that a second engine was a necessity since it ensured that the printer would be running, even at slow speed, in the event of a breakdown of one engine until help arrived from the company.

There was growing evidence that customer-led innovation was becoming a fountainhead of new ideas at Xerox. For example, the PARC ethnographic researchers had noticed during client visits that 44 per cent of printed documents were being disposed of as garbage within a day.[28] They were now researching a process they called re-usable paper (or on-the-spot recycling) by which the print could be erased and the paper used again.

Innovation was also being internalized at Xerox, aimed at finding ways of increasing the productivity of different categories of employees based on an understanding of not only the nature of work they performed but also their interactions with one another. For example, a researcher at XIG noticed that service technicians often made it a point to spend time not with customers but with each other. They would hang out in common areas like store rooms. Based on the perception that a service technician worked alone, a common first reaction would be that this was a drain on productivity. But the researcher, who had an anthropology background, noticed that field service was a social activity and that technicians were not slacking off while being together. They were doing some of the most valuable work in terms of sharing insights on how to repair machines quicker and better.[29]

ISSUES AT HAND

There were two areas that needed attention: reinforcing customer focus among XIG researchers and reinvigorating a platform-based research and development approach.

Customer Focus Among XIG Researchers

Xerox was traditionally known for its customer focus with initiatives like Key Accounts Management wherein every large customer had dedicated sales and support staff serving its needs. Customer focus was seen as a key success factor in the launch of new product-service combinations.

Said Vandebroek:

> Customer focus would be a good motivation for researchers at XIG because it improves the success rate of transferring research ideas into products and solutions that the customer would want to buy. Development usually follows a funnel model in which only a few products make it to the market. When you now start creating new services, the funnel dynamic changes. The research and development cycle for a printer, for example, spans across several years. A service, on the other hand, can be created more rapidly because it requires mostly reinforcements in terms of software and people. Depending on the complexity and modularity of the software, this could happen much more rapidly.

As she examined her options in helping researchers in XIG truly understand the customers' pain points and dreams, Vandebroek also wondered whether it was time for Xerox to open a new research centre dedicated to services and whether it could be located in an emerging market. The company's four existing research centres, focused on technology products, were all based in the developed world. The United States, which housed two of its centres, continued to be the global leader in innovation in 2007 with a score of 5.8 on the Global Innovation Index (GII) (see Exhibit 5).[30] GII was compiled annually on the basis of five input elements (institutions and policies; human capacity; infrastructure; technological sophistication; and business markets & capital) and three output elements (knowledge; competitiveness; and wealth).

The dilemma was about the choice of a new location in emerging markets. There was an opportunity to locate a new lab in a country of the BRIC (Brazil, Russia, India and China) quartet (see Exhibit 6). India and China had already shown innovation potential on elements like manufacturing and IT. Efforts were under way by respective governments to make the BRIC markets a "formidable"[31] part of the global innovation network.

Competency Alignment

The product-service combination had to be holistic; that is, it had to be built around the entire business of the customer. XIG had to develop domain expertise in different verticals like healthcare, banking, insurance and retail.

Said Vandebroek:

> It is the willingness to move beyond our core competencies that is critical to the success of creating new product-service combinations. Once we build modular and scalable platforms, we will be able to replicate them across different verticals while tailoring [them] to the needs of different customers in each vertical. For example, once we develop software infrastructure that links all output devices in customer premises, we can deploy solutions at customer sites anywhere in the world. Once the sites are connected to a uniform software platform, end users can print any document on any device. They don't need to know the print driver specifics for example. That is a competency we needed to build.

There was also an issue on the sales side. Product salespeople at Xerox were used to meeting with the purchase managers of customer companies. Selling product service combinations required them to be meeting with senior executives like chief information officers or chief financial officers. The sales process would become complex because the presentation techniques would be different at different levels. The time taken for closure of a sale would also be longer because salespeople had to address questions at different levels.

Emerging markets, which offered renewed growth potential to Xerox, presented additional problems. For example, while English was a universal language in North America and (to a lesser extent) in Europe, an emerging market like India had 178 "vigorous" languages.[32] This brought its own complexity for XIG in three areas: finding an interface between researchers, salespersons and customers; developing software platforms; and deploying product-service combinations at customer sites.

As Vandebroek sat in her virtual office in Boston and pondered over the strategic and organizational issues coming up at XIG, she wondered how she should address them.

Appendix: Cases

EXHIBIT 1: XEROX CORP – CONSOLIDATED INCOME STATEMENT

Year ending December ($millions)	2006	2005	2004	2003	2002
Revenue					
-Sales	7,464	7,400	7,259	6,970	6,752
-Service, outsourcing and rentals	7,591	7,426	7,529	7.734	8,097
-Finance income	840	875	934	997	1,000
Total revenue	15,895	15,701	15,722	15,701	15,849
Less Expenditure					
-Cost of sales	4,803	4,695	5,545	4,436	4,233
-Cost of service, outsourcing and rentals	4,328	4,207	4,295	4,311	4,494
-Equipment financing interest	305	326	345	362	401
-R&D costs	922	943	914	868	917
-Selling, admin and general expenses	4,008	4,110	4,203	4,249	4,437
-Restructuring charges	385	366	86	176	670
-Acquisition related costs	-	-	-	-	-
-Amortization of intangible assets	-	-	-	-	-
-Others	336	224	369	863	593
Total expenditure	15,087	14,871	14,757	15,265	15,745
Net income	1,210	978	859	360	91

Source: Company annual report 2006 (p. 50) and 2003 (p. 38).

EXHIBIT 2: XEROX CORP – REVENUE BREAKDOWN

Year ending December ($millions)	2006	2005	2004	2003	2002
Geographies					
-USA	8,406	8,388	8,346	8,547	9,096
-Europe	5,378	5,226	5,281	4,863	4,425
-Others	2,111	2,087	2,095	2,291	2,328
Total	15,895	15,701	15,722	15,701	15,849
Business segments					
-Equipment sales	4,457	4,519	4,480	4,250	3,970
-Service, outsourcing and rentals	7,591	7,426	7,529	7,734	8,097
-Finance income	840	875	934	997	1,000
-Supplies, paper and other sales	3,007	2,881	2,779	2,720	2,782
Total	15,895	15,701	15,722	15,701	15,849

Source: Company annual reports.

Appendix: Cases

EXHIBIT 3: NUMBER OF PATENTS GRANTED TO XEROX YEAR-WISE 1976-2006

Year	Number	Year	Number	Year	Number
1976	647	c/f	4,334	c/f	11,260
1977	585	1987	384	1997	1,057
1978	517	1988	430	1998	1,445
1979	216	1989	497	1999	1,284
1980	242	1990	477	2000	1,128
1981	322	1991	559	2001	1,313
1982	302	1992	758	2002	1,257
1983	310	1993	853	2003	1,190
1984	355	1994	936	2004	1,044
1985	464	1995	923	2005	975
1986	374	1996	1,109	2006	1,227
Subtotal	4,334	Subtotal	11,260	**Grand Total**	**23,180**

Source: http://appft.uspto.gov/netahtml/PTO/search-bool.html, accessed December 12, 2013.

Appendix: Cases

EXHIBIT 4: INNOVATION PROJECTS

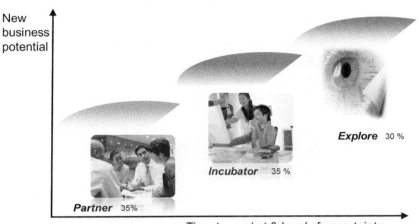

Source: Company files.

Appendix: Cases

EXHIBIT 5: GLOBAL INNOVATION INDEX 2007

Rank	Country	Score
1	US	5.80
2	Germany	4.89
3	UK	4.81
4	Japan	4.48
5	France	4.32
6	Switzerland	4.16
7	Singapore	4.10
8	Canada	4.06
9	Netherlands	3.99
10	Hong Kong	3.97
23	India	3.57
29	China	3.21
40	Brazil	2.84
54	Russian Federation	2.60

Source: www.globalinnovationindex.org/userfiles/file/GII-2007-Report, accessed December 10, 2013.

Appendix: Cases

EXHIBIT 6: BRIC MARKETS – PROFILE 2007

Country and Metrics	Unit	Actual			Forecast		
		2005	2006	2007	2008	2009	2010
BRAZIL							
Global Innovation Index		NA	NA	2.84	-	-	-
Population	Million	184.2	186.8	189.3	191.9	194.4	196.8
GDP	$billion	882.0	1,067.0	1,291.0	1,350.0	1,333.0	1,398.0
Consumer Price Inflation	%	6.9	4.2	3.5	3.9	4.0	3.8
Personal disposable income	$billion	403.5	457.8	539.2	534.1	496.2	512.9
RUSSIA							
Global Innovation Index		NA	NA	2.60	-	-	-
Population	Million	143.1	142.6	142.3	141.8	141.4	141.0
GDP	$billion	764.0	985.0	1,183.0	1.355.0	1,494.0	1,642.0
Consumer Price Inflation	%	12.7	9.7	7.8	7.6	7.4	7.0
Personal disposable income	$billion	443.0	552.0	694.0	819.0	930.0	1,054.0

EXHIBIT 6: *Continued*

Country and Metrics	Unit	Actual			Forecast		
		2005	2006	2007	2008	2009	2010
INDIA							
Global Innovation Index		NA	NA	3.57	-	-	-
Population	Million	1,080.0	1,095.0	1,110.0	1,125.0	1,140.0	1,155.0
GDP	$billion	806.0	916.0	1,141.0	1,325.0	1,513.0	1,721.0
Consumer Price Inflation	%	4.2	6.2	5.9	5.2	5.0	5.0
Personal disposable income	$billion	631.0	723.0	872.0	1,003.0	1,134.0	1,273.0
CHINA							
Global Innovation Index		NA	NA	3.21	-	-	-
Population	Million	1,308.0	1,314.0	1,323.0	1,331.0	1,337.0	1,342.0
GDP	$billion	2,278.0	2,720.0	3,250.0	3,832.0	4,481.0	5,231.0
Consumer Price Inflation	%	1.8	1.7	3.0	3.0	3.3	3.3
Personal disposable income	$billion	902.0	956.0	1,050.0	1.170.0	1,320.0	1,497.0

Sources: www.globalinnovationindex.org/userfiles/file/GII yearly report for 2007, www.eiu.com.proxy1.lib.uwo.ca/default.aspx country reports mid-2007, accessed October 25, 2013.

Appendix: Cases

Notes

1 *2003 Annual Report, p. 3*

2 *J Lundy, "Rightsizing Output Fleets: The Hidden Goldmine," DF-13-2054, March 2001, www.fujixerox.co.nz/library/01245375-d161-410d-aab9-2227fed978e0.cmr, accessed September 21, 2013.*

3 *Francois Ragnet, "The Less Paper Office," www.xerox.com/downloads/usa/en/t/ TL_whitepaper_less_paper_ office_Francois_Ragnet.pdf, accessed September 20, 2013.*

4 *Simon Mingay, "Green IT: The New Industry Shock Wave," Gartner Ras Core Research Note, G00153703, December 2007.*

5 *Net Generation was identified as comprising those born between January 1977 and December 1997. Dan Tapscott, "How the Net Generation is Changing Your World," McGraw-Hill, Columbus OH, 2009.*

6 *"The Office of the Future: An in-depth view of how word processing will reshape the corporate office," Business Week 30 June 1975, Executive Briefing, pp 48-71.*

7 *Generation Next was identified as comprising those born after January 1998. Dan Tapscott, "How the Net Generation is Changing Your World," McGraw-Hill, Columbus OH, 2009.*

8 *www.youtube.com/watch?v=8rC1pzgoRNU, accessed September 28, 2013.*

9 *P&G had a total of 55,000 office devices in its 400 locations around the globe. It took Xerox 18 months to roll out its Managed Print Services at P&G worldwide at the end of which P&G had 6,000 devices. Only about 10 per cent of the original devices were Xerox devices. Xerox marginally increased its footprint while eliminating competition altogether at P&G.*

10 *All currencies are in US dollars unless otherwise stated.*

11 *http://fr.slideshare.net/adampage1976/global-print-markets-to-2016 accessed November 3, 2013*

12 *Xerox annual report 2006 page 15*

13 *One petabyte equaled 1,000 terabytes; 1000 petabytes equaled one exabyte and 1,000 exabytes equaled one zettabyte www.whatsabyte.com accessed September 28, 2013*

14 *John F Gantz et al, "The Expanding Digital Universe: A Forecast of Worldwide Information Growth Through 2010," www.emc.com/collateral/analyst-reports/ expanding-digital-idc-white-paper.pdf March 2007 accessed September 22, 2013*

15 *www.businessweek.com/innovate/content/apr2007/id20070418_025021_ page_3.htm accessed May 30, 2012*

16 *www.parc.com/about_us, accessed June 20, 2012.*

17 *http://articles.economictimes.indiatimes.com/2010-03-22/news/27586848_1_ innovation-hub-innovation-lab-open-innovation, accessed September 23, 2013.*

18 *Henry Chesbrough, "Open services Innovation: Rethinking your Business to grow and Compete in a new era," Jossey-Bass USA 2011 pp115-118, accessed August 15, 2013.*

19 *Xerox Annual Report 2002 page 4.*

20 *Xerox Annual Report 2006 page 3.*

21 *Ibid.*

22 *Ibid, p. 5.*

23 *Ibid, p. 37.*

24 *Ibid, p. 6.*

25 *Connie Moore, "Best Practices: Eureka! Xerox discovers way to grow community knowledge. And customer satisfaction," KM World, October 1999, Volume 8 Issue 10,*

www.kmworld.com/Articles/Editorial/Features/Best-Practices-Eureka!-Xerox-discovers-way-to-grow-community-knowledge.-.-And-customer-satisfaction-9140.aspx, accessed February 16, 2014.

26 Sarah L. Roberts-Witt, "A Eureka moment at Xerox!"www.pcmag.com/article2/0, 2817,28792,00.asp, accessed June 03, 2012.

27 www.xerox.ca/innovation/enca.html, accessed September 27, 2013.

28 Nanette Byrnes, "Xerox refocuses on its customers" Business Week April 18, 2007, www.businessweek.com/innovate/content/apr2007/id20070418_025021_page_3.htm, accessed May 30, 2013.

29 John Seely Brown and Estee Solomon Gray, "The People Are the Company: How to build your company around your people," Fast Company October 31, 1995, www.fastcompany.com/magazine/01/people.html?page=0%2C3, accessed June 03, 2012.

30 www.globalinnovationindex.org/userfiles/file/GII-2007-Report.pdf, accessed December 10, 2013.

31 "The World's Top Innovators", January-February 2007, p. 33, http://www.world businesslive.com, accessed October 21, 2013.

32 http://www.ethnologue.com/country/IN, accessed December 12, 2013.

References

Achcaoucaou, F., Miravitlles, P. and León-Darder, F. (2014) 'Knowledge sharing and subsidiary R&D mandate development: A matter of dual embeddedness' *International Business Review*, 23(1): 76–90.

Acworth, E.B. (2008) 'University–industry engagement: The formation of the Knowledge Integration Community (KIC) model at the Cambridge-MIT Institute' *Research Policy*, 37(8): 1241–1254.

Ahuja, G. and Morris Lampert, C. (2001) 'Entrepreneurship in the large corporation: A longitudinal study of how established firms create breakthrough inventions' *Strategic Management Journal*, 22(6–7): 521–543.

Almeida, P. (1996) 'Knowledge sourcing by foreign multinationals: Patent citation analysis in the US semiconductor industry' *Strategic Management Journal*, 17(S2): 155–165.

Alvarez, S.A. (2007) 'Entrepreneurial rents and the theory of the firm' *Journal of Business Venturing*, 22(3): 427–442.

Alvarez, S.A. and Busenitz, L.W. (2001) 'The entrepreneurship of resource-based theory' *Journal of Management*, 27(6): 755–775.

Alvarez, S.A., Ireland, R.D. and Reuer, J.J. (2006) 'Editorial: Entrepreneurship and strategic alliances' *Journal of Business Venturing*, 21(4): 401–404.

Ambos, B. and Mahnke, V. (2010) 'How do MNC headquarters add value?' *Management International Review*, 50(4): 403–412.

Ambos, T.C., Andersson, U. and Birkinshaw, J. (2010) 'What are the consequences of initiative-taking in multinational subsidiaries?' *Journal of International Business Studies*, 41(7): 1099–1118.

Anand, J., Capron, L. and Mitchell, W. (2005) 'Using acquisitions to access multinational diversity: Thinking beyond the domestic versus cross-border M&A comparison' *Industrial and Corporate Change*, 14(2): 191–224.

Andal-Ancion, A., Cartwright, P. and Yip, G.S. (2003) 'The digital transformation of traditional business' *MIT Sloan Management Review*, 44(4): 34–41.

Andersson, U., Björkman, I. and Forsgren, M. (2005) 'Managing subsidiary knowledge creation: The effect of control mechanisms on subsidiary local embeddedness' *International Business Review*, 14(5): 521–538.

Andersson, U. and Forsgren, M. (1996) 'Subsidiary embeddedness and control in the multinational corporation' *International Business Review*, 5(5): 487–508.

Andersson, U., Forsgren, M. and Holm, U. (2002) 'The strategic impact of external networks: Subsidiary performance and competence development in the multinational corporation' *Strategic Management Journal*, 23(11): 979–996.

Andersson, U. and Pahlberg, C. (1997) 'Subsidiary influence on strategic behaviour in MNCs: An empirical study' *International Business Review*, 6(3): 319–334.

Ankrah, S. and Al-Tabbaa, O. (2015) 'Universities–industry collaboration: A literature review' *Scandinavian Journal of Management*, 31(3): 387–408.

Ardichvili, A., Cardozo, R. and Ray, S. (2003) 'A theory of entrepreneurial opportunity identification and development' *Journal of Business Venturing*, 18(1): 105–123.

Barney, J.B. (1991) 'Firm resources and sustained competitive advantage' *Journal of Management*, 17(1): 99–120.

Baron, R.A. (1998) 'Cognitive mechanisms in entrepreneurship: Why and when entrepreneurs think differently than other people' *Journal of Business Venturing*, 13(4): 275–294.

Baron, R.A. (2004) 'The cognitive perspective: A valuable tool for answering entrepreneurship's basic "why" questions' *Journal of Business Venturing*, 19(2): 221–239.

Barrick, M.R., Bradley, B.H., Kristof-Brown, A.L. and Colbert, A.E. (2007) 'The moderating role of top management team interdependence: Implications for real teams and working groups' *Academy of Management Journal*, 50(3): 544–557.

Bartlett, C. and Ghoshal, S. (1989) *Managing Across Borders: The Transnational Solution*. Harvard Business School Press, Boston.

Bartlett, C. and Ghoshal, S. (2003) 'Managing in a transnational network: New management roles, new personal competencies' in McKern, B. (ed.) *Managing the Global Network Corporation*, Routledge, London, pp. 260–283.

Beamish, P.W. and Roberts, M. (2010) 'Lundbeck Korea: Managing an International Growth Engine' (Ivey Publishing, product number: 9B10M012).

Bengtsson, M. and Kock, S. (2014) 'Coopetition—Quo vadis? Past accomplishments and future challenges' *Industrial Marketing Management*, 43(2): 180–188.

Berman, S.J. (2012) 'Digital transformation: Opportunities to create new business models' *Strategy & Leadership*, 40(2): 16–24.

Berry, H. (2014) 'Global integration and innovation: Multicountry knowledge generation within MNCs' *Strategic Management Journal*, 35(6): 869–890.

Berry, H., Guillén, M.F. and Zhou, N. (2010) 'An institutional approach to cross-national distance' *Journal of International Business Studies*, 41(9): 1460–1480.

Billington, C. and Davidson, R. (2010) 'Using knowledge brokering to improve business processes' *McKinsey Quarterly*, McKinsey&Company, January: 1–9.

Birkinshaw, J. (1997) 'Entrepreneurship in multinational corporations: The characteristics of subsidiary initiatives' *Strategic Management Journal*, 18(3): 207–229.

Birkinshaw, J. (2000) *Entrepreneurship in the Global Firm*. SAGE, London.

Birkinshaw, J. and Ridderstråle, J. (1999) 'Fighting the corporate immune system: A process study of subsidiary initiatives in multinational corporations' *International Business Review*, 8(2): 149–180.

Brandenburger, A.M. and Nalebuff, B.J. (2011) *Co-opetition*. Doubleday, New York.

Brown, S.L. and Eisenhardt, K.M. (1997) 'The art of continuous change: Linking complexity theory and time-paced evolution in relentlessly shifting organizations' *Administrative Science Quarterly*, 42(1): 1–34.

Buckley, P.J. and Casson, M. (1976) *The Future of the Multinational Enterprise*. MacMillan, London.

Buckley, P.J., Clegg, L.J., Cross, A.R., Liu, X., Voss, H. and Zheng, P. (2007) 'The determinants of Chinese outward foreign direct investment' *Journal of International Business Studies*, 38(4):499–518.

Burgelman, R. (1983) 'A process model of internal corporate venturing in the diversified major firm' *Administrative Science Quarterly*, 28(2): 223–244.

Burgelman, R. and Sayles, L.R. (1986) *Inside Corporate Innovation: Strategy, Structure, and Management Skills*. The Free Press, New York.

Burt, R. (1997) 'The contingent value of social capital' *Administrative Science Quarterly*, 42(2): 339–365.

Cantwell, J. and Mudambi, R. (2005) 'MNE competence-creating subsidiary mandates' *Strategic Management Journal*, 26(12): 1109–1128.

Cantwell, J.A. and Santangelo, G.D. (1999) 'The frontier of international technology networks: Sourcing abroad the most highly tacit capabilities' *Information Economics and Policy*, 11(1): 101–123.

Champion, D. (2001) 'Mastering the value chain: An interview with Mark Levin of Millennium Pharmaceuticals' *Harvard Business Review*, 79(6): 108–115.

Chandler, A.D. (1962) *Strategy and Structure*. The MIT Press, Cambridge, MA.

Chapman, G. (2013) *The Land Rover Story*. The History Press, Stroud.

Chen, T-J., Chen, H. and Ku, Y-H. (2004) 'Foreign direct investment and local linkages' *Journal of International Business Studies*, 32(3): 401–419.

Chesbrough, H.W. (2006) 'Open innovation: A new paradigm for understanding industrial innovation' in Chesbrough, H.W., W. Vanhaverbeke and J. West (eds.) *Open Innovation: Researching a New Paradigm*, Oxford University Press, Oxford, pp. 1–12.

Chesbrough, H.W. and Garman, A.R. (2009) 'How open innovation can help you cope in lean times' *Harvard Business Review*, 87(12): 68–76.

Ciabuschi, F., Dellestrand, H. and Martín, O.M. (2011) 'Internal embeddedness, headquarters involvement, and innovation importance in multinational enterprises' *Journal of Management Studies*, 48(7): 1612–1639.

Cohen, W.M. and Levinthal, D.A. (1990) 'Absorptive capacity: A new perspective on learning and innovation' *Administrative Science Quarterly*, 35(1): 128–152.

Colovic, A. and Lamotte, O. (2014) 'The role of formal industry clusters in the internationalization of new ventures' *European Business Review*, 26(5): 449–470.

Cooper, R.G. (2008) 'Perspective: The Stage-Gate® idea-to-launch process—Update, what's new, and NexGen systems' *Journal of Product Innovation Management*, 25(3): 213–232.

Cooper, R.G., Edgett, S.J. and Kleinschmidt, E.J. (2002) 'Optimizing the stage-gate process: What best-practice companies do—II' *Research-Technology Management*, 45(6): 43–49.

Corbett, A.C. (2007) 'Learning asymmetries and the discovery of entrepreneurial opportunities' *Journal of Business Venturing*, 22(1): 97–118.

Coviello, N.E., McDougall, P.P. and Oviatt, B.M. (2011) 'The emergence, advance and future of international entrepreneurship research—An introduction to the special forum' *Journal of Business Venturing*, 26(6): 625–631.

Covin, J.G. (1991) 'Entrepreneurial versus conservative firms: A comparison of strategies and performance' *Journal of Management Studies*, 28(5): 439–462.

Covin, J.G. and Lumpkin, G.T. (2011) 'Entrepreneurial orientation theory and research: Reflections on a needed construct' *Entrepreneurship Theory and Practice*, 35(5): 855–872.

Covin, J.G. and Miller, D. (2014) 'International entrepreneurial orientation: Conceptual considerations, research themes, measurement issues, and future research directions' *Entrepreneurship Theory and Practice*, 38(1): 11–44.

Crant, M.J. (2000) 'Proactive behaviour in organizations' *Journal of Management*, 26(3): 435–462.

da Rocha, A., Simões, V.C., de Mello, R.C. and Carneiro, J. (2017) 'From global start-ups to the borderless firm: Why and how to build a worldwide value system' *Journal of International Entrepreneurship*, 15(2): 121–144.

De Clercq, D., Castañer, X. and Belausteguigoitia, I. (2011) 'Entrepreneurial initiative selling within organizations: Towards a more comprehensive motivational framework' *Journal of Management Studies*, 48(6): 1269–1290.

Deal, T.E. and Kennedy, A.A. (1982) *Corporate Cultures: The Rites and Rituals of Corporate Life*. Addison Wesley, Reading, MA.

Delany, E. (2000) 'Strategic development of the multinational subsidiary through subsidiary initiative-taking' *Long Range Planning*, 33(2): 220–244.

Dess, G., Ireland, R., Zahra, S., Floyd, S., Janney, J. and Lane, P. (2003) 'Emerging issues in corporate entrepreneurship' *Journal of Management*, 29(3): 351–378.

Dess, G.G. and Lumpkin, G.T. (2005) 'The role of entrepreneurial orientation in stimulating effective corporate entrepreneurship' *The Academy of Management Executive*, 19(1): 147–156.

References

Dess, G.G., Lumpkin, G.T. and Covin, J.G. (1997) 'Entrepreneurial strategy making and firm performance: Tests of contingency and configuration models' *Strategic Management Journal*, 18(9): 677–695.

Dhanaraj, C., Lyles, M. and Lai, Y. (2007) 'Innovation without Walls: Alliance Management at Eli Lilly and Company' (Ivey Publishing, product number: 9B07M015).

Dimitratos, P. and Plakoyiannaki, E. (2003) 'Theoretical foundations of an international entrepreneurial culture' *Journal of International Entrepreneurship*, 1(2): 187–215.

Dimitratos, P., Plakoyiannaki, E., Pitsoulaki, A. and Tüselmann, H.J. (2010) 'The global smaller firm in international entrepreneurship' *International Business Review*, 19(6): 589–606.

Dittrich, K., Duysters, G. and de Man, A-P. (2007) 'Strategic repositioning by means of alliance networks: The case of IBM' *Research Policy*, 36(10): 1496–1511.

Dooley, L. and O'Sullivan, D. (2007) 'Managing within distributed innovation networks' *International Journal of Innovation Management*, 11(3): 397–416.

Dörrenbächer, C. and Gammelgaard, J. (2006) 'Subsidiary role development: The effect of micro-political headquarters–subsidiary negotiations on the product, market and value-added scope of foreign-owned subsidiaries' *Journal of International Management*, 12(3): 266–283.

Dörrenbächer, C. and Geppert, M. (2006) 'Micro-politics and conflicts in multinational corporations: Current debates, re-framing, and contributions of this special issue' *Journal of International Management*, 12(3): 251–265.

Doz, Y. and Prahalad, C.K. (1984) 'Patterns of strategic control within multinational corporations' *Journal of International Business Studies*, 15(2): 55–72.

Du, J. and Williams, C. (2017) 'Innovative projects between MNE subsidiaries and local partners in China: Exploring locations and inter-organizational trust' *Journal of International Management*, 23(1): 16–31.

Dunning, J. (1981) *International Production and the Multinational Enterprise*. Allen and Unwin, London.

Dunning, J. (1988) 'The eclectic paradigm of international production: A restatement and some possible extensions' *Journal of International Business Studies*, 19(1): 1–31.

Dunning, J. (1994) 'Multinational enterprises and the globalization of innovatory capacity' *Research Policy*, 23(1): 67–89.

Dunning, J. (2000) 'The eclectic paradigm as an envelope for economic and business theories of MNE activity' *International Business Review*, 9(2): 163–190.

Dunning, J.H. (2002) *Regions, Globalization, and the Knowledge-Based Economy*. Oxford University Press, Oxford.

Dyer, J.H., Powell, B.C., Sakakibara, M. and Wang, A.J. (2007) 'The determinants of success in R&D alliances' *Academy of Management Proceedings*, 2007(1): 1–6.

Ecker, B., van Triest, S. and Williams, C. (2013) 'Management control and the decentralization of R&D' *Journal of Management*, 39(4): 906–927.

Eckhardt, J.T. and Shane, S.A. (2003) 'Opportunities and entrepreneurship' *Journal of Management*, 29(3): 333–349.

Edström, A. and Galbraith, J.R. (1977) 'Transfer of managers as a coordination and control strategy in multinational organizations' *Administrative Science Quarterly*, 22(2): 248–263.

Egelhoff, W.G. (2010) 'How the parent headquarters adds value to an MNC' *Management International Review*, 50(4): 413–431.

Eisenhardt, K.M. (1985) 'Control: Organizational and economic approaches' *Management Science*, 31(2): 134–149.

Eisenhardt, K.M. (1989a) 'Agency theory: An assessment and review' *Academy of Management Review*, 14(1): 57–74.

Eisenhardt, K.M. (1989b) 'Making fast strategic decisions in high velocity environments' *Academy of Management Journal*, 32(3): 543–577.

Eisenhardt, K.M. and Martin, J.A. (2000) 'Dynamic capabilities: What are they?' *Strategic Management Journal*, 21(10/11): 1105–1121.

Ethiraj, S., Kale, P., Krishnan, M.S. and Singh, J. (2005) 'Where do capabilities come from and how do they matter? A study in the software services industry' *Strategic Management Journal*, 26(1): 25–45.

Etzkowitz, H. (2010) *The Triple Helix: University-Industry-Government Innovation in Action*. Routledge, New York.

Etzkowitz, H., Webster, A., Gebhardt, C. and Terra, B.R.C. (2000) 'The future of the university and the university of the future: Evolution of ivory tower to entrepreneurial paradigm' *Research Policy*, 29(2): 313–330.

Evans, J. and Mavondo, F.T. (2002) 'Psychic distance and organizational performance: An empirical examination of international retailing operations' *Journal of International Business Studies*, 33(3): 515–532.

Evans, W.R. and Davis, W.D. (2005) 'High-performance work systems and organizational performance: The mediating role of internal social structure' *Journal of Management*, 31(5): 758–775.

Fombrun, C.J. and Ginsberg, A. (1990) 'Shifting gears: Enabling change in corporate aggressiveness' *Strategic Management Journal*, 11(4): 297–308.

Forsgren, M. (2016) 'A note on the revisited Uppsala internationalization process model—The implications of business networks and entrepreneurship' *Journal of International Business Studies*, 47(9): 1135–1144.

Freeman, C. (1995) 'The "National System of Innovation" in historical perspective' *Cambridge Journal of Economics*, 19(1): 5–24.

Frost, T. and Zhou, C. (2000) 'The geography of foreign R&D within a host country: An evolutionary perspective on location-technology selection by multinationals' *International Studies of Management and Organization*, 30(2): 10–43.

References

Galán-Muros, V. and Plewa, C. (2016) 'What drives and inhibits university-business cooperation in Europe? A comprehensive assessment' *R&D Management*, 46(2): 369–382.

Gammelgaard, J. and Hobdari, B. (2013) 'Subsidiary strategic responsibilities and autonomy in Carlsberg' in Gammelgaard, J. and C. Dörrenbächer (eds.) *The Global Brewing Industry: Markets, Strategies and Rivalries*, Edward Elgar Publishing, Cheltenham, UK, pp. 199–222.

Garcia-Pont, C., Canales, J.I. and Noboa, F. (2009) 'Subsidiary strategy: The embeddedness component' *Journal of Management Studies*, 46(2): 182–214.

Garud, R. and Van de Ven, A.H. (1992) 'An empirical evaluation of the internal corporate venturing process' *Strategic Management Journal*, 13(S1): 93–109.

Gassmann, O. and Enkel, E. (2004) 'Towards a theory of open innovation: Three core process archetypes' *R&D Management Conference (RADMA)* Lisbon, Portugal.

George, G., Wiklund, J. and Zahra, S.A. (2005) 'Ownership and the internationalization of small firms' *Journal of Management*, 31(2): 210–233.

George, G., Zahra, S.A. and Wood, D.R. (2002) 'The effects of business–university alliances on innovative output and financial performance: A study of publicly traded biotechnology companies' *Journal of Business Venturing*, 17(6): 577–609.

Ghemawat, P. (2011) *World 3.0: Global Prosperity and How to Achieve it*. Harvard Business Press, Boston, MA.

Ghoshal, S. and Bartlett, C.A. (1988) 'Creation, adoption and diffusion of innovations by subsidiaries of multinational corporations' *Journal of International Business Studies*, 19(3): 365–388.

Ghoshal, S. and Nohria, N. (1989) 'Internal differentiation within multinational corporations' *Strategic Management Journal*, 10(4): 323–337.

Gilbert, B.A., McDougall, P.P. and Audretsch, D.B. (2008) 'Clusters, knowledge spillovers and new venture performance: An empirical examination' *Journal of Business Venturing*, 23(4): 405–422.

Global Competitiveness Report (2015) www.weforum.org/reports/global-competitiveness-report-2014-2015 accessed 21 June 2017.

Granovetter, M. (1983) 'The strength of weak ties: A network theory revisited' *Sociological Theory*, 1: 201–233.

Guest, R. (2011) *Borderless Economics: Chinese Sea Turtles, Indian Fridges and the New Fruits of Global Capitalism*. Macmillan, London.

Gulati, R. (1998) 'Alliances and networks' *Strategic Management Journal*, 19(4): 293–317.

Gupta, A.K., Govindarajan, V. and Malhotra, A. (1999) 'Feedback-seeking behaviour within multinational corporations' *Strategic Management Journal*, 20(3): 205–222.

Gupta, A. and Govindarajan, V. (2000) 'Knowledge flows within multinational corporations' *Strategic Management Journal*, 21(4): 473–496.

Guth, W.D. and Ginsberg, A. (1990) 'Guest editors' introduction: Corporate entrepreneurship' *Strategic Management Journal*, 11(Special Issue: Corporate Entrepreneurship): 5–15.

Haas, M.R. and Cummings, J.N. (2015) 'Barriers to knowledge seeking within MNC teams: Which differences matter most?' *Journal of International Business Studies*, 46(1): 36–62.

Hart, S.L. (1992) 'An integrative framework for strategy-making processes' *Academy of Management Review*, 17(2): 327–351.

Haskell, N., Veilleux, S. and Béliveau, D. (2016) 'Functional and contextual dimensions of INVs' alliance partner selection' *Journal of International Entrepreneurship*, 14(4): 483–512.

Hayek, F.A. (1945) 'The use of knowledge in society' *The American Economic Review*, 35(4): 519–530.

Hayward, M.L.A. (2002) 'When do firms learn from their acquisition experience? Evidence from 1990–1995' *Strategic Management Journal*, 23(1): 21–39.

Hedlund, G. (1980) 'The role of foreign subsidiaries in strategic decision-making in Swedish multinational corporations' *Strategic Management Journal*, 1(1): 23–36.

Hedlund, G. (1994) 'A model of knowledge management and the N-form corporation' *Strategic Management Journal*, 15(S2): 73–90.

Hedlund, G. and Rolander, D. (1990) 'Action in heterarchies—New approaches to managing the MNC' in Bartlett, C.A., Y.L. Doz and G. Hedlund (eds.) *Managing the Global Firm*, Routledge, London, pp. 15–46.

Hennart, J.F. (1982) *A Theory of Multinational Enterprise*. University of Michigan Press, Ann Arbor.

Hicks, J. and Lehmberg, D. (2012) 'Collision Course: Selling European High Performance Motorcycles in Japan' (Ivey Publishing, product number: 9B12M025).

Hines, J.L. (2004) 'Characteristics of an entrepreneur' *Surgical Neurology*, 61(4): 407–408.

Hitt, M.A., Ireland, R.D., Camp, S.M. and Sexton, D.L. (2001) 'Guest editors' introduction to the special issue—Strategic entrepreneurship: Entrepreneurial strategies for wealth creation' *Strategic Management Journal*, 22(6–7): 479–491.

Hofstede, G.H. (1997) *Cultures and Organizations: Software of the Mind*. McGraw-Hill, New York.

Horak, S. and Yang, I. (2016) 'Affective networks, informal ties, and the limits of expatriate effectiveness' *International Business Review*, 25(5): 1030–1042.

Hsieh, C., Nickerson, J.A. and Zenger, T.R. (2007) 'Opportunity discovery, problem solving and a theory of the entrepreneurial firm' *Journal of Management Studies*, 44(7): 1255–1277.

Hurmelinna-Laukkanen, P. and Ritala, P. (2010) 'Protection for profiting from collaborative service innovation' *Journal of Service Management*, 21(1): 6–24.

Inkpen, A.C. and Tsang, E.W. (2005) 'Social capital, networks, and knowledge transfer' *Academy of Management Review*, 30(1): 146–165.

Ireland, R.D., Hitt, M.A. and Sirmon, D.G. (2003) 'A model of strategic entrepreneurship: The construct and its dimensions' *Journal of Management*, 29(6): 963–989.

Isenberg, D.J. (2008) 'The global entrepreneur' *Harvard Business Review*, 86(12): 107–111.

Jensen, R. and Szulanski, G. (2004) 'Stickiness and the adaptation of organizational practices in cross-border knowledge transfers' *Journal of International Business Studies*, 35(6): 508–523.

Johanson, J. and Vahlne, J.E. (1977) 'The internationalization process of the firm—A model of knowledge development and increasing foreign market commitments' *Journal of International Business Studies*, 8(1): 23–32.

Johanson, J. and Vahlne, J.E. (2009) 'The Uppsala internationalization process model revisited: From liability of foreignness to liability of outsidership' *Journal of International Business Studies*, 40(9): 1411–1431.

Jones, M.V., Coviello, N. and Tang, Y.K. (2011) 'International entrepreneurship research (1989–2009): A domain ontology and thematic analysis' *Journal of Business Venturing*, 26(6): 632–659.

Kanter, R.M. (1983) *The Change Masters: Innovation and Entrepreneurship in the American Corporation*. Simon and Schuster, New York.

Keil, T. (2002) *External Corporate Venturing: Strategic Renewal in Rapidly Changing Industries*. Greenwood Publishing Group, Westport.

Keohane, R.O. and Nye Jr, J.S. (1998) 'Power and interdependence in the information age' *Foreign Affairs*, 77(5): 81–94.

Keupp, M.M. and Gassmann, O. (2009) 'The past and the future of international entrepreneurship: A review and suggestions for developing the field' *Journal of Management*, 35(3): 600–633.

Kirzner, I.M. (1973) *Competition and Entrepreneurship*. University of Chicago Press, Chicago.

Klein, A. (2011) 'Corporate culture: Its value as a resource for competitive advantage' *Journal of Business Strategy*, 32(2): 21–28.

Knight, G.A. (1997) 'Cross-cultural reliability and validity of a scale to measure firm entrepreneurial orientation' *Journal of Business Venturing*, 12(3): 213–225.

Knight, G.A. (2001) 'Entrepreneurship and strategy in the international SME' *Journal of International Management*, 7(3): 155–171.

Kogut, B. and Zander, U. (1993) 'Knowledge of the firm and the evolutionary theory of the multinational corporation' *Journal of International Business Studies*, 24(4): 625–645.

Kolk, A. and van Tulder, R. (2010) 'International business, corporate social responsibility and sustainable development' *International Business Review*, 19(2): 119–125.

Koruna, S. (2004) 'Leveraging knowledge assets: Combinative capabilities— Theory and practice' *R&D Management*, 34(5): 505–516.

Kostova, T., Marano, V. and Tallman, S. (2016) 'Headquarters–subsidiary relationships in MNCs: Fifty years of evolving research' *Journal of World Business*, 51(1): 176–184.

Kostova, T. and Roth, K. (2002) 'Adoption of an organizational practice by subsidiaries of multinational corporations: Institutional and relational effects' *Academy of Management Journal*, 45(1): 215–233.

Kuemmerle, W. (1999) 'The drivers of foreign direct investment into research and development: An empirical investigation' *Journal of International Business Studies*, 30(1): 1–24.

Kumar, K., Kumar, M. and Alsleben, M. (2009) 'SAP: Establishing a Research Centre in China' (University of Hong Kong, product number: HKU817).

Lam, A. (1997) 'Embedded firms, embedded knowledge: Problems of collaboration and knowledge transfer in global cooperative ventures' *Organization Studies*, 18(6): 973–996.

Lam, A. (2003) 'Organisational learning in multinationals: R&D networks of Japanese and US MNEs in the U.K.' *Journal of Management Studies*, 40(3): 673–703.

Lamotte, O. and Colovic, A. (2015) 'Early internationalization of new ventures from emerging countries: The case of transition economies' *Management*, 18(1): 8–30.

Laursen, K. and Salter, A. (2006) 'Open for innovation: The role of openness in explaining innovation performance among U.K. manufacturing firms' *Strategic Management Journal*, 27(2): 131–150.

Lee, C. and Beamish, P.W. (1995) 'The characteristics and performance of Korean joint ventures in LDCs' *Journal of International Business Studies*, 26(3): 637–654.

Lee, J-H. and Venkataraman, S. (2006) 'Aspirations, market offerings, and the pursuit of entrepreneurial opportunities' *Journal of Business Venturing*, 21(1): 107–123.

Lee, S.H. and Williams, C. (2007) 'Dispersed entrepreneurship within multinational corporations: A community perspective' *Journal of World Business*, 42(4): 505–519.

Lévesque, M. and Minniti, M. (2006) 'The effect of aging on entrepreneurial behaviour' *Journal of Business Venturing*, 21(2): 177–194.

Leydesdorff, L. and Meyer, M. (2006) 'Triple helix indicators of knowledge-based innovation systems: Introduction to the special issue' *Research Policy*, 35(10): 1441–1449.

Lockett, A. and Wright, M. (2005) 'Resources, capabilities, risk capital and the creation of university spin-out companies' *Research Policy*, 34(7): 1043–1057.

Low, M.B. (2001) 'The adolescence of entrepreneurship research: Specification of purpose' *Entrepreneurship Theory and Practice*, 25(4): 17–25.

Lumpkin, G.T. and Dess, G.G. (1996) 'Clarifying the entrepreneurial orientation construct and linking it to performance' *Academy of Management Review*, 21(1): 135–172.

Lyon, D.W., Lumpkin, G.T. and Dess, G.G. (2000) 'Enhancing entrepreneurial orientation research: Operationalizing and measuring key strategic decision making process' *Journal of Management*, 26(5): 1055–1085.

MacMillan, I.C., Block, Z. and Narasimha, P.N.S. (1986) 'Corporate venturing: Alternatives, obstacles encountered, and experience effects' *Journal of Business Venturing*, 1(2): 177–191.

March, J.G. (1991) 'Exploration and exploitation in organizational learning' *Organization Science*, 2(1): 71–87.

Martinez, J.I. and Jarillo, J.C. (1989) 'The evolution of research on coordination mechanisms in multinational corporations' *Journal of International Business Studies*, 20(3): 489–514.

McDougall, P.P. (1989) 'International versus domestic entrepreneurship: New venture strategic behavior and industry structure' *Journal of Business Venturing*, 4(6): 387–400.

McKern, B. and Naman, J. (2003) 'The role of the corporate center in diversified international corporations' in McKern, B. (ed.) *Managing the Global Network Corporation*, Routledge, London, pp. 220–259.

Meyer, G.D. and Heppard, K.A. (2000) 'Entrepreneurial strategies: The dominant logic of entrepreneurship' in Meyer, G.D. and K.A. Heppard (eds.) *Entrepreneurship as Strategy: Competing on the Entrepreneurial Edge*, Sage Publications, Thousand Oaks, CA, pp. 1–22.

Meyer, K.E., Mudambi, R. and Narula, R. (2011) 'Multinational enterprises and local contexts: The opportunities and challenges of multiple embeddedness' *Journal of Management Studies*, 48(2): 235–252.

Miles, M.P. and Covin, J.G. (2002) 'Exploring the practice of corporate venturing: Some common forms and their organizational implications' *Entrepreneurship: Theory and Practice*, 26(3): 21–41.

Miller, D. (1983) 'The correlates of entrepreneurship in three types of firms' *Management Science*, 29(7): 770–791.

Miller, D. and Friesen, P.H. (1982) 'Innovation in conservative and entrepreneurial firms: Two models of strategic momentum' *Strategic Management Journal*, 3(1): 1–25.

Minbaeva, D.B. and Michailova, S. (2004) 'Knowledge transfer and expatriation in multinational corporations: The role of disseminative capacity' *Employee Relations*, 26(6): 663–679.

Minbaeva, D., Pedersen, T., Björkman, I., Fey, C.F. and Park, H.J. (2003) 'MNC knowledge transfer, subsidiary absorptive capacity, and HRM' *Journal of International Business Studies*, 34(6): 586–599.

Minniti, M. and Bygrave, W. (2001) 'A dynamic model of entrepreneurial learning' *Entrepreneurship: Theory and Practice*, 25(3): 5–16.

Minocha, S. and Stonehouse, G. (2006) 'The "learning trap": A Bollywood frame for strategic learning' *Management Decision*, 44(10): 1344–1362.

Mintzberg, H. (1985) 'The organization as political arena' *Journal of Management Studies*, 22(2): 133–154.

Mitchell, R.K., Busenitz, L.W., Bird, B., Gaglio, C.M., McMullen, J.S., Morse, E.A. and Smith, J.B. (2007) 'The central question in entrepreneurial cognition research 2007' *Entrepreneurship Theory and Practice*, 31(1): 1–27.

Monteiro, L.F., Arvidsson, N. and Birkinshaw, J. (2008) 'Knowledge flows within multinational corporations: Explaining subsidiary isolation and its performance implications' *Organization Science*, 19(1): 90–107.

Moore, K. (2001) 'A strategy for subsidiaries: Centres of excellences to build subsidiary specific advantages' *Management International Review*, 41(3): 275–290.

Morgan, G. and Kristensen, P.H. (2006) 'The contested space of multinationals: Varieties of institutionalism, varieties of capitalism' *Human Relations*, 59(11): 1467–1490.

Morgan, G. and Whitley, R. (2003) 'Introduction' *Journal of Management Studies*, 40(3): 609–616.

Mortara, L., Napp, J.J., Slacik, I. and Minshall, T. (2009) *How to Implement Open Innovation: Lessons from Studying Large Multinational Companies.* University of Cambridge, IFM.

Mu, S.C., Gnyawali, D.R. and Hatfield, D.E. (2007) 'Foreign subsidiaries' learning from local environment: An empirical test' *Management International Review*, 47(1): 79–102.

Müller-Seitz, G. (2012) 'Leadership in interorganizational networks: A literature review and suggestions for future research' *International Journal of Management Reviews*, 14(4): 428–443.

Nahapiet, J. and Ghoshal, S. (1998) 'Social capital, intellectual capital, and the organizational advantage' *Academy of Management Review*, 23(2): 242–266.

Naldi, L., Achtenhagen, L. and Davidsson, P. (2015) 'International corporate entrepreneurship among SMEs: A test of Stevenson's notion of entrepreneurial management' *Journal of Small Business Management*, 53(3): 780–800.

Narula, R. (2001) 'Choosing between internal and non-internal R&D activities: Some technological and economic factors' *Technology Analysis and Strategic Management*, 13(3): 365–387.

Nell, P.C., Puck, J. and Heidenreich, S. (2015) 'Strictly limited choice or agency? Institutional duality, legitimacy, and subsidiaries' political strategies' *Journal of World Business*, 50(2): 302–311.

Nelson, R.R. and Winter, S.G. (1982) *An Evolutionary Theory of Economic Change.* Harvard University Press, Cambridge, MA.

Nerkar, A. and Roberts, P.W. (2004) 'Technological and product-market experience and the success of new product introductions in the pharmaceutical industry' *Strategic Management Journal*, 25(8–9): 779–799.

Ning, L. and Sutherland, D. (2012) 'Internationalization of China's private-sector MNEs: An analysis of the motivations for foreign affiliate formation' *Thunderbird International Business Review*, 54(2): 169–182.

Nobel, R. and Birkinshaw, J. (1998) 'Innovation in multinational corporations: Control and communication patterns in international R&D operations' *Strategic Management Journal*, 19(5): 479–496.

Nohria, N. and Ghoshal, S. (1994) 'Differentiated fit and shared values: Alternatives for managing headquarters–subsidiary relations' *Strategic Management Journal*, 15(6): 491–502.

Nohria, N. and Ghoshal, S. (1997) *The Differentiated Network: Organizing Multinational Corporations for Value Creation.* Jossey-Bass, San Francisco.

Nonaka, I. (1988) 'Toward middle-up-down management: Accelerating information creation' *Sloan Management Review*, 29(3): 9–18.

Nonaka, I., Von Krogh, G. and Voelpel, S. (2006) 'Organizational knowledge creation theory: Evolutionary paths and future advances' *Organization Studies*, 27(8): 1179–1208.

North, D. (1990) *Institutions, Institutional Change and Economic Performance.* Cambridge University Press, New York.

Obregón, M. (2001) *Beyond the Edge of the Sea: Sailing with Jason and the Argonauts, Ulysses, the Vikings, and other Explorers of the Ancient World.* Random House, New York.

Oviatt, B.M. and McDougall, P.P. (1994) 'Toward a theory of international new ventures' *Journal of International Business Studies*, 25(1): 45–64.

Oviatt, B.M. and McDougall, P.P. (2005) 'Defining international entrepreneurship and modeling the speed of internationalization' *Entrepreneurship Theory and Practice*, 29(5): 537–554.

Padula, G. and Dagnino, G.B. (2007) 'Untangling the rise of coopetition: The intrusion of competition in a cooperative game structure' *International Studies of Management and Organization*, 37(2): 32–52.

Paterson, S.L. and Brock, D.M. (2002) 'The development of subsidiary-management research: Review and theoretical analysis' *International Business Review*, 11(2): 139–163.

Penrose, E.T. (1959) *The Theory of the Growth of the Firm.* Oxford University Press, Oxford.

Pfeffer, J. (1998) 'Seven practices of successful organizations' *California Management Review*, 40(2): 96–124.

Pfeffer, J. and Veiga, J.F. (1999) 'Putting people first for organizational success' *The Academy of Management Executive*, 13(2): 37–48.

Pisano, G.P. and Verganti, R. (2008) 'Which kind of collaboration is right for you?' *Harvard Business Review*, 86(12): 78–86.

Polanyi, M. (1966) *The Tacit Dimension.* Doubleday, New York.

Porter, M.E. (1986) 'Competition in global industries: A conceptual framework' in Porter, M.E. (ed.) *Competition in Global Industries*, Harvard Business School Press, Boston, MA, pp. 15–60.

Porter, M.E. (1998) 'Clusters and the new economics of competition' *Harvard Business Review*, 76(6): 77–90.

Powell, W.W. and DiMaggio, P.J. (2012) *The New Institutionalism in Organizational Analysis*. University of Chicago Press, Chicago.

Prahalad, C.K. and Doz, Y.L. (1981) 'Strategic control—The dilemma in headquarters–subsidiary relationships' in Otterbeck, L. (ed.) *The Management of Headquarters–Subsidiary Relationships in Multinational Corporations*, Gower Publishing, Aldershot, Hampshire, pp. 187–203.

Pu, M. and Soh, P-H. (2017) 'The role of dual embeddedness and organizational learning in subsidiary development' *Asia Pacific Journal of Management*, doi:10.1007/s10490-017-9513-4.

Rauch, A., Wiklund, J., Lumpkin, G.T. and Frese, M. (2009) 'Entrepreneurial orientation and business performance: An assessment of past research and suggestions for the future' *Entrepreneurship Theory and Practice*, 33(3): 761–787.

Ritala, P. and Hurmelinna-Laukkanen, P. (2009) 'What's in it for me? Creating and appropriating value in innovation-related coopetition' *Technovation*, 29(12): 819–828.

Roberts, E.B. and Berry, C.A. (1985) 'Entering new businesses: Selecting strategies for success' *Sloan Management Review*, 26(3): 3–17.

Rothaermel, F.T. (2001) 'Incumbent's advantage through exploiting complementary assets via interfirm cooperation' *Strategic Management Journal*, 22(6–7): 687–699.

Rugman, A.M. (1980) 'Internalization as a general theory of foreign direct investment: A re-appraisal of the literature' *Review of World Economics*, 116(2): 365–379.

Rugman, A.M. and Verbeke, A. (2003) 'Extending the theory of the multinational enterprise: Internalization and strategic management perspectives' *Journal of International Business Studies*, 34(2): 125–137.

Schumpeter, J.A. (1934) *The Theory of Economic Development*. Harvard University Press, Cambridge, MA.

Scott, W.R. (1995) *Institutions and Organizations*. SAGE, Thousand Oaks, CA.

Sen, S. and Bhattacharya, C.B. (2001) 'Does doing good always lead to doing better? Consumer reactions to corporate social responsibility' *Journal of Marketing Research*, 38(2): 225–243.

Senge, P. (1990) *The Fifth Discipline: The Art and Science of the Learning Organization*. Currency Doubleday, New York.

Seppänen, R., Blomqvist, K. and Sundqvist, S. (2007) 'Measuring inter-organizational trust—A critical review of the empirical research in 1990–2003' *Industrial Marketing Management*, 36(2): 249–265.

Shane, S. and Venkataraman, S. (2000) 'The promise of entrepreneurship as a field of research' *Academy of Management Review*, 25(1): 217–226.

Shepherd, D.A. (2003) 'Learning from business failure: Propositions of grief recovery for the self-employed' *Academy of Management Review*, 28(2): 318–328.

Shepherd, D.A., Williams, T.A. and Patzelt, H. (2015) 'Thinking about entrepreneurial decision making: Review and research agenda' *Journal of Management*, 41(1): 11–46.

Shook, C.L., Priem, R.L. and McGee, J.E. (2003) 'Venture creation and the enterprising individual: A review and synthesis' *Journal of Management*, 29(3): 379–399.

Song, J. (2014) 'Subsidiary absorptive capacity and knowledge transfer within multinational corporations' *Journal of International Business Studies*, 45(1): 73–84.

Srivastava, A., Bartol, K.M. and Locke, E.A. (2006) 'Empowering leadership in management teams: Effects on knowledge sharing, efficacy, and performance' *Academy of Management Journal*, 49(6): 1239–1251.

Srivastava, A. and Lee, H. (2005) 'Predicting order and timing of new product moves: The role of top management in corporate entrepreneurship' *Journal of Business Venturing*, 20(4): 459–481.

Stach, G. (2006) 'Business alliances at Eli Lilly: A successful innovation strategy' *Strategy & Leadership*, 34(5): 28–33.

Stark, D. (1999) 'Heterarchy: Distributing intelligence and organizing diversity' in Clippinger, J.H. III (ed.) *The Biology of Business: Decoding the Natural Laws of Enterprise*, Jossey-Bass, San Francisco, CA, pp. 153–179.

Stopford, J.M. and Baden-Fuller, C.W.F. (1994) 'Creating corporate entrepreneurship' *Strategic Management Journal*, 15(7): 521–536.

Strutzenberger, A. and Ambos, T.C. (2014) 'Unravelling the subsidiary initiative process: A multilevel approach' *International Journal of Management Reviews*, 16(3): 314–339.

Teece, D.J. (2014) 'A dynamic capabilities-based entrepreneurial theory of the multinational enterprise' *Journal of International Business Studies*, 45(1): 8–37.

Teece, D.J. and Pisano, G. (1994) 'The dynamic capabilities of firms: An introduction' *Industrial and Corporate Change*, 3(3): 537–556.

Teece, D.J., Pisano, G. and Shuen, A. (1997) 'Dynamic capabilities and strategic management' *Strategic Management Journal*, 18(7): 509–533.

Tödtling, F., Prud'homme van Reine, P. and Dörhöfer, S. (2011) 'Open innovation and regional culture—Findings from different industrial and regional settings' *European Planning Studies*, 19(11): 1885–1907.

Tomiura, E. (2007) 'Effects of R&D and networking on the export decision of Japanese firms' *Research Policy*, 36(5): 758–767.

Tregaskis, O. (2003) 'Learning networks, power and legitimacy in multinational subsidiaries' *International Journal of Human Resource Management*, 14(3): 431–447.

Tsai, W. and Ghoshal, S. (1998) 'Social capital and value creation: The role of intrafirm networks' *Academy of Management Journal*, 41(5): 464–476.

Tsang, E.W. (1999) 'The knowledge transfer and learning aspects of international HRM: An empirical study of Singapore MNCs' *International Business Review*, 8(5): 591–609.

Turunen, H. and Nummela, N. (2017) 'Internationalisation at home: The internationalisation of location-bound service SMEs' *Journal of International Entrepreneurship*, 15(1): 36–54.

Tushman, M.L. (1977) 'Special boundary roles in the innovation process' *Administrative Science Quarterly*, 22(4): 587–605.

Van de Ven, A.H. (1986) 'Central problems in the management of innovation' *Management Science*, 32(5): 590–607.

Van de Vrande, V., Vanhaverbeke, W. and Duysters, G. (2009) 'External technology sourcing: The effect of uncertainty on governance mode choice' *Journal of Business Venturing*, 24(1): 62–80.

Van Rooij, A. (2005) 'Why do firms acquire technology? The example of DSM's ammonia plants, 1925–1970' *Research Policy*, 34(6): 836–851.

Venkataraman, S. (1997) 'The distinctive domain of entrepreneurship research' *Advances in Entrepreneurship, Firm Emergence and Growth*, 3(1): 119–138.

Verbeke, A. (2003) 'The evolutionary view of the MNE and the future of internalization theory' *Journal of International Business Studies*, 34(6): 498–504.

Verbeke, A., Chrisman, J.J. and Yuan, W. (2007) 'A note on strategic renewal and corporate venturing in the subsidiaries of multinational enterprises' *Entrepreneurship Theory and Practice*, 31(4): 585–600.

Wasserman, S. and Faust, K. (1994) *Social Network Analysis: Methods and Applications*. Cambridge University Press, New York.

Wassmer, U. (2010) 'Alliance portfolios: A review and research agenda' *Journal of Management*, 36(1): 141–171.

Weber, B. and Weber, C. (2007) 'Corporate venture capital as a means of radical innovation: Relational fit, social capital, and knowledge transfer' *Journal of Engineering and Technology Management*, 24(1): 11–35.

Welch, C., Marschan-Piekkari, R., Penttinen, H. and Tahvanainen, M. (2002) 'Corporate elites as informants in qualitative international business research' *International Business Review*, 11(5): 611–628.

Wiersema, M.F. and Bantel, K.A. (1992) 'Top management team demography and corporate strategic change' *Academy of Management Journal*, 35(1): 91–121.

Wiklund, J. (1999) 'The sustainability of the entrepreneurial orientation–performance relationship' *Entrepreneurship Theory and Practice*, 24: 37–48.

Williams, C. (2009) 'Subsidiary-level determinants of global initiatives in multinational corporations' *Journal of International Management*, 15(1): 92–104.

Williams, C. and Du, J. (2014) 'The impact of trust and local learning on the innovative performance of MNE subsidiaries in China' *Asia Pacific Journal of Management*, 31(4): 973–996.

Williams, C. and Kumar, M. (2012) 'Subsidiary initiatives in multinational enterprises: National and organizational determinants' EIBA conference, Brighton, UK, December 2012.

Williams, C. and Lee, S.H. (2009a) 'Resource allocations, knowledge network characteristics and entrepreneurial orientation of multinational corporations' *Research Policy*, 38(8): 1376–1387.

Williams, C. and Lee, S.H. (2009b) 'International management, political arena, and dispersed entrepreneurship in the MNC' *Journal of World Business*, 44(3): 287–299.

Williams, C. and Lee, S.H. (2009c) 'Exploring the internal and external venturing of large R&D-intensive firms' *R&D Management*, 39(3): 231–246.

Williams, C. and Lee, S.H. (2011a) 'Entrepreneurial contexts and knowledge coordination within the multinational corporation' *Journal of World Business*, 46(2): 253–264.

Williams, C. and Lee, S.H. (2011b) 'Political heterarchy and dispersed entrepreneurship in the MNC' *Journal of Management Studies* (Special Issue: Revitalizing Entrepreneurship), 48(6): 1243–1268.

Williams, C. and Lee, S.H. (2016) 'Knowledge flows in the emerging market MNC: The role of subsidiary HRM practices' *International Business Review*, 25(1): 233–243.

Williams, C. and Nones, B. (2009) 'R&D subsidiary isolation in knowledge-intensive industries: Evidence from Austria' *R&D Management*, 39(2): 111–123.

Williams, C., Takeshita, S., Gilles, M., Ruhe, C., Smith, J. and Troll, S. (2013) 'Leadership and preparedness to internationalize in the brewing industry: The case of Asahi Breweries of Japan' in Gammelgaard, J. and C. Dörrenbächer (eds.) *The Global Brewing Industry: Markets, Strategies and Rivalries*, Edward Elgar Publishing, Cheltenham, UK, pp. 247–268.

Williams, C. and van Triest, S.P. (2009) 'The impact of corporate and national cultures on decentralization in multinational corporations' *International Business Review*, 18(2): 156–167.

Williams, C. and Vossen, J. (2014) 'How open do MNCs need to be to extract value in open innovation?' *International Journal of Innovation Management*, 18(5) doi: 10.1142/S1363919614500352.

Williams, C., Zhu, J. and Colovic, A. (2016) 'Foreign market knowledge, country sales breadth and innovative performance of emerging economy firms' *International Journal of Innovation Management*, 20(6) doi: 10.1142/S1363919616 500596.

Williamson, O.E. (1991) 'Comparative economic organization: The analysis of discrete structural alternatives' *Administrative Science Quarterly*, 36(2): 269–296.

World Bank (2016) http://web.worldbank.org/WBSITE/EXTERNAL/TOPICS/EXTEDUCATION/0,,contentMDK:20161496~menuPK:282412~pagePK:148956~piPK:216618~theSitePK:282386,00.html accessed 5 October 2016.

Young, S. and Tavares, A.T. (2004) 'Centralization and autonomy: Back to the future' *International Business Review*, 13(2): 215–237.

Zahra, S.A. and Garvis, D.M. (2000) 'International corporate entrepreneurship and firm performance: The moderating effect of international environmental hostility' *Journal of Business Venturing*, 15(5): 469–492.

Zahra, S.A. and George, G. (2002) 'International entrepreneurship: The current status of the field and future research agenda' in Hitt, M.A., R.D. Ireland, S.M. Camp and D.L. Sexton (eds.) *Strategic Entrepreneurship: Creating a New Mindset*, Blackwell Publishers, Oxford, pp. 255–288.

Zahra, S.A., Sapienza, H.J. and Davidsson, P. (2006) 'Entrepreneurship and dynamic capabilities: A review, model and research agenda' *Journal of Management Studies*, 43(4): 917–955.

Zhou, L., Wu, W.P. and Luo, X. (2007) 'Internationalization and the performance of born-global SMEs: The mediating role of social networks' *Journal of International Business Studies*, 38(4): 673–690.

Zott, C., Amit, R. and Massa, L. (2011) 'The business model: Recent developments and future research' *Journal of Management*, 37(4): 1019–1042.

Index

Figures are shown in italics
Tables are shown in bold

3M Taiwan: case study 3, 119, 229–251;
  and cross-contextualization of
  initiatives 87; and entrepreneurial
  knowledge 9, 10, 95; and local
  embeddedness 74, 78–79; and
  organizational culture 35; and
  recognition of international
  opportunity 7–8; and subsidiary-driven
  venturing 46–47, 52, 89; and
  technology 107; and venturing
  workforce 92

absorptive capacity 91, 98
ad-tech industry 7, 30
Affiliated Computer Services (ACS)
  63, 88
aggressiveness *see* corporate aggressiveness
alliances: and entrepreneurial knowledge
  60–62, 93–94; and headquarters-driven
  venturing 20–21, 54–56, 57–59, 66–67;
  local 72–73; strategic partners 89; and
  subsidiary-driven venturing 80
Asahi Breweries of Japan 24–25
assets: and headquarters-driven venturing
  27–28, 33, 57–59; for open innovation
  58; and subsidiary-driven venturing
  42–43, 73–75
autonomy of work units 12, 104–105

boundary porosity 90–91, 98
Bruno, Julio 30–31, 33, 46, 87
business models 26–27

capabilities: for creation of entrepreneurial
  knowledge 19–20 *see also* external
  capabilities; internal capabilities

careers 111–113
Carlsberg 48, 59
cognition theory 40, 100
collaboration: benefits 20–21; and
  entrepreneurial knowledge 60–61, 65,
  67–68, 76; and headquarters-driven
  venturing 54–55, 56–59; national
  innovation system 71, 74–75; and
  subsidiary-driven venturing 71, 74
coopetition 64–65
corporate aggressiveness: and
  entrepreneurial knowledge 28,
  101–102, 103; and entrepreneurial
  orientation (EO) 18, 25; and
  headquarters-driven venturing 59
corporate culture 27–28, 31, 43, 46–47,
  52, 58, 74, 87, 95, 102, 104–105; and
  headquarters-driven venturing 34–35
corporate social responsibility (CSR)
  110–111
corporate strategy: and corporate
  aggressiveness 102; and entrepreneurial
  component 24–27; and entrepreneurial
  knowledge 17–18, 29; and external
  capabilities 55–57
credibility, and subsidiary-driven
  venturing 42–43
cross-contextual strategy: cases in point
  86–88; and corporate social
  responsibility (CSR) 110–111; and
  digital transformation 107; and
  dynamic capabilities 95–104; and the
  eclectic (or OLI) paradigm 109–110;
  and emerging and non-traditional
  markets 110; and entrepreneurial
  knowledge co-ordination 90–91; and

293

Index

ethical concerns 110–111; and
international venturing 85–86,
117–118; and internationalization
process 108

differentiated fit 49
digital transformation *see* technology
dispersed entrepreneurship 19, 70–71
driving forces: and entrepreneurial
knowledge 17–19, *97*; multiplicity of
88–89, 94–95 *see also* headquarters-
driven external venturing;
headquarters-driven internal venturing;
subsidiary-driven external venturing;
subsidiary-driven internal venturing
DSM 59
dynamic capabilities, and cross-contextual
strategy 95–104

eclectic (OLI) paradigm 109–110
economic trust 74
Eli Lilly 55, 57–58, 66, 113
emerging markets 110
'empire-building' entrepreneurs 59
employees *see* venturing workforce
entrepreneurial culture, and headquarters-
driven venturing 34–35
entrepreneurial internationalization 4–5
entrepreneurial knowledge: benefits 6;
channelling 96, *97*, 98–99;
contexts 116–117; co-ordination across
contexts 90–91; creation 19–22; and
dynamic capabilities 95–104; and
headquarters-driven venturing 28–30,
60–62; and heterarchy 11–15; processes
97; search for 6–11, 17–19; and
subsidiary-driven venturing 43–45,
75–77; and venturing workforce 91–95
entrepreneurial orientation (EO) 18,
25–26, 28, 36–37, 101, 103
entrepreneurial resource allocation
adjustment 96, *97*, 101–104
entrepreneurship: and corporate culture
27–28; dispersed 19, 70–71;
international 2–5; knowledge-based
view of 5; and multiplicity of driving
forces 88–89; research 5, 15–16;
strategic 17–18
ethical concerns 110–111
Expatica: case study 3, 119, 121–137; and
entrepreneurial knowledge 14; and
external capabilities 55, 62; and
headquarters-driven venturing 16, 33,
62, 93; and heterarchy 104–105; and

knowledge of opportunities 8–9; and
technology 107
expatriate management, and
entrepreneurial knowledge 77
experimentation in a heterarchical
firm 12
exploration and exploitation 10, 60,
66, 75; and headquarters-driven
venturing 66
external capabilities: and corporate
strategy 55–57; and headquarters-
driven venturing 54–57; and
subsidiary-driven venturing 70–71,
73–75; and venturing 15–17, *17*
external corporate venturing (ECV)
20–21
external investment opportunities 59

failure, learning from 9–10, 29, 113
finance, and subsidiary-driven venturing
42–43
formalization, and headquarters-driven
venturing 66–67

General Motors Overseas Operations
29–30

headquarters' managers: challenges of
subsidiary-driven venturing 48–50; and
entrepreneurial knowledge
co-ordination 93; in heterarchical firm
12–14; importance of 105; role 88; and
subsidiary-driven venturing 42–43 *see
also* strategic leadership
headquarters-driven external venturing:
challenges for leaders 63–64; challenges
for managers 64–68; challenges of
research 68; context of 15–17, *17*, **120**;
and entrepreneurial knowledge 60–62;
and external assets 57–59; and external
capabilities 54–57
headquarters-driven internal venturing:
challenges for leaders 32–34; challenges
for managers 33–37; context of 15–17,
17, **120**; and entrepreneurial
component 24–27; and entrepreneurial
knowledge 28–30; and internal
capabilities 23–24, 27–28, 33, 37–38
Hedlund 13–14
heterarchy: and entrepreneurial
knowledge 11–15, 22n2; features of 12;
and international venturing 5, 104–105
hierarchy: and entrepreneurial knowledge
14, 22n2; importance of 105

Index

high performance work system (HPWS) 51, 81

human resource management (HRM) 27, 51, 81;

IBM 55, 60, 61, 64

Infusion Development Corporation: alliance with Microsoft 62–63; case study 3, 119, 172–195; and entrepreneurial knowledge 10–11, 14; and headquarters-driven venturing 33, 62–63, 112; and internationalization process 108–109; and learning from outcomes 10; and recognition of international opportunity 7, 9; and subsidiary-driven venturing 46, 52; and venturing workforce 92

Infusion Poland: case study 196–213; and entrepreneurial knowledge 33, 95; and heterarchy 105; and local embeddedness 74, 77–78, 80, 94; and subsidiary-driven venturing 47, 77–78

initiative, and subsidiary-driven venturing 19

initiative filtering 96, *97*, 99–101

innovation 8, 27, 31, 48, 50, 63, 71, 72, 74, 75, 87, 99; and open innovation 55, 56–57, 58, 65–66

integration, normative 12

internal capabilities: and headquarters-driven venturing 23–24, 27–28; and subsidiary-driven venturing 39–40, 42–43; and venturing 15–17, *17*

Internal Corporate Venturing (ICV) 20, 27

international entrepreneurship *see* entrepreneurship

international opportunities *see* opportunities

international solutions *see* solutions

international venturing: careers in 111–113; contexts 15–17, *17*, 116–117, **120**; cross-contextual strategy 85–88, 117–118; definition 2–3; entrepreneurial knowledge processes *97*; and heterarchy 104–105; multiplicity of driving forces 88–89; orientation 20–21; theory 4; and venturing workforce 91–92 *see also* headquarters-driven external venturing; headquarters-driven internal venturing; subsidiary-driven external venturing; subsidiary-driven internal venturing

internationalization: and cross-contextual strategy 108; entrepreneurial 4–5

investment, external opportunities 59

knowledge: entrepreneurial *see* entrepreneurial knowledge

knowledge flows 56–57, 61–62, 65–66, 90–91 *see also* entrepreneurial knowledge

knowledge of opportunities: and headquarters-driven venturing 28–29, 60; and international venturing 6–8; and local embeddedness 75–76; and subsidiary-driven venturing 44, 75–76

knowledge of solutions: and headquarters-driven venturing 29, 60–61; and international venturing 8–9; and local embeddedness 76; and subsidiary-driven venturing 44–45, 76

knowledge transportation 86

knowledge-based view of entrepreneurship 5

Land Rover 2

leaders: challenges of headquarters-driven venturing 32–34, 63–64; challenges of subsidiary-driven venturing 47, 79–80; and entrepreneurial component 24–27; and entrepreneurial knowledge 95–96, 97, 98–99; and entrepreneurial resource allocations 101–104; and external capabilities 55–57; and initiative filtering 99, 101

learning from outcomes: and headquarters-driven venturing 29–30, 61; and international venturing 9–10; and local embeddedness 76–77; and subsidiary-driven venturing 45, 76–77

learning traps 9

Lehman Brothers 7, 9

local actors: role 89; and subsidiary-driven venturing 70–71

local embeddedness: cases in point 77–79; challenges for leaders and managers 79–82; and entrepreneurial knowledge 75–77, 93; and external capabilities 73–75; research 81–83; and subsidiary managers 71–73; and subsidiary-driven venturing 71–73, 93; and venturing workforce 92

'local-for-global' initiatives 19, 42

'local-for-local' initiatives 19

295

managers: challenges of headquarters-driven venturing 33–37, 64–68; challenges of subsidiary-driven venturing 47–51; and entrepreneurial knowledge co-ordination 93–95; and subsidiary-driven venturing 40–41 *see also* headquarters' managers; subsidiary managers

Microsoft 62–63, 88

Millennium Pharmaceuticals 57, 61

multiple centers, in heterarchical firm 12

Musk, Elon 32, 33

national innovation system 71, 74–75

N-form of international firm 13

non-traditional economies 110

normative integration, in heterarchical firm 12

Oakley Capital 87

OLI theory 109–110

open innovation 55, 56–57, 58, 65–66

opportunities *see* knowledge of opportunities

organization, and headquarters-driven venturing 66–67

organizational culture *see* corporate culture

outcomes *see* learning from outcomes

Panasonic 64

Penrose 59

Poland 7, 10–11, 33, 77–78

political arena, and headquarters-driven venturing 35–36

PPG 66–67

proactivity, and subsidiary-driven venturing 40–41

Reed, Richard 1–2

research: and challenges 36–37, 51–52, 68, 82–83, 105–111; and entrepreneurial knowledge 106; and headquarters-driven venturing 36–37, 68; in international venturing 105–111; need for more holistic 106–107; and subsidiary-driven venturing 49–52, 81–83

responsiveness, importance of 9

Roq.ad: case study 3, 119, 138–152; and entrepreneurial knowledge 14; and headquarters-driven venturing 30, 33; and heterarchy 105; and recognition of international opportunity 7; and technology 107; venturing workforce 92

SAP 26

shared values approach 49

social networks 4, 6, 82, 90–92, 99, 106

sociological trust 74

solutions *see* knowledge of solutions

strategic leadership *see* leaders

strategy *see* corporate strategy

subsidiary managers: challenges of subsidiary-driven venturing 50–51, 81–82; and entrepreneurial knowledge co-ordination 93; and headquarters-driven venturing 67–68; and local embeddedness 71–73; role 89

subsidiary-driven external venturing: cases in point 77–79; challenges for leaders 79–80; challenges for research 81–83; challenges for subsidiary managers 81–82; context of 15–17, *17*, **120**; co-participation in heterarchical firm 12; and entrepreneurial knowledge 75–77; and external capabilities 70–71, 73–75; involvement in strategic decision-making 13–14; and local embeddedness 71–73

subsidiary-driven internal venturing: and ambition and proactivity 40–41; challenges for leaders 47; challenges for managers 47–51; challenges for research 51–52; context of 15–17, *17*, **120**; co-participation in heterarchical firm 12; and entrepreneurial knowledge 43–45; and internal capabilities 39–40, 42–43; involvement in strategic decision-making 13–14

tacit knowledge 98

tangible and intangible assets: and headquarters-driven venturing 27–28, 33; for open innovation 58; and subsidiary-driven venturing 42–43, 73–75

technology: and cross-contextual strategy 107–108; and entrepreneurial knowledge 77; and headquarters-driven venturing 59

Tesla: case study 119, 214–228; and headquarters-driven venturing 31–32, 33, 64, 89; and heterarchy 15, 105; and international venturing 15; and technology 107–108

testing ideas, in heterarchical firm 12

Time Out Group: case study 3, 119, 153–171; cross-contextualization of initiatives 86–87; entrepreneurial

296

component to strategic direction 25; and entrepreneurial knowledge 15, 16, 95; and headquarters-driven venturing 30–31, 33; and heterarchy 105; and local embeddedness 16, 78, 93; and subsidiary-driven venturing 45–46; and technology 107; Time Out Market (TOM) initiative 45–46, 86–87, 103; venturing of 16
Tommasi Motorcycles 77
Travel 15, 112, desire for 1–2
trust 49, 61, 65, 82, 90, 108; between subsidiary managers and local agents 73–74
Twinning 62

Vandebroek, Sophie 63
Veldhuizen, Antoine van 33
venturing workforce 91–95

Welling, Mark 33
workforce *see* venturing workforce

Xerox Innovation Group (XIG): case study 3, 119, 252–274; cross-contextualization of initiatives 87–88; and headquarters-driven venturing 27, 63; and heterarchy 105; and international venturing 15; and subsidiary-driven venturing 47–48, 63